The Inertia of Fear and the Scientific Worldview

The Inertia of Fear and the Scientific Worldview

Valentin Turchin

Translated by Guy Daniels

Columbia University Press New York · 1981

Columbia University Press
New York

Printed in the United States of America

Thanks is due to the following publishers for their kind permission to reprint certain passages.

Alfred A. Knopf, and editions Gallimard for Albert Camus, *L'Homme révolté* (Paris: Gallimard, 1951). English translation: *The Rebel,* translated by Anthony Bower (New York, 1956). Copyright © 1956 by Alfred A. Knopf, Inc.

Random House for Alvin Toffler, *Future Shock* (New York, 1970). Copyright © 1970 by Random House, Inc.

Library of Congress Cataloging in Publication Data

Turchin, Valentin Fedorovich.
The inertia of fear and the scientific worldview.

Includes bibliographical references and index.
1. Science—Social aspects—Russia. 2. Science—Philosophy. 3. Turchin, Valentin Fedorovich. 4. Physicists—Russia—Biography. 5. Dissenters—Russia—Biography. I. Title.
Q175.52.R9T87 947.085′3 80–36818
ISBN 0–231–04622–7

Contents

To My American Readers

When I was leaving the Soviet Union a friend, an American journalist, said to me: "In America, you will be a dissident, too." I laughed in disbelief but said, just in case: "May be. But I understand you do not jail your dissidents."

"No," he said, which we agreed makes a big difference.

It does indeed; but my friend was right. On some important points I found myself a dissident in this country. This can be seen in particular, in some of the responses to my manuscript from American experts who read it.

In the Soviet Union my book was declared anti-Soviet, and I faced trial and imprisonment for spreading it in *Samizdat*. In America it will be found—not anti-American, of course, but in a very real sense *un*-American.

To begin with, an American reader will not know how to pigeonhole my book. Is it an academic work to be read by specialists during their working hours, or is it for the general reader to be read as entertainment in leisure time? This dichotomy is firmly established in America and seems self-evident. Books written for leisure time may have educational value, but they should be read without effort; nobody expects that they will be studied as one would study a book one needs professionally.

My book, however, ignores this dichotomy. It is addressed to the general reader, even if he happens to be a specialist in one of the problems discussed; at the same time, it is far from being an entertainment. The book is written on the assumption that the reader will think over it—I might even say study it—and compare its ideas with his own ideas on the subject. And it is assumed that when he meets a difficult place he will not throw down the book with indignation, but will make an effort to understand it.

To assume this is to assume that the reader is seriously and sincerely interested in the subject of the book. Then what is the subject?

I would like to stress that although written by a Soviet dissident, this book *is not a book on Soviet dissent;* neither is it a book on the Soviet Union primarily. I take the situation in the USSR only as a starting point for discussing much more general things, which should be important to every human being: the meaning of life, the way to live in a society, and the present confrontation between totalitarianism and freedom with its effects on the future of mankind. I approach these problems from the positivistic viewpoint, relying on contemporary philosophy of science, and using general concepts of cybernetics (systems theory).

In Russia, it seemed natural and important to write (and read!) a book on this theme. In America, it hardly occurs to anybody that this *may* be the theme. Thus the readers for the publishing houses were figuring out: will the book be interesting to Sovietologists?

I tried to have this published in English through the kind help of Mr. Hedrick Smith when I was still in Moscow. The book was rejected by the first publisher approached with the following conclusion by the expert whom that publisher consulted:

> In sum, I think it is a good and interesting manuscript, certainly deserving of publication—even demanding publication—but my guess is that a university press would be more suitable. . . .

The reason for this dialectical verdict was, as it turned out, that the reader had been asked by the publisher to evaluate the book from a very narrow angle. One reads on in the review:

> I do not believe that Turchin's book will attract as much attention as Roy Medvedev's *On Socialist Democracy* (which was probably only modestly successful). It is a more theoretical work than the latter, more scientific in orientation by far, and more distant from the normal dialogue about the Soviet Union. It is also probably more important than Medvedev's work, since Turchin asks hard questions which Medvedev avoided, and tries to give independent answers.

A short but thoughtful description of the contents of the book follows. Then the review ends as follows:

> I very much want to see the "Inertia of Fear" published, but have come up with a negative recommendation because of the way you put the question to me, at least in part. You asked me in your letter whether I thought it would play as large a role as Medvedev's *On Socialist Democracy*, and I must admit that I do not think that it will because of the somewhat esoteric characteristics I have described. Medvedev's book is more interesting to European and American students of politics. Turchin's work would appeal to that smaller circle of people interested in scientific analysis of political processes, models of political behaviour, and the influence of science on politics.

I could not have imagined it in Russia, but having lived two and a half years in America, I agree that against the current cultural background my book does look "somewhat esoteric."

The reviewer also found my manuscript to be "too intellectualized to reveal the purely human aspects and too close to the events and personal sufferings to be considered a philosophical treatise. . . ." My goal in writing this book was to synthesize certain distinct elements. It is not an academic work dedicated to a detailed and thorough investigation of a certain special topic; it is rather a philosophical and political credo of a contemporary Russian scientist. As such, it is inseparable from the present political conditions in

Russia, the author's personal history, and other "human aspects." There is neither need nor possibility to sever "human aspects" from the kind of philosophy I am concerned with, which is not any special branch of it, but what is in German called *Weltanschauung,* and is translated into Russian as *mirovozzreniye,* and into English as *worldview.*

From this unorthodox nature of the book, a rather unorthodox literary style results. Some parts are easy to read, others will require effort. You will find abrupt changes from a journalistic account to a treatise on philosophy and general science. The unity of this book is not achieved by a systematic coverage of topics in a certain field of knowledge; it results from the coverage of the factors contributing to the worldview of a certain person, the author. In this quality it is fairly systematic. I believe that if one keeps this in mind when reading my book, one will see its logic as it develops from the first to the last page.

By stressing the personal character of the worldview presented here, I do not mean to suggest that I propose it only as a personal document. If it were, I should not have begun this work. The origins of whatever we try to create are always personal, but the outcome is intended to be of universal significance. I believe that my reasoning, which I begin with the characterization of the totalitarian Soviet society, must be compelling for human beings, everywhere—regardless of where they live and their personal experience.

The cultural stratum that nourished my work is easily identified. The reviewer cited above called me "a typical Russian *intelligent*"; another wrote: "Although developed in a personal way, I think it [the book] reflects the opinions of a considerable number of the scientific intelligentsia in the Soviet Union, although few would go so far in advancing what is clearly a dissident platform."

True enough. *Intelligentsia,* as it emerged in Russia in the last century, is the community of those broadly educated people who believe in Reason and Knowledge, and that those lucky enough to obtain more knowledge have a duty to carry it on to the less lucky; they believe also that critical intelligence enhances human freedom and dignity; they oppose tyranny and obscurantism, whether coming from the tsar and the priests, or from the Communist dictators. The reader will see that I do not hold a high opinion of the contemporary Soviet intelligentsia as a whole; neither do I idealize the intelligentsia in the old Russia. But the noble tradition of Russian intelligentsia has survived in the most significant phenomena of contemporary Russian culture. The underground readership of my book in the Soviet Union is among the intelligentsia.

A Russian coming to live in America is surprised to discover that *there is no intelligentsia in this country.* Of course, there are many well-educated intellectuals who share the ideals with the Russian *intelligent,* but they do not constitute a community, do not amount to a phenomenon of public life, as they still do in Russia. Members of each of the multitude of religious denominations do constitute a community. Hippies did. Yippies did. Homosexuals do. But intellectuals do not. They do not even constitute a readership upon which a publishing house could count.

I am surprised at how easily the scientists of America surrender everything that is outside of their special fields of knowledge to the charlatans of various kinds who compete for the mind of the public. I believe that critical scientific thought should lend its method, style, and specific knowledge to the exploration of all parts and aspects of life, starting with the problem of ultimate values. This is not a terribly popular view in America at the present time, but I believe that it will prevail, and that every contribution to its prevalence is important. Thus I will be still satisfied even if only few will read my book.

I wish to thank most cordially Mr. Hedrick Smith for his help, and also Mr. Guy Daniels, who did the difficult job of translating my Russian into English.

Valentin Turchin
New York, September 1980

Preface to the Russian Edition

Every time I undertake to write about social problems in the Soviet Union, I come up against the following contradiction. On the one hand, I am a confirmed evolutionist and reformist. Or to put it more precisely, using a word that has little currency in Russia, I am a gradualist—a person who favors unhurried reforms effected in parallel with the evolution of social consciousness. And I am not alone in this position. To the contrary, so far as I can judge, the majority of educated people in the Soviet Union take the same view toward social phenomena. Although it is said that the only thing we learn from history is that we never learn anything from history, this is hardly the case—fortunately. One result of the Bolshevik Revolution was that we learned not to believe in ardent appeals to achieve three things at one stroke: to destroy the ruling class, to wreck the state machinery, and to build a new society: just and flourishing. Hence the last thing I want is to adopt, vis-à-vis the existing Soviet regime and ruling class, that posture of categorical rejection taken by the Bolsheviks in their day. We need a critical analysis of the situation, but one that is also constructive. In my view, the task of critics is not to treat the ruling class as an opposing, inimical force but rather to find a way out of the impasse—one leading to long-overdue reforms. Such a way will necessarily be a compromise to one degree or another: it must not threaten the interests of the ruling class to such an extent that it makes the latter an implacable enemy of reform. Plainly, any criticism pursuing the kind of aims mentioned above must be rather moderate. One who works toward compromise must not dry up the soil from which it might grow.

On the other hand, social conditions in the Soviet Union are such that if a citizen merely calls things by their right names, he becomes, in the eyes of the ruling class, a desperate extremist with whom no compromise whatsoever is possible. Probably never in human history has there been such a constant, omnipresent disparity between words and reality as in the USSR in the past fifty years—a disparity, moreover, that is accepted by the entire society. When one says white is white, or black is black, he is punished for it: one becomes an outcast, a dissident.

In the autumn of 1968 I wrote a short monograph called *The Inertia of Fear,* which at the time was rather widely circulated in *samizdat.* The present book, although written from scratch and therefore a new work with the same title, is based on the same ideas as was the first version. Among the most important of those ideas are positivism in the area of philosophy, and socialism (but not Marxism) as a view of society; a conviction as to the leading role of a world view in social movements; basic democratic freedoms and individual rights as the main prerequisites to the normal development of society; gradualism in politics; a view of the intelligentsia as that force which in principle can—and hence must—achieve democratic reforms; a very critical appraisal of the existing intelligentsia; an appeal to overcome the inertia of fear that took root in the Stalin era and is inhibiting social initiative.

Yet in some ways the present book differs from the first version, owing to the hiatus of seven years between them. The year 1968 marked the high point of the era of *podpisantstvo* ("signerism"),[1] when the names of Yuly Daniel and Andrei Sinyavsky became widely known—as did, right after them, those of Alexander Yesenin-Volpin, Andrei Sakharov, Pyotr Yakir, Alexander Ginzburg, Pavel Litvinov, and others. There seemed reason to hope that there was a socially significant minority in the country that would make a vigorous attempt to achieve democratic reforms. And, like other *samizdat* authors in those days, I saw my own task as primarily one of sketching out the ideological basis for those people to recognize one another and join their efforts. Writing from a gradualist position, I made certain concessions in phrasing, emphasized the points at which my own system of views intersected with the official Soviet ideology, and excluded from consideration many important aspects on which there was disagreement. I reasoned that what had gone unmentioned could be tacitly understood, if there was a wish to understand.

But it turned out that a basis for any substantial widening of the circle of "signers" was lacking—as it still is. If any changes are to be made in a society, a vigorous minority must strive for them. In terms of a percentage, that minority may be very small. For example, 0.1 percent of the population may be very influential if there is a question of long-overdue changes that are passively favored by broader strata (as is the case at present). But that tiny minority must consist of people who are actually striving for change—who are ready to risk their lives for that goal, in one way or another. And there is no such 0.1 percent in the Soviet Union—the few such people there can be counted one by one. The decline of culture in the Soviet Union and the totalitarian destruction of the individual have both gone much further than could have been believed in 1968. Those people who came forth in the late 1960s have been scattered by the authorities: some have been sent to prison or to psychiatric hospitals; others have been compelled to emigrate; and most of them, frightened, have fallen silent. There have been almost no replacements. Thus in 1970, Andrei Sakharov, Roy Medvedev, and I made one more attempt, in an open letter to the leaders of the Soviet Union, to formulate a minimum of conditions that might (so it seemed) serve as a rallying point for those people who realized the necessity for democratic reforms. No one responded.

It is now clear that the work must be begun at an even earlier stage. It is no longer a question of rallying the proponents of democracy capable of social action, and concerting their efforts, but merely of creating some sources of thought and feeling which (one might hope) will foster the growth of the requisite socially committed minority.

In this situation, what matters most of all is to call things by their right names and strive for an integral system of views, not leaving anything left unsaid. Apparently, the only correct course is the following: to combine uncompromising analysis on the level of facts and principles with a cautious strategy of gradualism on the level of conclusions and actions. To be a gradualist does not mean that one must be guided by half-truths, or that one does not have definite political ideals. To the contrary, gradualism presupposes a firmly held ideology: it is only on that basis that one can proceed to make compromises, or to engage in politics. (Actually, of course, we dissidents have never had occasion to engage in politics. The authorities simply pay no heed to us. So that there is no one to compromise with, even if we tried.)

I should like to conclude this brief foreword with a quotation from Gandhi, which I have always tried to follow and which I did in fact follow in writing this book:

> Man and his deed are two distinct things. Whereas a good deed should call forth approbation and a wicked deed disapprobation, the doer of the deed, whether good or wicked, always deserves respect or pity as the case may be. "Hate the sin and not the sinner" is a precept which, though easy enough to understand, is rarely practised, and that is why the poison of hatred spreads in the world.[2]

Valentin Turchin
Moscow
June 1976

The Inertia of Fear and the Scientific Worldview

Part I
Totalitarianism

Going into the Steady State

> Maxim felt the kind of desperation he would have felt if he had suddenly discovered that his inhabited island was actually populated not by people but by puppets . . . Before him was a huge machine, too simple to evolve and too huge to allow any hope that it could be destroyed by small forces. There was no force in the country that could free that huge nation, which had no inkling that it was not free . . . The machine was invulnerable from within. It was stable with respect to any small perturbation.
>
> A. Strugatsky, B. Strugatsky[1]

To use the language of thermodynamics, the Soviet Union essentially is going into a *steady state*—into a phase where it can reproduce itself from generation to generation without substantial changes. The days of Lenin and Stalin were the heroic epoch of the new society, when it was still creating itself, and when its founders were faced with the difficult task of remaking the mentality of a human being and converting him or her into a cog in the machinery of the state. Solving this problem required oceans of blood and millions of victims. By the time of Khrushchev, however, the problem had been basically solved. It remained now merely to look after the new society, punctually pulling out the weeds but not making any strenuous efforts to effect major changes. But Khrushchev's methods were not the right ones for that purpose: they were too fanciful. So he was replaced by new rulers—the present ones—under whose dispensation dullness and impersonality have become the highest virtue of the statesman. Today the Soviet Union is marching "with a firm tread" toward the kind of social order described in the novels of Yevgeny Zamyatin, Huxley, Orwell, and Arkady and Boris Strugatsky.

Totalitarianism is usually understood to mean total control[2] by the state over all socially important aspects of citizens' lives, including their thinking. A totalitarian state establishes a standardized ideological system, and forcibly implants it in the minds of its citizens. Persons who declare they do not share the state's ideology are punished. Depending upon such factors as degree of divergence, the punishment ranges from blocked promotions to liquidation. Basic civil rights—freedom of association, the freedom to receive and disseminate information, and the freedom to exchange ideas—are abolished. The struggle among ideas gives way to the struggle *against* ideas by means of physical force. From the viewpoint of evolutionary theory, totalitarianism is a malformation, a degeneration, since a lower level of organization is distorting and suppressing a higher one. A totalitarian society loses the capacity to develop normally, and becomes ossified. This is an impasse—indeed, a pitfall—on the road of evolution.

Totalitarian traits were characteristic of many civilizations of the past; and in each case the result was that the society stagnated for many centuries. In the twentieth century, science and technology are providing means, unprecedented in their effectiveness, for manipulating human consciousness. So that the danger of falling into the pitfall, and the depth of that pit itself, are growing rapidly. Today, huge areas of the world are blighted by totalitarianism. They are like patches of necrotic tissue in a living organism. Modern civilization is rushing toward globalism. In a very real sense, it is already global. But if it becomes totalitarian, where is the cure to come from?

Don't Worry

There are certain significant differences between our time and the Stalin era which indicate that the totalitarian society is going into a steady state. First and most important, in Stalin's time no one was sure of what the next day would bring; even the most loyal supporter of the regime (and the most highly placed) could end up in the meat grinder of the Gulag Archipelago, and perish. Today you don't have to worry about a thing. If you obediently carry out all of the authorities' orders, and work toward the stabilization of totalitarianism, the authorities will not simply leave you alone; they will try to provide that (rather meager) prosperity they are capable of providing. This comparison is of course entirely in favor of the present regime: a system that destroys its own supporters cannot be regarded as perfected. Stalin's meat grinder was necessary in order to instill in people a Great Terror of the State—to reeducate them in the new, totalitarian spirit. And this was done on a grand scale—lavishly. Of course the bounds of what was strictly necessary were often overstepped, and so-called excesses were committed. Lord, how popular that word "excess" was! One "excess" here, another there . . . Today, however, the word has gone out of fashion: there are no more excesses. The authorities have acquired experience. They have learned how to combat ideas with a minimum of bloodshed. They try to avoid excessive repression. There appeared a new ruling class which distinguishes "our people" from "the outsiders." And they don't touch their "own people."

Foreign observers often talk about the gradual "softening" and "liberalization" of the political regime in the USSR, from which they draw the conclusion that in the final analysis, Soviet society is being "liberalized" to a point where it is becoming a society of the Western, democratic kind. Such conclusions have no basis in fact. On the contrary, everything indicates that the trend is toward perpetuating the totalitarian way of life. The level of violence drops in proportion as society becomes accustomed to that way of life, and is reconciled to it. If by "softening" we mean a decrease in the number of victims, the regime is indeed considerably "softer" than it was in Stalin's era. It is likewise true that Stalin's regime was softer in 1952 than in 1937. But these things are only a consequence (and an indication) of the stabilization of totalitarianism. The basic principles upon which the new system is built have not changed one iota: the utter rightlessness of the individual in the absence of elementary civil liberties; the bureaucratic system of government under which all decisions are discussed and made in secret; the cutting off of free exchange of information and ideas; the mass disinformation supplied to the public by the media; the elevation of lying and hypocrisy to the status of a social norm; the imperialistic foreign policy; and, for the unsubmissive, the same prisons as before—except that there are no shootings. (Of course, Yuri Galanskov was in fact killed in prison. And how many other cases have there been of which we know nothing?)

The Twilight of the Demigods

> Our iron fist knocks down all barriers.
> The Unknown Fathers are content!
>
> A. Strugatsky and B. Strugatsky[3]

Another typical indication that the totalitarian society is going into a steady state is the shifting of emphasis in propaganda from the worship of certain individuals (those heroes and demigods to whom we are indebted for our happy life) to the worship of things which, although more abstract, constantly reproduce themselves: the system, the Party, the

Central Committee. An American journalist once asked me: "Who are the heroes of Soviet children? Whom do they teach them in school to admire, and whom do they actually admire?"

I found that I could not give a good answer to that question. I suddenly realized that we no longer have the cult of heroes that was typical of the period when I was growing up. In the 1930s, Valery Chkalov[4] was the idol of every little boy in the country. For the present generation, the only comparable figure is Yuri Gagarin. But I am convinced that Chkalov was far more popular than Gagarin was, with respect not only to the number of emulators but to the depth and sincerity of the admiration instilled in the youngsters. And Chkalov was not the only hero. I am thinking, for instance, of the heroes of Admiral Papanin's expedition. I can still remember those four names: Papanin, Krenkel, Fyodorov, and Shirshov.[5] And then there were the civil war heroes.

In the 1930s, the names of aircraft designers were known to everyone: they were popularized as examples to be emulated. But more recently the name of Sergei Korolyov, who headed up our space program, did not become widely known until after his death. When the Soviet newspapers reported the launching of sputniks, or advances in the space program generally, they made mysterious mention of a certain "Chief Designer" and a "Chief Theoretician." Ostensibly, this was done for reasons of secrecy. Actually, however, foreign specialists were well aware that the "Chief Designer" was Sergei Korolyov and the "Chief Theoretician" was Mstislav Keldysh. But the Soviet public was not supposed to know this. So long as the Soviet leaders had been men who, in the eyes of the public, had been heroes of the Revolution and the Civil War, the existence of heroes in other fields of activity had not prejudiced the interests of the system. But in a time when the leaders are faceless, the existence of colorful figures with great prestige poses a certain threat. After all, Sergei Korolyov might well have said to any member of the Politburo, "I gave the world access to space. And just who are *you*?"

Actually, of course, he would never have said such a

thing. Yet the mere possibility of such a confrontation can hardly have been pleasant for the leaders. The main theme of the publicity about the space program was that success in space was an achievement of the Soviet system; that it had been possible only under socialism, and only under the leadership of the Communist Party and its Central Committee.

When, in the era of Khrushchevian liberalism, I first began to look into writings on the history of the CPSU, I learned to my amazement that in the 1920s the word *vozhd'* ("chieftain") was often—and perhaps more often than not—used in the plural: the *vozhdi* of the Party. I was born in 1931; and I had come to expect that there could be only one *vozhd'*: the Great and Wise Chieftain of all progressive mankind. The idea of *vozhdizm,* which had come into being and taken root during the Revolution, had by the time of my childhood and youth been concentrated in one man—into one blindingly bright point. Later, that point faded, and there were no more "chieftains"—only leaders.

The leaders of a totalitarian state in the phase of stability are perceived by the ordinary person as a single, undifferentiated mass. The speeches they make are completely standardized, quite undistinguishable from each other in style; and the disagreements which arise among them are never aired for public discussion. There may be outstanding individuals among them, and then again there may not be. It is possible that they are all the same; and it is equally possible that they are all different. We know nothing about them; and according to the structure of our social system, we are not *supposed* to know anything about them. All we are supposed to know is that they are the focus and personification of the "collective wisdom" of the Party and the system.

Overcoming the Vestiges of the Past

One generation follows another, and pretotalitarian times recede ever farther into the past. In the late 1960s we witnessed collective protests by prominent artists and scientists—in particular, by members of the Soviet Academy of Sciences—against the rehabilitation of Stalin and Stalinist methods. In official language, these protests could rightly be called "vestiges of capitalism," since the protesters were mostly products of older times who, through all the terrors of the Stalin era, kept their belief in pretotalitarian ideals, and in the possibility of realizing them. At the same time, they held high positions, and their collective protests amounted to a serious social phenomenon that could not be ignored. Since then, some of them have died, and others have ceased to believe that anything can be done. Of the first "academician-signers," only Andrei Sakharov has continued on the same path.

And then, in August 1973, we beheld a very different kind of protest: a shameful letter from forty Soviet academicians condemning Sakharov's activities—a letter that was printed in all the Soviet newspapers.

This letter, and the campaign of slander that followed it, marked a new era in the history of Soviet science. In his day, Stalin still had to resort to the services of "outsiders" if they were outstanding specialists in their field. A person of this kind was, to a certain extent, allowed to remain himself. And the bureaucrats accorded him special treatment, as if he were an oddity, or a relic of the past. Now all that has changed. Science has been absorbed into the state. It now occupies the position it is supposed to occupy in a totalitarian society that has gone into a steady state. The new academicians are people with a totalitarian mentality, and they have been put through the screening process of state control. Today, "outsiders" do not get into the Academy: the state now has more than enough of its own people. (Whether they are also good scientists is another question.) In the spring of 1968, Mstislav Keldysh, president of the Soviet Academy of Sciences, said of those scientists who had signed letters of protest against lawlessness and political repressions: "Soviet science can get along without them."

With a View toward Further Improvement

One of the prerequisites to the steady-state condition is self-reproduction. Under Stalin, the development of self-reproducing totalitarian political machinery had been completed. Today, the self-reproduction of totalitarianism in the field of science and culture has become an established fact. One special indicator of these processes is the mass campaigns against the enemies (real or imagined) of totalitarianism. To the outside observer, these campaigns are what earthquakes are to a geologist: by them, he can tell what processes of mountain-building in the earth's crust have not yet been completed. The political trials of 1937–39 were the last of the earthquakes. Since then, the formations have hardened; and about all that happens these days is an occasional landslide and the formation of small fissures—usually concealed. But getting totalitarianism to function smoothly in the realm of culture has taken longer. As recently as the last years of the Stalin era, we witnessed mass campaigns against "Mendelians," "cosmopolites," etc. Then these campaigns began steadily to diminish in scope, and became closer to scale. It may well be that those carried out against Solzhenitsyn and Sakharov in 1973 were the last of their kind. Such campaigns have gone out of fashion, like "excesses."

This is because control by the Party apparatus over the economy and culture has already encompassed all levels of the hierarchy. I have in mind the kind of control that does not permit access to positions of leadership (or indeed to any prominent posts) by people willing and able to fight for their convictions and basic civil rights—in short, people who are "outsiders" from the viewpoint of the totalitarian state. The technique of control has reached a high degree of perfection, and it continues to improve. From time to time the Party and government organs promulgate decrees which are usually called something like "Concerning Measures for the Further Improvement of . . ." For example, on November 9, 1974, *Pravda* published an account of a decree promulgated by the Party's central committee and the Soviet Council of Ministers entitled "Concerning Measures for the Further Improvement of the Certification of Scientific and Pedagogical Personnel." Two things in this decree catch one's eye. First, the Higher Certification Commission, which awards academic degrees and titles, has been shifted from the jurisdiction of the Ministry of Higher Education to that of the Council of Ministers. The second thing is evident from the following quotation:

> It is recommended that an invariable rule be established for the practical activity of the Higher Certification Commission, the learned councils of colleges and universities, and those of scientific institutes, so that only dissertations of both scientific and practical value be accepted, and [only] persons who have proven their worth in a positive manner in scientific, industrial, and social work be accepted as candidates for academic degrees.

So even if you're Isaac Newton, if you haven't proven your worth in a "positive manner in social work," you can't be a Candidate of Sciences.[6]

Nor does this apply only to graduate work. Potential nonconformists are often spotted when they are still in their youth; and they are not permitted to get a decent education. For the slightest show of nonconformity, students are expelled from college. And then they are scornfully labelled *nedouchka* (someone who has not completed his education).

Nedouchka! How that word is relished by newspaper hacks and Party workers, who are themselves only half-educated! The *nedouchka* Amalrik. The *nedouchka* Bukovsky . . .

On one occasion when I was still working at a respected academic institute, I arranged for a talk to be given there by G. S. Pomerants, a well-known *samizdat* author whose works were circulated throughout the Soviet Union. Pomerants is a very interesting thinker, and a brilliant and engaging essayist. He spoke to a packed audience at one of the seminars on philosophical methodology held at the institute. But the fact that a *samizdat* author had spoken at the institute did not pass unnoticed. Someone complained to the Party Bureau about an "incorrect ideological line" at the seminar, and I was summoned to give an explanation. At the session of the Party Bureau to which I was summoned, a good deal of fuss was raised by a certain person who was rather inconspicuous around the institute—a man who, strictly speaking, was not a scientist but merely something close to it. Nor was he, for that matter, a member of the Party Bureau. (Later, I was told that he was the one who, at an earlier session of the Bureau, had brought up the matter of the seminar.) Repeatedly, this person pestered me with the question: "Who is Pomerants—a candidate or a doctor?"[7]

Finally, I had to say that Pomerants was neither a candidate nor a doctor of sciences, but that he merely worked as a bibliographer at the Main Social Science Library.

You should have seen the expression, compounded of indignation and scorn, on the face of that paltry stool-pigeon! "What?" he exclaimed. "Not even a candidate?"

It was shortly before the war that Pomerants wrote his first substantial work—one that he wanted to submit as a dissertation. But the war intervened. Then he was imprisoned. Soon after his release from labor camp, he became a well-known *samizdat* author, and quite simply he was not given a chance to defend his dissertation. He wrote another, and submitted it to a certain institute; but it was returned without anyone's even having taken the trouble to come up with a decent excuse.

13 Further Improvement

In the twentieth century, respect for scientists and learning is great, as is respect for other professional achievements. But for the nonspecialists (who constitute, of course, the great majority in any given field) it is recognition by the state which constitutes certification of your professional level. And the state knows whom to certify and whom not to certify. Society is so highly integrated today that hardly any substantial achievement is possible without the collaboration of teams of people working at institutions. Perhaps it is only writers who can work alone today. Even a mathematician needs access to a computer, and can you imagine an amateur physicist who in his spare time dashes off to an accelerator to study collisions of elementary particles? An architect is not an architect so long as the building he has designed is not built; and a film director is not a director until his film is shown on the screen.

Under present-day conditions, raising one's professional qualifications requires a concomitant rise in the job hierarchy. In almost every field, a person who wants to carry out his creative projects, and who has the requisite skills and experience to do so, must have under him at least a small group of people. And it is here that the totalitarian state presents him with a difficult choice: either to sell one's soul to the Devil or to relinquish his projects and his professional growth. According to a basic principle of the Soviet state, a superior in any field must not only direct the work of his subordinates but educate them as well. This principle is endlessly repeated and stressed in Party theory, and serves as the basis of the Party's practical policies in the spheres of both economics and culture.

For a superior to educate his subordinates, it is by no means necessary that he give them lectures on the theory of Marxism-Leninism. No, something very different is expected of him. To educate one's subordinates means to set for them an example of the kind of behavior that meets with the approval of the authorities. At the very least, it means that one guarantees silence on those matters about which one is told to keep mum; and of course that one follows without demur the "recommendations" of Party organs. If one meets these requirements, one can mount to the first rung of the career ladder. And the same requirements must be met in order to receive any kind of award, bonus, etc.

Since the October Revolution, totalitarianism's attack on the arts and sciences (culture) has proceeded from the top downward; that is, "outsiders" have been pushed down to ever-lower levels of the hierarchy. By now this process apparently has reached its natural completion. In science, for instance, the "outsiders" may still hold positions as junior or senior research associates, but in no case may they head up a laboratory or department, or any structural unit whatsoever. A superior must educate his subordinates.

Everyone must solve in his own way the dilemma that the totalitarian society poses before anyone in a creative profession: conscience or work. Most of those people who are called "decent" sacrifice their work in part and their conscience in part. They try to keep their dealings with social problems to a minimum; they try to confine themselves to the purely professional aspects of their work, and to purely professional contacts. But those who have not retained an iota of decency will stoop to anything to get ahead. Sometimes, for instance, they take part in hideous masquerades in which they "freely and openly" exchange views on politics and ideology with people from the West.

Levels of Deprivation of Freedom[8]

> The latest discovery of State Science is the
> location of the center of imagination—a
> miserable little nodule in the brain in the
> area of the *pons varolii*. Triple X-ray
> cautery of this nodule—and you are cured
> of imagination—
> FOREVER.

15 Levels of Deprivation of Freedom

> You are perfect. You are machinelike.
> The road to 100 percent happiness is free.
> Hurry, then, everyone—old and young
> —hurry to submit to the Great Operation
>
> Yevgeny Zamyatin[9]

A person can be confined physically; for example, he can be chained in a galley or put behind bars. This is deprivation of freedom on the lowest level. Or a person can be blinded, so that although in a formal sense he is free, he must entrust himself to a guide. This is deprivation of freedom at a higher level—that of information. Finally, all of a person's senses—and, consequently, his capacity to receive information about the outside world—may be left intact, but at the same time his consciousness may be transformed, or his will paralyzed, by an operation on the brain, or by the administration of drugs to him. This is deprivation of freedom at the highest level—the kind that the inexperienced observer does not always notice. And he will of course not notice anything if he has never seen a normal person who has not been operated on.

Totalitarianism passes through corresponding stages in its taking over society. It moves from the outside inward, invading ever-deeper strata of societal life and disfiguring ever-higher levels in the organization of living matter.

During the first years after their seizure of power, the authorities of the Bolshevik regime depended exclusively on violence ("revolutionary" violence). Their attitude toward the dissemination of information was, from the viewpoint of later times, unpardonably frivolous. One example was the publication of memoirs by persons who had fought against the Red Army in the Civil War. It was assumed that the "class-conscious worker" would (with the help of a Preface) separate out the interesting historical facts from the enemy's wicked lies. Again, Party members had rather full information about what went on at the higher levels of the hierarchy.

And of course it never entered anyone's head to limit access to "bourgeois" philosophical works. To the contrary, it was felt that "you should know your enemy."

Later, however, it became plain that it was better not to know the enemy. Nor was it good to know what was going on at the higher levels, in places of incarceration, and in many other places. A closed society—closed, that is, for purposes of information—was created. It reached its fullest bloom in the last years of Stalin's life. Hundreds of thousands of informers eavesdropped on every word uttered by citizens. Any and all books having even a remote bearing on politics, sociology, or philosophy were sequestered in "special depositories." Contacts with foreigners were reduced to a minimum, and could be made only under strict monitoring by state security. The very word "foreigner" frightened the man in the street. The associations prompted by this word were: espionage, the secret police, the Lubyanka.

This was the stage in the development of the totalitarian society when the main emphasis was on the informational level, while the number of persons annihilated physically was beginnning to drop. Of course the consciousness of the citizenry had already been radically altered, but the authorities didn't put much faith in that. Hence they had an hysterical fear of information—of *knowledge*. The cynicism required by a totalitarian state in stable condition had not yet fully developed: it had not yet become part and parcel of the social consciousness. The assumption was that people *did not know* about the millions of innocent victims—about the monstrous meat grinder of Gulag. And in fact, many people did not know. They did not, needless to say, because they did not *want* to know, and were afraid to. There was a kind of tacit understanding between the regime and the people: the authorities set up the informational barriers; and the people rejoiced that they did not have to know.

In the third and final stage of totalitarianism, the emphasis is being placed on maintaining the totalitarian mentality of the citizens. In this stage it is presupposed that the altering of consciousness has been completed, and that the urge toward freedom has been totally suppressed. Under these conditions it becomes possible to reduce the scale of physical force further and partially (but only partially) to open up channels of information—to the greater joy of "surfeited, well-disposed foreigners with notebooks and ball-point pens in their hands." (Alexander Solzhenitsyn.)

In 1956, the old "Stalin falcons" protested against the exposure of Stalin's crimes, because they feared that if people found out, and realized what they had found out, it would upset the balance and might bring far-reaching consequences. But Khrushchev, who made a career out of exposing Stalin, felt that the system was stable enough so that nothing terrible would happen. And in general, he proved to be right. People *found out*, and nothing happened. Soviet man had become "rugged enough to cope." Serious troubles occurred only in Eastern Europe, where people had not had the Soviet kind of conditioning. The twelve years between the suppression of the Hungarian uprising in 1956 and the invasion of Czechoslovakia in 1968 constitute, essentially, the period of transition to the third stage of totalitarianism. Those years can be compared to the twelve years between 1922 and 1934—the period of the transition from naked force to the informationally closed society.

To Accept or Not To Accept?

Periods of transition can be distinguished from periods of stagnation in that something in any case is happening in periods of transition. At such times, people are faced with the problem of finding their own place in the changing circumstances. Soon after the Revolution of 1917, it became clear to most educated Russians that the Bolshevik regime was not what they had hoped for and expected from the Revolution. Hence the question to accept or not to accept? Of those who did not emigrate during the Civil War, most accepted the Revolution. The others were repressed, while a small number survived in the form of an "internal emigration." But since the state terror was rampant, one was left with the feeling that both the political regime and the way people thought had been imposed by force. And I believe one can unhesitatingly affirm that such was the case.

The rehabilitation of people who had been victims of the Stalinist terrorism entailed a partial rehabilitation of ideas as well. Books which had previously been banned began to appear. The intelligentsia began talking about the need for democratization, for the public disclosure of various official proceedings, for a freer exchange of information. Sooner or later this was bound to provoke a social movement. And that is what happened. A suitable mode of action was hit upon: sending petitions to the higher authorities. (As a matter of fact this was—and is—the only mode of action possible, under Soviet conditions, for an open political movement.) The people who signed such petitions were called "signers" (*podpisanty*).

For a while, the number of signers increased, and it looked as if the movement would encompass broad segments of the intelligentsia. Then the authorities began to take countermeasures. Compared with those of the Stalin era, the countermeasures were laughably mild: criticism and censure at meetings, cancellations of official trips abroad, demotions, and sometimes dismissal from employment. The steps taken against Party members (and there indeed were Party members among the signers) included reprimands or, for those who persisted, expulsion from the Party. In the case of many people, however, the authorities did nothing beyond taking note of their signing. For example, I was given no trouble at that time, although I had signed several collective protests.

But even these measures were enough to stop the movement. Signerism peaked in the months of February and March 1968. By the summer of that year, even before the occupation of Czechoslovakia, it had become apparent that the movement was rapidly declining. The events of August 21 only consolidated the victory of totalitarianism. The signers proved to be a minority—a very tiny minority. Most of the intelligentsia did not support them.

The educated Soviet citizen had again been faced with a choice, and he had again chosen totalitarianism; only this time he had done so under incomparably less pressure. Under Stalin, his mouth had been kept shut by a monstrous, implacable force. To offer any kind of opposition at all meant almost certain death. To the activists of the democratic movement it seemed that now, when one could do something to restore the basic rights of the individual, people would grasp that opportunity, and the movement would snowball—among the intelligentsia, at any rate. But this was an illusion, as became plain in the process of gathering signatures, and many activists simply gave up. The Great Fear of the Stalin era no longer existed, but the *inertia* of fear was still at work. The founders of the new system had not labored in vain: terror had left its mark. It lurked in the nooks and crannies of consciousness. It mutilated souls. It altered notions of ethical values—of good and evil.

More than any other segment of society, the intelligentsia needs basic democratic freedoms, and suffers from their lack. It needs them professionally, so that it can perform its social functions. Hence it is first and foremost the intelligentsia that should be concerned with whether the rights of the individual are being respected and should try to secure those rights if they are not. It is responsible to society for them. To combat prejudices and obscurantism, to work toward intellectual and spiritual freedom, is the plain duty of an educated person, just as it is a doctor's duty to keep a watchful eye on people's health.

I have already said that in a totalitarian society a person doing creative work is faced with a situation in which the demands of conscience conflict with the interests of the job. But that situation does not necessarily entail the kind of passivity on the part of the intelligentsia that we now see on every hand. The necessity of choosing, and that of compromising, have always existed—and always will exist—in any aspect of life. Life itself is a matter of constantly making compromises. And if the Soviet intelligentsia had possessed a strong drive toward doing its duty, compromising when necessary, the sociopolitical atmosphere in the country would have been very different. But that drive was lacking. Why?

This is what I wrote in the first version of *The Inertia of Fear* in the autumn of 1968.

The Philosophy of the Cow, Dogmatic Pessimism, and Other Theories

Among the horrible consequences of the Stalinist terrorism was both the physical destruction of people and the dehumanization of those left alive—their loss of a "human face." To one degree or another that process affected everyone; and because generations influence one another it even had its effect on young people who never experienced Stalin's times. The saddest thing is that we got used to that dehumanization: we learned to live with it; and we took our mangled mentality to be a norm.

When a thug aims a revolver at an unarmed person, the latter has only two choices: to submit or to die on the spot. And no one can pass judgment on the person who submits under those circumstances. But the thug is no longer here. Isn't it time to put on a human face again?

We have become so accustomed to the massive, systematic lie that we accept it completely, considering it as natural and necessary to maintain the social order. We find it quite normal to say one thing at home, or among friends, and the opposite thing in public. And we teach our children to do the same. We feel no shame when, at a meeting, we vote for a resolution that we consider wrong and, after leaving the auditorium, roundly abuse that same resolution. We do not regard it as a shameful act of betrayal when we fail to stand up for an associate who has been unjustly accused. And sometimes, when our conscience demands the merest nothing of us, we refuse to grant it even that much. We are cowardly and unprincipled.

There are hardly any dodges we will not resort to, hardly any paltry arguments we will not invent, to justify ourselves in our own eyes and in those of our friends.

Many of our scientists shelter themselves behind an excuse whose simplicity bears the stamp of genius. "That's not my business," they say. "My business is science, and nothing else concerns me. I'll do anything at all, just so long as nobody interferes with my work. In that way, I'll make the biggest possible contribution to society."

This is the philosophy of the cow, who can do nothing but give milk, and who will give it to anybody and everybody. A scientist, when he reasons in this way, is laying claim to the unquestionable exclusiveness of both his profession and his own person. And as a matter of fact, when such a claim is made by a scientist, it seems to be better founded than if it had been made by someone in another profession. Often, we put science in a special category, assigning to it a higher value that is independent of other values more directly involved with the life of society. In the early stages of science's development, and perhaps even in the past century, such a viewpoint could be regarded as to some extent justified. In those days, science was developing more or less autonomously; and it had to build up its strength in order to become an important social phenomenon. Given the belief that ultimately science would change society for the better, this buildup of strength was perhaps tactically correct. But today science is closely bound up with the life of society as a whole: the overall, global problems of science are indivisible from those of society. Can one, without indulging in self-deception, defend the viewpoint that the solution of problems affecting everyone must be sacrificed so that some particular, narrow problems can be solved a bit more quickly? Usually, behind such views, lurk purely selfish motives.

Finally, setting up an opposition between one's concern for social problems and one's activity in a narrow field is itself simply not justified. The person who wants to do his duty toward society will always find ways to do it which do not fatally affect his work. The philosophy of the cow, though, is indispensable to those who want to shirk their duty, buying their way out of it with milk. And incidentally, even the milk of such people is most often thin . . .

"But what can you do?" another member of the intelligentsia asks. "Everywhere you look, you find nothing but lies and baseness. If you stick your neck out, they'll get you, period. And nothing is going to change, except maybe for the worse. No, it's better to sit still and keep your mouth shut."

It's no use pointing out to him all the changes which are constantly taking place in our lives. It's no use asking him how, in his opinion, progress takes place in the world generally. He will either paint a dark picture of everything or simply walk away. His pessimism is a dogma that he has no intention of subjecting to doubt, and which is therefore invulnerable. The conviction that nothing can be done is one he needs for his self-justification. When the forces of reason and good win a victory, he merely shrugs. But when evil and ignorance get the upper hand, he doesn't miss a single opportunity to gloat: "See? I told you! I warned you!" And he rejoices that no one managed to "provoke" him into an "imprudent" act.

Then there is another theory which might be summed up in the phrase "it will happen by itself."

"Why, sure!" the proponent of this theory says. "Of course there will be improvement. But it will happen only slowly, under the action of objective laws. It can neither be stopped nor speeded up. We just have to wait. In due time, everything will be fine."

As if that improvement would happen by itself, in some mystical manner, without any input from people! As if we were not indebted for improvement to those very people who are giving to it their health, their energies, even their lives!

Of course we *can* simply wait. For that matter, if you fall into the water, you can simply wait, without even struggling, until somebody pulls you out. And it's possible that, finally, somebody *will* pull you out (there are some good people in the world, after all), but it's also possible that they *won't* pull you out—not because they don't want to, but because they can't.

And there are many other excuses that help members of the intelligentsia to avoid taking the actions that conscience demands. People in high positions say that such actions are all right for "ordinary people," because they have nothing to lose. "Ordinary people" say such things are all right for those in high places, because nobody will give them any trouble. One person says he's just finishing his dissertation. Another doesn't want to make things hard on his boss. And yet another is afraid his official trip abroad might be cancelled. Finally, the young person says he's too young, and the oldster says he's too old.

None of these excuses is worth a plugged nickel: every one of them falls apart the very first time it is subjected to serious and honest scrutiny. But the *intelligent*[10] does not want to scrutinize the issue seriously and honestly. He prefers to keep those stage props which conceal his own fear and deep spiritual malaise. He cautiously picks his way among them so that he will not accidentally bump into them and wreck them. And he sometimes feels a real hatred toward anyone who sets an example of courageous behavior and honorably confronts him with a moral choice. He hates such people because they disturb his peace and quiet. Not only does he lie and feel afraid, he does not want to stop lying and feeling afraid: he's become quite used to it, and things are more convenient and reassuring that way. This is the worst possible moral degradation.

Morality. Conscience. Honor. We have a strange attitude toward these notions. Not that we deny them entirely, setting them down to bourgeois prejudices. But we do regard them as somehow trivial, old-fashioned, "non-Marxist." The smelting of iron and steel, we say, is a serious matter. In Marxist-Leninist terminology it is the "base," and hence important to society. But stuff like morality and ethics is the "superstructure." Yet sometimes it is precisely while things are going more or less well with iron-smelting and the rest of the "base," that certain elementary moral principles have been forgotten on a massive scale, thus obstructing the normal development of society.

Such is the case in the Soviet Union. So long as we value foreign finery above a clear conscience, so long as we are capable of betraying a fellow-worker because we're afraid of damaging our careers, we are not worthy of being called human beings, and we do not deserve the destiny of human beings.

We certainly need not demand of one another some kind of heroism—some kind of unusual courage. But is it not true that we ourselves are the source of the lying and hypocrisy? Surely, honorable people, if they really wanted to, could agree among themselves simply to be honorable. Can't we at least do what is fully within our power? But no. We prefer to find excuses. We prefer to sink without a trace into petty, selfish concerns and forget about duty and honor, life and death. We prefer to vote for a falsehood and then, when we come home in the evening, complacently tell our children the lie that we are honorable persons.

Moral and Political Unity

> The most insignificant Soviet citizen, freed of the chains of capitalism, stands head and shoulders above any big foreign bureaucrat bearing the yoke of capitalist enslavement.
>
> Joseph Stalin [11]

The years after 1968 were years of polarization. Those people (a small minority) who refused to accept the basic principle of totalitarianism—suppression of the individual's rights—crystallized their views, and they were given a name imported from the West: "dissidents." (Russian: *dissidenty.*) The others returned to the bosom of the totalitarian majority. Mutely and apathetically, society watched how the authorities dealt with the dissidents.

I remember that in the autumn of 1972 I asked Academician X, a well-known astrophysicist, to help the astronomer Cronid Lubarsky, who was soon to go on trial. Lubarsky, the author of several dozen scientific studies and a former president of the Moscow Astronomical Society, had been arrested for taking part in publishing *The Chronicle of Current Events,* a well-known *samizdat* bulletin. What I asked of Academician X was very little: to write for the court a testimonial evaluating Lubarsky as a scientist. I knew from what had happened in other political trials—in particular, from the trial of the mathematician R. I. Pimenov—that such a testimonial, if signed by a prominent scientist who was a member of the Academy, might help to mitigate the sentence. X had been among the first "academician signers," and this fact gave me reason to hope for a positive result from my *démarche.* But my hopes proved to be unjustified. Times had changed. The academician refused to sign the testimonial.

Cronid Lubarsky was sentenced to five years in a strict-regimen labor camp. He was a sick man, and most of his stomach had been removed. Every day he spent in the labor camp was torture for him.

Not long ago an incident occurred which, although insignificant in itself, is very typical of the atmosphere of recent years. Professor Yuri Orlov, a physicist and associate member of the Armenian Academy of Sciences, telephoned Academician Y (also a physicist) to arrange for the two of them to meet and discuss certain problems. Unfortunately, Orlov is known not only as a physicist but also as one of the most active dissidents. The moment Y found out with whom he was speaking, and before he had learned what Orlov wanted to talk about, he hastened to warn him: "Just remember: I'm not interested in the forward movement of humanity!"

Yet there had been a time when Y had signed a protest against the use of Stalinist methods. But dissidents were no longer in fashion. Because "whatever you say, you just can't do anything." It didn't matter to the academician whether humanity moved forward or backward. All he cared about was not getting dragged into this or that action in defense of innocent people who had been put behind bars, and other such trivia.

With respect to individual cases—and any dissident can cite a great many of them—it is always possible to object that they are only individual cases and not statistics. But there is one kind of public activity that involves the automatic gathering of statistics: voting at the meetings and sessions of such groups as the learned councils of scientific institutes. Efim Etkind, a literary critic and historian from Leningrad, was dismissed from his job[12] after his superiors had been informed by the KGB that they considered him to be disloyal. At a scientific institute, dismissal of a person who obtained his post via competitive examination requires that the learned council enact (by secret ballot) a resolution to this effect. In Etkind's case, such a resolution was passed; the members of the learned council voted for it *unanimously!* The foreign correspondents in Moscow who relayed this news abroad were amazed. How could it be that among over fifty persons, voting secretly, not a single one opposed this politically motivated firing? How could it have happened?

It can happen. It is not for nothing that Soviet propaganda shouts to the whole world about the moral and political unity of Soviet society. Naturally, the propagandists use sleight-of-hand and shift the meanings of words; but what they say is not altogether a lie. In its disdain for the rights of the individual, its lack of self-respect, and its servility toward the regime, Soviet society *is* unified, both morally and politically.

I have been told that the members of the learned council had it in for Etkind for some reason. If so, this may partially explain (although of course it does not justify) the results of the voting. But here is another case. Among the staff members at a certain institute was the physicist A, a kind-hearted man of irreproachable honesty with a ruddy, round face—a living symbol of Russian good nature and sociability. I believe there was not a single person in the institute who bore him any ill will. Then one day A committed an "offense." As a Party member, he had written a letter to some high Party authorities that was not to their liking. In writing the letter, A was in fact complying with the Party rules, which state that a Communist must inform higher authorities of acts on the part of lower authorities which, from his viewpoint, are incorrect. Moreover, the letter, as was proper, was not an "open" one. But it was written toward the end of 1968, at the time of a "complicated situation" (as Party jargon has it) at the institute. So orders came down from above to condemn the freethinker. In a trice, they held a Party meeting, found him guilty, and gave him a strict reprimand. Then came the session of the learned council. The physicists sat there thinking: the matter is trifling, but the situation is complicated, so A must be punished. Otherwise you don't know *what* kind of thing might happen. A motion was offered to demote A from senior research associate to junior research associate. This would mean a drop in salary of more than one-third, and A had a wife and two children.

Only one person found the motion unjust. This was B,

who was head of a laboratory. He took the floor and said, "Why demote him? After all, he's doing very good work, and we have no complaints against him. He's already been reprimanded by the Party, and that's enough."

At this, the others all started shouting at B, saying such things as: "What kind of idea is that? We must think of the good of the institute!" And so on.

Then came the balloting. Result: it was unanimously decided that A should be demoted. B, too, had voted in favor of the resolution. After all, if there had been only one vote against it, everyone would have known it was his. (The way he voted did not save him, though: Some time later he was demoted from laboratory director to senior research associate.

As a rule, repressions against people in the creative professions—either penalties or actual dismissal from the job—are carried out in a completely legal, "democratic" way. Society emasculates itself. And this tradition is passed on to the next generation.

Not long before I was dismissed from the institute where I was working (in the summer of 1974), A. M. Gorlov, a Candidate of Technical Sciences, was dismissed from the same institute. He was guilty of nothing other than the fact that he was acquainted with Alexander Solzhenitsyn, and that one day, having gone to the latter's dacha when Solzhenitsyn was not at home, he ran into some KGB agents who were either searching the premises or setting up a stakeout. Gorlov was duly beaten and then threatened that if he didn't keep his mouth shut things would go badly with him. But he did not keep mum, and the incident became known. Naturally, he began to have trouble on the job, and ultimately he was dismissed by means of a secret vote. He had worked at the institute for fifteen years.

Personal Experience

My personal experience is likewise rather edifying. In August 1973, when the libelous press campaign against Academician Sakharov was launched, I issued a brief statement in his defense. Within a week, I found myself at a general meeting of the institute's staff—a meeting called in order to condemn my unworthy act. Some of the speakers protested that a person like me could not be head of a laboratory and in charge of other people. (The fact was that for some six months, owing to an oversight by the authorities when I was being transferred from one institute to another, I had—*mirabile dictu!*—been head of a laboratory.) Others demanded that I be thrown out of the institute altogether, since there was no place for me in a healthy collective. One elderly lady exclaimed with great feeling: "I've seen how all the students go to him! Tell me, Comrades: How can we entrust the education of our children to a man like him?"

The resolution censuring my behavior was passed unanimously. Of the 300 persons at the meeting, not a single one voted against it, or even abstained.

Shortly thereafter, I was informed by the Sovetskaya Rossiya Publishing House, where my book, *The Phenomenon of Science,* was being prepared for publication (it had already been set in type), that work on the book had been stopped because of "shortage of paper." The manuscript of another book of mine, *Programming in the Refal Language,* which had been sent to the Nauka Publishing House, was at that time in the hands of a publisher's reader. He returned it to the publishing house, declaring that he was "not entitled morally" to evaluate a book by an author with my political leanings.

Moral and political unity . . .

When I was censured at the meeting of the institute's staff, the voting was by a show of hands. But I have also had some experience with a secret ballot. In September 1973, shortly after the meeting, my laboratory was disbanded; but I remained at the institute as a senior research associate. For the next few months I worked undisturbed, and I had hopes that I could combine my dissent with my professional work. Not at all. In the spring of 1974, the question of my confirmation in the position I then held came up before the institute's learned council. At first the matter was postponed: apparently my superiors didn't know what to do, and were asking for instructions. Then the departmental triangle (*treugolnik*)[13] was instructed to prepare an evaluation report on me.

The professional part of the report, written within the department, had only good things to say about me. But the last paragraph of the report as a whole read as follows: "At the same time, being closely associated with Academician Sakharov, V. F. Turchin in September 1973 issued a statement to members of the bourgeois press in which he justified Sakharov's behavior. This act by V. F. Turchin was unanimously censured by the institute's staff."

The session at which the learned council took up the question of my confirmation was held in July 1974. The deputy director, who chaired the session, did not read the professional part of the evaluation report on me. He read only that final paragraph. Then he expressed the hope that the members of the learned council would "draw the correct conclusions" from the final paragraph. Not a single word more was said on the subject. There was no discussion of my work. Although a month earlier, at a departmental session, it had been resolved to recommend to the learned council that I be confirmed in my position, the head of the department, who was present at the session of the learned council as a member, did not feel it necessary to rise and convey this information. The result of the balloting was: five for confirmation, and nineteen against. So I was fired.

When I told an acquaintance of mine about this incident, he exclaimed: "Ah! Five people out of twenty-four voted against firing you! Here, give me your slide rule for a moment. That's almost 21 percent. You have far more than the usual number of decent people at that institute!"

After my dismissal I tried to get work at several other research institutes, but without success. The pattern was always the same: the head of a laboratory would want to hire me; but when the matter reached the level of the Party Bureau and the director of the institute, the answer was always no. Sometimes I was told: "Now if you'd just promise to behave differently, we could try to hire you." And at one place a man who wanted to take me on told me despondently that the director and several others who were interested in me as a specialist had said that nonetheless they were against hiring me. They didn't want any trouble.

Let me conclude this tale of academicians with one little anecdote. An acquaintance of mine asked Academician Z if he could help me get a job. Now, not only had I known Academician Z for more than fifteen years but we had collaborated on research projects. His reply, however, was clear and concise: "No. Those people are against society."

That's the way things are.

The Heretics[14]

> I'm an unacknowledged brother—
> a heretic in the family of my people.
>
> Osip Mandelstam

I have no illusions about the matter: my conflict is not merely one with the authorities but one with society as well, and perhaps even more with the latter. That is not a conflict of purposes or opinions. I want pretty much the same things, and look at things in pretty much the same way, as other people in the circle to which I belong. That is a conflict of values. But it is our system, our hierarchy of values—what we regard as more important, and what we regard as less important—that ultimately determines how we act. Whether we go with the majority or fall into heresy depends upon that system of values.

It is not that I object to heresy as such. Every nation, and humanity as a whole, needs its heretics. It needs people who do not behave like the majority, who experiment on themselves (and on those close to them, alas!). Without them, there would be no development—no forward movement. Everything new has its beginnings among a minority. After all, even the proof of a theorem is conceived in the head of an individual before it becomes an acknowledged fact. For me, dissent, like my scientific work, is a part of my lifelong task.

In and of itself, the existence of heretics is natural. And it is evident that people who violate prevalent norms of behavior cannot count on having an easy life in society. That, too, is natural. But the line that divides Soviet dissidents from society is unnatural. In order to be labelled a heretic it suffices merely that you refuse to lie (if only by remaining silent), or that you speak out just once for an innocent person who is being tormented before your very eyes. And even less is required for you to be labelled a quasi-dissident and suspect: a spirited remark or a refusal to be a part of vigorous, systematic obscurantism. And this in the twentieth century, when (so it would seem) the basic principles of humanism and the rights of the individual have long since been recognized by the civilized world!

The humanists of the sixteenth century were no doubt sustained by the conviction that they were blazing the trail to a new social order. But the Soviet dissidents are merely calling upon people to remember truisms. They are merely trying to build defenses against the impending darkness.

Everybody Knows About Everything

An American once said to me, as the two of us were discussing the influence of technology on societal life: "In America we feel that technological progress in the Soviet Union is of great importance in making society more democratic. For example, today your country is not producing enough automobiles to meet the demand. But production will be increased. Then anybody will be able to get into a car and drive around the country. And he will see, for instance, that in many cities there is no meat, and that in general the newspapers print lies."

I must say that I found this idea amusing. It is by no means necessary to have a car in order to realize that the newspapers print lies. Everyone has eyes and ears, plus friends and relatives in different parts of the country. Basically, everybody knows about everything. Everyone knows that there is no meat; that the newspapers lie; that the words about freedom and democracy are pure rubbish; and that in fact the leaders do whatever they deem fit. Also, that you have to sit still and keep quiet or you'll end up in a labor camp; that blue-collar workers in America live better than professors do here; and much else besides.

All of us know about everything; and we all admit that we do. This fact marks the difference between totalitarianism's third stage—that of consciousness—and its second, or informational, stage. Today the emphasis is on accepting the inevitable: on the necessity of the regime. Just as in Stalin's time there was a tacit understanding between the regime and the citizens that the latter supposedly "didn't know about anything," today it is mutually understood that the citizens supposedly "can't do anything," although they know about almost everything. In official jargon this is called the "Communist consciousness of the Soviet people."

Official Soviet phraseology is quite an amusing thing: It does not directly and overtly employ words in a sense opposite to what they really mean; rather, there is a shift in the meaning—a shift that takes place not on the surface but at a certain depth. The complex, abstract concepts presuppose the existence of a kind of ladder, or hierarchy, of concepts by means of which they are decoded and deciphered down to the level of simple, observed reality. At some halfway point in this hierarchy, the meaning changes into its opposite, which results in a shift in the concept being deciphered. Orwellian doublethink, so typical of totalitarianism, becomes possible because the conversion of meaning takes place not on the surface but at a deeper level. Words crucial to the life of society are used in two senses: "theoretical" (the basic, unslanted meaning) and "practical" (the slanted meaning). The theoretical sense has positive emotional connotations but, alas, no relationship to reality. The "practical" sense accurately reflects reality. Of this is born a certain hybrid—or centaur—that totalitarians successfully use in their thinking.

According to the theory, "Communist consciousness" means free choice of the Communist ideology in a free society—as the result of competition among ideas where there is free access to information and to opposing viewpoints. Actually, Communist consciousness is a mentality formed under the pressure of a monstrous machine for propaganda and violence, so that one must extract with difficulty each crumb of information, all the while in constant dread of arrest. What is of interest here, however, is not the difference between the theoretical and the practical meanings of Communist consciousness, but their similarity. When we recall how hideous was the terrorism under Stalin and compare it with the way things are today, we can still say that today Soviets accept totalitarianism voluntarily and consciously. Therein lies the tragedy.

The authorities still have the same panicky fear of information that they had before. Blocking the exchange of information is still, of course, one of their most important tasks, and a foundation stone of totalitarianism; but today the authorities know that, given the "Communist consciousness" of the masses, no serious threat is posed if a few droplets of information leak out. What does in fact pose a threat, what does influence people's consciousness, is an idea—so the authorities give the top priority to maintaining an ideational vacuum.

In 1974, the *Herald of the Russian Christian Student Movement*, a Russian-language journal published in France, printed an article signed "XY." The author analyzed, among other things, the causes in the drop in *samizdat* circulation as compared to the late 1960s. The suggested explanation, with which I am in total agreement, was that in the 1960s, the wave of *samizdat* writings consisted mostly of exposés dealing both with the Stalin era and with the contemporary one. Now that wave has passed: society has had its fill of "self-exposés." We need new ideas. And ideas, unlike mere information, require a dialogue. But *samizdat* conditions are much less favorable for fostering ideas than for exposing evils.

Totalitarian consciousness is primarily nihilistic and corrupt. In combatting totalitarianism, the aim is not destruction but creation; it is not a struggle *against* but a struggle *for*. Actually, there is nothing to destroy; everything is in ruins already. We need positive ideals. We need the belief that they can be realized. We need a program for the gradual democratization of society.

We all know that it's hard to build and easy to destroy, but to prevent building is easier yet. That is what the state's huge, powerful machine for propaganda and punishment is used for. No wonder the obscurantists feel so confident. The past few years have witnessed a systematic attack on culture. The era of "Khrushchevian liberalism" is now remembered as a kind of golden age when, occasionally, *books were still published*. Since then, there has been a fundamental, basic purge of all institutions having to do with the mass media. Every fresh idea is viewed as potentially dangerous, and is ruthlessly excised. One might ask whether it makes sense to be so vigilant about details when a Soviet citizen can hear much more dangerous things on the radio—on the *Deutsche Welle* broadcasts, for instance.

This does make sense, however, because a nonconformist remark made by a living person and appearing in print, may legitimately seem to be a rallying point for dissidents. A special breed of people, professional obscurantists, have been given the job of seeing to it that this kind of thing does not occur. And they know their job, these scorched-earth strategists, experts in high-vacuum technique.

Marxist-Leninist Theory

But what are the thoughts of "Soviet man"? Is the Marxism-Leninism that is officially preached his real ideology? Or is the former only the ideology of the Party-government hierarchy? Or does the hierarchy itself perhaps not believe in what it preaches in millions of printings and broadcasts over the radio in all the languages of the world?

In the Soviet Union, Marxism-Leninism is called an advanced and uniquely scientific theory of social development. Whatever answers might be given to the questions I have just asked, one thing can be said at the outset: Marxism-Leninism is plainly not a theory in the sense of making predictions and planning; and no one regards it as such. Even the Party bureaucrats are not that naïve.

A middle-ranking acquaintance of mine told the following true-life story. He had received a promotion and with it a new office. The office had been renovated, and the newly painted walls had of course to be adorned with portraits of the "chieftains." My acquaintance went to the storeroom, where the first thing that met his eye was a portrait of Marx. He gave instructions for it to be hung in his office. The next day, he was visited at his office by his boss, a man very high up in the hierarchy. When the latter saw the portrait of Marx, he made a wry face. "Ugh! Why did you put up a portrait of that Jew? You should've told me, and I'd have given you one of Lenin."

The interesting thing in this anecdote is not the anti-Semitism (that speaks for itself) but the fact that in it one gets a glimpse of the contempt for the doctrine founded by "that Jew." A Soviet bureaucrat is above all a realist; and as such he knows full well that the Party's pragmatic policies have nothing to do with Marxist theory. As for the boss's attitude toward the portrait, it was determined by strictly human factors. Marx was a Jew—an outsider. Lenin was one of us—the founder of the state.

It is a curious fact that foreign observers—even those who are very familiar with life in the Soviet Union—are inclined to overestimate the role of theoretical principles or dogmas in determining the specific practical steps taken by Soviet leaders. Recently, I read an article by Robert Conquest,[15] the author of *The Great Terror*, one of the first basic studies of the Stalin era. On the whole it is a very interesting article, with an analysis of relations between the Soviet Union and the West which I feel is absolutely correct. But it seems to me that Conquest overrates the role of theory. He writes:

> . . . No one, I imagine, thinks that Brezhnev recites the *Theses on Feuerbach* every night before retiring. The point is rather, that "Marxist-Leninist" belief is the sole justification for him and his regime—and further, not simply belief in a particular political theory, but belief in the transcendental, overriding importance of that political theory. As George Kennan has remarked: "It is not so much the actual content of the ideology . . . as the absolute value attached to it."

True enough. But then he says:

> But we can in fact document—and without much difficulty—the attachment to actual dogma of the Soviet leadership. The invasion of Czechoslovakia was a nota-

> ble example of doctrinal discipline. Another striking example was the extraordinary and clearly long-considered advice given to the Syrian Communists in 1972, and leaked by nationalist members of the local leadership. In two separate sets of conversations with Soviet politicians and theoreticians respectively, even the former group, two of whom have been identified as Suslov and Ponomarev in person, advised in the most scholastic terms on the impossibility, according to Marxist principles, of recognizing the existence of "an Arab nation." Or, to take a more important matter, the Soviet agricultural system is based on, and rendered grossly inefficient by, nothing but dogma.

I can in no way agree with this. Doubtless the reply made to the Syrians with respect to "an Arab nation" was pondered and discussed for a long time. But there is even less doubt that the discussion was conducted on a strictly political plane, the issue being whether the integration of the Arabs would serve the interests of the Soviet Union at the moment. Obviously, they reached the conclusion that it would not. Having done so, they told some *apparatchiki* to formulate that conclusion "in the most scholastic terms," and to round up the requisite quotations, etc. In the case of Czechoslovakia, the Soviet leaders were intent upon avoiding a contagious example—likewise from a political point of view. As for the *kolkhoz* system, it was set up by Stalin to serve a very practical purpose: to centralize the administration and sweat the peasantry. And in its social aspect, the system is not novel: it is what the Soviet Marxists call "the Asiatic mode of production."

Marxism-Leninism is taught in each and every college, and the students' attitude toward that wisdom tells us a great deal. They all know that they shouldn't try to *understand* it; that all they have to do is say the words they are told to say. Sometimes, however, a conscientious novice will tackle the subject seriously, as he would a science. He then finds inconsistencies and discrepancies with reality. So he starts asking the teacher questions that the latter either answers in a confused and incomprehensible manner, or doesn't answer at all. For the others in the class this provides an amusing diversion from the boring lessons in the "social sciences." But this diversion soon comes to an end when the curious student discovers that his curiosity is by no means helping him to get good grades. To the contrary, he gets a reputation for "ideological immaturity"—something that can have very unpleasant consequences. But most often, one of his classmates, wanting to help him, intervenes (spoiling the fun) and tells him the right approach to Marxist-Leninist theory.

Theory and Reality

Is it at all possible to deal with Marxist-Leninist theory when it is in flagrant conflict with reality?

In theory, a proletarian revolution should long ago have taken place in the industrially developed countries, but nothing of the kind has happened; and, as is plain to everyone, it is not likely to happen in the foreseeable future.

In theory, the working class in a capitalist society should be constantly in a state of both relative and absolute impoverishment. In reality, the living standard of blue-collar workers has constantly risen; and it is much higher than in the so-called socialist countries.

In theory (and this is a famous dictum of Lenin's) it is labor productivity that in the final analysis determines the progressiveness of the sociopolitical system and ensures the ultimate victory of socialism. In reality, productivity in the Soviet Union is much lower than in the advanced capitalist countries. Soviet industrial productivity is at least two or three times lower than it is in the United States, and in agriculture it is at least ten times lower.

In theory, people are groaning under the yoke of capitalism in West Germany and yearn to be in East Germany. In reality, millions of East Germans have fled Westward, and only machine guns and barbed wire can stop this exodus.

In theory, the freest and most democratic country in the world is the Soviet Union. In reality? One is reluctant to say anything there. "Everybody knows about everything."

Over and over again, we have seen Marxist theory used to justify completely opposite conclusions: Stalin discovered that as one got closer to socialism, the class struggle, instead of diminishing, grew more intense; Lenin's concept of breaking world capitalism's chain at its weakest link became Lenin's concept of peaceful coexistence between countries with differing social systems, and Lenin's policy of a new "conscious" attitude toward work was transformed into Lenin's principle of monetary incentives.

Only someone stupid or naïve would actually try to find answers to specific problems in such a theory. And the Soviet leaders, whatever else they may or may not be, are certainly not naïve. They do not expect Marxism-Leninism to predict anything, or to give answers to their problems.

It would nevertheless be a grave mistake to conclude that the huge sums of money spent on implanting Marxist-Leninist theory in the minds of all Soviet citizens are spent to no purpose. And the intensive training in that theory that is undergone by workers in the Party apparatus does have a definite effect on them. The relationship between theory and practice is by no means a simple one.

Every theory, before it is used to predict events in the world around us, gives us a conceptual apparatus—a language for describing reality. Whether or not the predictions later turn out to be accurate, the language of the theory remains with us; and we see reality through the prism of that language and those concepts.

I again quote, with complete agreement this time, from the aforementioned article by Robert Conquest:

> The Marxist-Leninist language used by the ruling Party is not merely some sort of formula. It is the only way in which the leaders are able to represent to themselves the

> phenomena with which they deal. "Each language cuts out its own segment of reality. We live our life as we speak it . . .": this fairly typical comment by a prominent student of language (George Steiner) is certainly applicable to the use in politics, from birth onward, of a particular political dialect. Soviet leaders are, it seems clear, simply unable to think in any other categories.

And not just the leaders, unfortunately. This language and way of thinking are foisted upon all citizens of the totalitarian state, from the day they are born.

In the functions performed by Marxist-Leninist theory in the Soviet state, one can distinguish between a formal aspect and a substantive one. In the twentieth century, a state simply cannot get along without a "theory." After all, one has to say and write *something* to explain to the citizens, in one way or another, what is happening. A state ideology which is sole and exclusive is an indispensable element of totalitarianism. It is a symbol of faith. Its unquestioning acceptance is Heinrich Böll's "Communion with the Host of the Beast." In this respect, the ideology serves as a kind of military uniform distinguishing the in-group from the outsiders. Here, the content of the theory plays no role. It is this formal function of theory that is reflected in the remark by George Kennan that Robert Conquest quoted above.

But there is more to Marxism-Leninism than just its formal function. In terms of its content, too, this theory is eminently suitable, and necessary, to totalitarianism. In particular, I should like to stress the importance of historical materialism's basic principle: "Social being determines consciousness." This is the cornerstone upon which the totalitarian mentality is erected. It is the theoretical justification for the easy submission of the Soviet man to this social order, for his belief that he "cannot change it anyway." Later, we shall come back to this aspect of Marxism to examine it in more detail.

It would seem that the clear contradiction between theory and reality should discredit the former in the eyes of the Soviet people. This contradiction does not of course vitiate the formal aspect of the theory. But what about the substantive aspect? How can one reconcile an awareness that the theory contradicts reality with a belief in the theory as a whole? Is this not in itself pathological?

In justice to "Soviet man," it must be acknowledged that such is not the case. For with the exception of purely mathematical ones, no theory is completely formalized. A theory contains a hierarchy of concepts and principles; and the transition from the higher levels to the lower ones is by no means always effected via unique, strictly formal conclusions or computations. To the contrary, in going from the higher principles down to directly observed phenomena, one must make additional assumptions, approximations, etc., and one must allow for error. For example, when a physicist discovers a discrepancy between the results of his experiment and the theoretical predictions, he does not promptly raze the whole edifice of theoretical physics. First he checks to see whether he has not made a simple arithmetical error in his calculations. Then he tries to find out whether all the factors affecting the results of the experiment were taken into account. Next, he questions the accuracy of his simplifications (which, as a theoretical physicist, he almost certainly used in his computations), the accuracy of the results obtained by others in their experiments (which results, likewise, he almost certainly used), etc.

If this is the way things are even in physics, what can we expect of a social science? It is hardly surprising that a conflict with reality on the lowest level of the hierarchy does not lead to the immediate destruction, in people's minds, of the entire hierarchy.

The Ideological Hierarchy

In the Soviet ideological system, which taken together is called Marxism-Leninism, one can distinguish the following four levels.

1. *The philosophical level.* Dialectical materialism. Matter as primary, consciousness as secondary. Development as a conflict between opposites. Historical materialism. Social existence determines social consciousness.

2. *The socioeconomic level.* The doctrine of social classes. The class struggle. Socioeconomic formations. The inevitable transition from capitalism to socialism by means of a proletarian revolution. (Recent emendation: the revolution may be peaceful.) Dictatorship of the proletariat.

3. *History of the CPSU and the Soviet State.* The necessity for a Party of the new, Leninist type. Democratic centralism. Party history in detail (polished to a high sheen, needless to say, and transformed with a view to the interests of the moment). The October Revolution of 1917 as the revolution predicted by Marx. Mankind's age-old dream come true.

4. *Current policies.* Armed with Marxist-Leninist theory, which alone is scientific, the heroic Soviet people is performing glorious feats of labor under the wise leadership of the Communist Party of the Soviet Union and its Leninist (?) Central Committee. With a firm tread, . . . etc.

I am completely convinced that a great part of the Soviet people sees the falsehood in the propaganda of the fourth level, and reacts to it accordingly. But I am equally convinced that a majority in the Soviet Union accept the third level entirely. Tentatively, this mentality might be characterized as drawing a line between Lenin and Stalin—between principles and their implementation. The principles may well be valid, but because of various mistakes ("excesses," bad people, etc.) things don't turn out very well in practice. This is the mentality of mass man, who has not learned (who, indeed, is prevented from learning) how to make his own analysis of the connection between principles and reality.

A minority have managed to make such an analysis. They have thought seriously about the history of their country—and what is happening around them—and have come to reject the third level of the official ideological hierarchy. There are undoubtedly millions of such people, although only a very few of them have reached the point of deciding that they must reevaluate the principles of the second and first levels. Especially favorable is the status of the principle which holds that "social existence determines consciousness"—totalitarian Marxism-Leninism's holy of holies. I have often had occasion to realize the tenacity with which that principle clings to its purchase in the minds even of highly educated people. It is so persuasive because of its seeming "realism" and "scientificness." The opposing viewpoint seems like unfounded idealism—like wishful thinking. Also, there is a special kind of screening of the first level by the second, which proclaims the noble goals of building a just society, and the possibility of attaining those goals—even the necessity of their final triumph, as if it flowed from that same principle of historical materialism.

The concept of screening is in general very important in understanding the way the ideological hierarchy functions. The lower levels serve as screens for the upper levels in the sense that they absorb some of a person's "rejection energy." A person who rejects certain ideas accepted in his milieu when confronted by the facts usually feels it necessary to prove to others (and to himself) that he is rejecting those ideas only because of that pressure from the facts and not because he revels in rejection for its own sake. Hence he wants to stop somewhere. His "rejection energy" is exhausted as he moves up the ladder from specific facts to more abstract concepts. The propagandistic function of the fourth level is to screen out as much rejection energy as possible. The result, paradoxical as it may seem, is that falsehood does not so much weaken the theory as strengthen it.

The words of the fourth level—the soldier-words—charge into the fray by the millions. No one believes them. And without ever reaching their goal, they perish in huge numbers, seemingly in vain. But behind the heaps of their corpses, one catches sight of more important words: the officer-words; the general-words. And it is for the sake of these, the highest-ranking words, that the entire ideological hierarchy is built. These general words (and the concepts behind them) indoctrinate the totalitarian masses. The process is not outwardly discernible but it does go on—constantly and unremittingly.

But let us return to our comparison between the Marxist-Leninist ideological hierarchy and theoretical physics. We have already noted the similarity in the hierarchical structure, and in the indirect, tortuous pathway that connects principles with observed facts. The difference, however, is in the purpose for which the theories were built. A physical theory is built in order to predict facts. Hence an accumulation of discrepancies between the theory and the facts necessarily leads, sooner or later, to a restructuring of the theory at all levels. But the ideological system of a totalitarian state is built for its own sake—in order to preserve its basic principles. Hence a discrepancy between it and reality cannot even begin to change it. What we have here is therefore a compound of the worst elements of theories in general. This theory does not have the capacity to predict events, yet it imposes a conceptual apparatus that is dead and incapable of development. Marxist-Leninist theory is a mannikin that takes up the space a living being should occupy. It is the sawdust that is stuffed into people's heads so that no room is left for living ideas.

Religious people, however, reject the Marxist-Leninist ideology on principle—from the top downward. They constitute what might be called an ideological minority, although a rather large one. According to official statistics, there were 32 million believers in the Soviet Union in 1974.[16] All of them are being harassed in one way or another. Especially harsh persecution is reserved for those who try to prevent informers and other persons bearing the state's stamp of approval from infiltrating their groups. The believers' struggle for their rights elicits sympathy and support from all those defending the basic rights of the individual, and the courage of many, as well as their persistent refusal to abandon their own convictions, set an example for the population in general. The existence of minorities (whether ideological or national) who are defending their rights is a significant social phenomenon. But in terms of a worldview, their influence is slight. And contrary to what is sometimes claimed, I do not see that it has grown.

It is natural to judge others in terms of oneself; despite all the inadequacies of this approach, there is no getting away from it. Although I share many of the Christian ideas, recognize their importance for modern civilization, and revere deeply the person of Christ, I cannot understand how, in our time, Christianity *as a whole* can be accepted as a faith and a system of thought. Having only just rejected one dogmatic, obsolete system, how can one accept another system which, although more worthy, is even more dogmatic and obsolete? It seems to me that in order to do this, one would have to do some kind of violence to oneself—perhaps of a masked or unconscious variety. And the same thing of course applies to other traditional religious systems.

No, the only alternative to the counterfeit state ideology is to analyze it from the position of a critical, scientific worldview, and to create positive ideals based on that same position. The first part of this task is relatively simple, while the second incredibly difficult. Indeed, the very phrase "positive ideals" suggests something obsolete and unsuccessful. On the other hand, even modest results in this direction count for a lot.

Does Social Existence Determine Consciousness?

Many people are won over by the apparent "sober realism" of this basic principle of historical materialism. Even people who oppose Marxist totalitarianism sometimes find this principle to be the least controversial aspect of Marxism.[17] Yet that principle—along with the concepts of the individual, of society, and of history, that derive from it—constitutes the very cornerstone of totalitarianism.

> Lenin writes:
>
> Social consciousness *reflects* social existence: that is what Marx's doctrine consists in. . . . Consciousness in general reflects existence: that is the general principle of all materialism. Not to see its direct and *indissoluble* connection with the tenet of historical materialism—that social consciousness *reflects* social existence—is something quite impossible.[18]

But what does materialism consist in? According to Marxism-Leninism, philosophers of all times and all nations have been—and always will be—faced with the question: Which is primary, matter or consciousness? If you say it is matter, you are a materialist and a good guy, because your answer is correct and scientific. If you say that consciousness is primary, you are an idealist and a bad guy. And if you say you don't know, you are an agnostic and likewise a bad guy.

To a philosopher with a modern, scientific worldview, the very question—in the form in which it is posed by Marxism-Leninism—is meaningless. But it doesn't follow that it shouldn't be asked. Meaningless questions *should* be asked. But then they should be analyzed, so that one can find out what makes them meaningless. The greatest achievement of philosophy in the twentieth century consists precisely in the depth analysis of abstract concepts which had previously seemed to be somehow primordial, and to be taken for granted. This school of thought, whose founders include the physicist Ernst Mach, is totally rejected by Marxism-Leninism. In his notorious *Materialism and Empirio-criticism,* Lenin excommunicates Mach and his followers from socialism. To this very day, for the Communists there are no greater enemies than the Machists. A Leninist does not need critical philosophy. All he needs is to look his superior in the eye and reply (without any doubts or anxieties): "Yes, matter is primary, Comrade General."

In rejecting the critical analysis of concepts, Marxism-Leninism has remained on the level of the naïve realism of earlier centuries. But it doesn't need anything more, because naïve realism is perfectly adequate for propaganda. In fact, it is the most convenient angle of vision for propaganda. Philosophical concepts are used in an inaccurate, approximate, and distorted sense. They are emotionally charged with associations from daily life; and in this form they serve very well to inculcate "class-consciousness" in the masses.

And yet, if by "materialism" we mean a program for investigating those phenomena we call "spiritual" through phenomena that we call "material," I am all for such materialism; because in that approach lies the essence of science. And I can also agree with the Marxist idea that the scientific approach to the phenomena of spiritual life (and in particular to consciousness) means regarding them as *forms of the movement of matter.*

But what connection is there between materialism in this sense and the basic principle of Marxist historical materialism? None whatsoever. We are dealing with two groups of phenomena: social existence and social consciousness. Both are associated with humanity—with our bodies and our minds. And both must be regarded as forms of the movement of matter. But by no means do the phenomena of one group determine the phenomena of the other.

In the passage quoted above, Lenin links historical materialism to the tenet that consciousness *reflects* existence. And, true enough, it *does* reflect existence. But to proceed from that to the thesis that *existence determines conscious-*

ness, one must make a much bigger assumption; namely, that consciousness does not simply *reflect* existence (i.e., that it comprises some kind of reflection) but that it *is* a reflection—and nothing more. What kind of idea is that? It is an idea according to which the entire so-called spiritual life of man is merely an aggregate of reflections—reflexes; i.e., direct, one-to-one responses to the stimulation of nerve-endings by the environment. Is such a view worth refuting? In our day, not even a Marxist-Leninist would publicly subscribe to it. He would call such a view a "vulgar-materialist" one. Yet on the sly, it has been made the basis of a philosophy of history.

It was Descartes who introduced the concept of reflexes. But for him, reflexes merely indicated the structure of our corporeal machine. The human being, according to him, also had a *soul.* Descartes even set forth some definite ideas as to which part of the brain is the organ of the soul. By way of emphasizing the difference between reflexes and the soul, he gave the following example. Let us suppose that someone raises his hand before our eyes, as if to strike us. Although we know he is doing it only as a joke, and has no intention of harming us, it is still hard for us not to close our eyes.

> And this shows that it is not by the agency of the soul that they close, since it is against our will, which is the only—or at any rate the principal—function of the soul. But it is because the machine of our body is so constituted that the movement of that hand toward our eyes excites another movement in our brain, which conducts the animal spirits into the muscles which cause the eyelids to close.[19]

If we reject the existence of the soul as "idealism and priestly superstition" (a favorite expression of Lenin's), we are left with nothing but reflexes.

Thinking in the Light of Cybernetics

What is the soul?
A pensive homunculus.

Bulat Okudzhava

René Descartes was a scientist. A scientist builds models of phenomena that are little understood and have been little studied, making use of phenomena that have been better studied. But when he is confronted by a phenomenon for which he can build no model that is in any way convincing, he says: "Wait a minute! I can't say anything sensible about this." And so, in order to describe such phenomena he uses the same words and concepts that were used before, and that make no claim to being scientific.

For example, "soul."

A fine word.

Since the time of Descartes, science has made considerable progress in understanding how people think. And even though our models of the thought process will in the future make scientists smile, just as we smile at some of Descartes's mechanical models, what we already know is very substantial as regards the question at hand.

Even as recently as Pavlov's time, the reflex was, to all intents and purposes, the only scientific concept used to describe the behavior of living organisms. Today, however, cybernetics uses several new concepts. The most important of these are the goal, feedback, and regulation.

When one brings a spoonful of soup to one's mouth, one's brain registers (or "reflects") not only the current situation—the position of the spoon—but also the ideal, desired situation: the spoon in the mouth. That is the *goal*. The mechanism that makes possible the achievement of the goal may be schematized as follows. The current situation is compared with the ideal one; as a result, nervous impulses are triggered which contract the muscles in such a way as to bring the current situation closer to the ideal one. The altered situation is perceived by the sense organs, and again compared with the ideal one. Thus the flow of information comes full circle. This is called *feedback*. The continuous correction of the action with a view to the goal, by means of feedback, is called *regulation*.

What material structures in the brain store the goals? How is the comparison of the goal with the current situation effected? How does the brain fix the algorithm for generating the nervous impulses as a result of the comparison? About all this we know next to nothing. Beyond doubt, however, these processes are effected by means of certain material formations; and we can envisage these formations as kinds of programs or *plans* of behavior,[20] by analogy with the program stored in the memory of a computer.

Another important concept of cybernetics essential to describe behavior is that of the *hierarchy*. The goals and plans of behavior form a hierarchy; in it the more complex and general goals require, for their achievement, the setting and achievement of several simpler, subsidiary goals. The corresponding plans of behavior comprise—or bring into play—simpler plans, just as a computer program may activate several auxiliary programs.

To return to our example, before eating the spoonful of soup, one must first learn to hold the spoon, to spoon up the soup from the bowl, and to lift the spoon in such a way that the soup does not spill out. The plans for carrying out these actions are constituent parts of the plan "eat soup." In its turn, the eating of the soup is a part of a more complex plan. One must first make it; and for that one must have foodstuffs, to obtain which one must have money. In order to have money, one must work; and in order to work, one must first study for or be trained to do the job. In this way we reach the goals and plans of the highest level.

As one moves up in the hierarchy of goals and plans, the goals become more and more general. The same thing applies to plans of behavior; their effectuation requires increasingly general and abstract concepts. As the time scale expands, the spatial scale expands correspondingly. When you are dashing to catch a bus that has not yet left a bus stop, and your only goal is to get there in time to board the bus, you think of nothing else. Your plan involves seconds or minutes. But when you are planning on a scale of hours and days, your interests and plans are indivisible from those of your family and other persons close to you. Plans involving years and decades are indivisible from group and national interests; and when you think on the scale of generations, you must think of humankind as a whole.

That the brain fixes goals creates, *ipso facto,* a wide breach in the idea that "social existence determines consciousness." A bird starting to build a nest is guided by its own instinct; as yet there is no "existence" of the nest. But even more important is the question of the genesis of goals and plans. I shall examine that question in the spirit of the approach I took as a basis for my book *The Phenomenon of Science*—that is, on the basis of the concept of the "metasystem transition."

The Metasystem Transition

The language and concepts of cybernetics are becoming a part of general education, like arithmetic; and I think this is a very promising thing. I shall therefore offer a concise presentation, based upon the fuller discussion that has appeared in *The Phenomenon of Science.*[21]

Let us, then, imagine a certain system S. Let us further imagine that a certain number of systems S, or systems of the S type, are joined into a whole, and are equipped with a system that controls them. The system S′ that is formed in this manner we call a *metasystem* as compared with the system S. The metasystem S′ contains a number of systems S as its subsystems. Thus it has the means of *controlling* those subsystems in the broadest sense: coordinating their functions, modifying them, generating them, etc. The transition from the system S to the metasystem S' we call the *metasystem transition.*

The account given here concerns only the structural aspect. Very often, we do not know the detailed cybernetic structure of the complex systems we are dealing with, but we can observe the external manifestations of the activity or functioning of these systems. How does the metasystem transition look to us in its functional aspect? Let the system S manifest a certain activity A. If we observe the activity of the metasystem S', we shall find a new type of activity A' which consists in *controlling the activity A.*

In *The Phenomenon of Science,* I view the metasystem transition as the basic unit or *quantum* of evolution. All qualitative steps along the path of evolution are metasystem transitions of greater or lesser scope. Under the action of natural selection, all existing formations may be improved within certain limits by means of small quantitative changes. But radical shifts in the structure of a living organism can take place in only one way: via a metasystem transition whereby the existing formations are used by nature as building blocks for a new structure. Natural selection is of course operative here, too. (Nature always proceeds by trial and error.) But now it is directed toward building the metasystem S' out of the subsystem S. What is formed is a new level of the hierarchy of control—a new level of the organization of organic—or inorganic—matter! Because man, in designing and making more complex the things he creates, uses the same method—the only one in existence.

Examples of the metasystem transition include the development of multicellular organisms from single-celled ones; the formation of a nervous system to control movement; the transition from the unconditioned to the conditioned reflex; the making of tools, plus the making of tools to make tools, etc.; the formation of societies from individuals; the division of government into legislative, executive, and judicial branches; the automatic machine tool; the development of the concept of proof in mathematics; and the development of the mathematical theory of proofs in mathematics (metamathematics).

Let us compare the conditioned reflex with the unconditioned reflex. In the case of the unconditioned reflex, associations of representations[22] are inborn and fixed; they do not depend upon the individual experience of the animal. In the case of the conditioned reflex, the associations are controlled; they appear and disappear as a result of the environment's action on the given subject. The process of *associating* arises. This is a metasystem transition.

The transition from higher animals to human beings is yet another metasystem transition, and one of decisive importance: the capacity to *control associating* arises. In higher animals, *associations* are controlled but the process of *associating* (the formation of new associations) is not. (I.e., associations in the animal's brain arise according to certain fixed laws governed by the actions in the environment.) But a human being has the ability to create new associations at will. This ability is manifested as imagination, the development of language, planning, remembering, and self-teaching. In short, it is what we usually call *thinking*. It is this ability which makes it possible for humans to overcome the absolute power of instinct.

We Are Free

As the ability to learn increases, instincts become more and more abstract, and an increasingly greater share of behavior plans are learned by the living organism, either via imitation or through trial and error. In the case of nonhuman animals, however, instinct remains the supreme judge and director of behavior. Every hierarchy has its supreme level. An animal's goals and behavior plans are instinctive and cannot be changed in its lifetime, but, only through the species' evolution.

Humans are the first living beings capable, on their own, of setting their own goals and elaborating plans—including those on the highest level. Of course we learn most behavior plans by imitating our elders. But in the course of thinking about those plans we may reject them, modify them, or create new ones from scratch. And those new behavior plans may run directly counter to the most stable, basic instincts: those of self-preservation and reproduction. Owing to this capacity to control associating, the hierarchy of behavior plans has proven not to be closed—but to be open for experimentation.

We are free. Only humans possess absolute freedom of behavior. We inherit that as other creatures inherit their instincts. Like any other capacity, it may remain undeveloped. And it may be repressed, just as an animal's instincts may be represessed by potent means. But it exists. We *are* free.

The emergence of humanity has opened up a new era in the evolution of life. The trial-and-error method has always been, and still is, the chief instrument of evolution. But whereas before the emergence of man that instrument was used on the carriers of heredity, the genes, and evolution was merely biological, the evolution of human culture has now arisen. This is a process whereby the trials and the errors take place in the imagination and the acts of human beings. We are capable of conscious creativity. We can do what once only nature as a whole could do. Therefore, we bear responsibility for life on this planet—and perhaps in the universe.

What is consciousness? What is will?[23] How can we relate our felt free will (which belongs to the category of "spiritual phenomena") to the physical laws of nature and to our knowledge of the structure of the brain? For the time being, we cannot give intelligible answers to these questions. Hence we cannot deny that we have souls.

The soul exists. And it is indissolubly bound up with the most astounding and most important aspect of the reality we see around us: that aspect which is reflected in the concepts of creativity, of the metasystem transition, of evolution.

The Transposition of the Upper Levels

Let us, however, return to the basic tenet of historical materialism. Social consciousness consists of the most general social norms of behavior, expressed in the most general concepts, and defining what is good and what is bad. In other words, these are plans which, together with the most general plans of biological origin (the instincts of self-preservation and reproduction), make up the highest level in the hierarchy of behavior plans. And what is social existence? It comprises, first of all, the material component of civilization: those objects with which we deal in daily life and in "production." It also comprises definite behavior plans: skills in handling objects; social relations into which we enter in the production process (relations of production); and forms of participation in the process of the distribution of material wealth. In short, these behavior plans may be called *economic*. They too are very general plans; and they may be said to form the second level of the hierarchy, right under the plans on the highest, or *ethical*, level.

What is the relationship between these levels? Can it be said that either of them *determines* the other? Of course not. The relationship between them is one of *control*, as in any hierarchy. Generals, for example, do not "determine" their troops: they do not reproduce them in their own image, or even at their own discretion. They *command* troops. However, this does not mean that they determine each act, each movement, of their soldiers. Command is exercised by way of definite general concepts; and within the limits of the mission, the choice of means is left to the soldiers' own discretion. In just the same way, the general biological and ethical behavior plans "command" the available economic plans, selecting from among them, including or excluding them, or partially modifying them.

But Marxism contends that social existence *determines*

social consciousness. In a recent Soviet textbook on historical materialism, we find:

> Karl Marx and Friedrich Engels demonstrated the total untenability of those idealistic views of society that had previously held sway in sociology. They proved scientifically that the chief and decisive aspect of social life is not the ideal but the material factor, and above all the production of material wealth. According to the doctrine of Marxism-Leninism, material production is the basis of, and the decisive force in, social development. And in the final analysis it determines all other aspects of social life. Not only is consciousness not primary with respect to the material life of society: to the contrary, it depends upon the latter, and is determined by it.[24]

Three pages later we find the following curious explanation:

> People's thoughts, desires, and moods arise from, and change in accordance with, their practical requirements. And in the final analysis they depend upon the degree of development of their material life—on their economic status in society.

Thus we have here a transposition of the two upper levels of the hierarchy: it is claimed that those behavior plans which seem to us to be the highest are actually dependent upon the behavior plans—and, in general, upon the practicability—of the economic level. But where is the scientific proof of this very strong claim—a proof allegedly provided by Marx and Engels? Needless to say, we do not find it in the textbook; no such proof exists, of course—nor did it ever exist. The most one can find in the writings of the founders of Marxism, is a reference to certain parallels between the development of material production and the ideas dominant in society.

But these parallels (the existence of which is incontrovertible, and was noted by others before Marx) proves nothing. That ideas and material production are interdependent and develop in a very close relationship with each other is beyond doubt. But the question is: What is the nature of that relationship? No one would deny that the actions of generals largely depend upon—and in some ways are determined by—the kind of troops they have. But does that mean that in the final analysis, the troops command the generals? that the outcome of the battle does not depend upon the general's skill?

It is typical of control relationships that the lower level does not determine but only limits the possibilities. The upper, controlling level determines the choice among various possibilities. Not even the greatest general can defeat an army if he has only one platoon of soldiers. It is only in this trite sense that one can say that existence determines consciousness. As for development, its mainsprings must be sought in the sphere of what controls, not of what is controlled.

In Marxist terminology economic life is called the *base* and the institutions expressiing social consciousness are called the *superstructure*. This terminology is quite acceptable. But why does it follow that the base has a determining significance, whereas the superstructure is something secondary and derivative? Such a conclusion can be drawn only if one limits one's thinking to the medieval categories of substance, quantity and quality, primary and secondary, etc. This is precisely the style of the Marxists' thinking. However, those who think in terms of systems and relationships, upon discovering a base and a superstructure in a complex system, would instead conclude that it is the superstructure which plays the controlling, determinant role. After all, even a person's head is a superstructure above the body! And what is the chief difference between humans and other animals? The details of the digestive apparatus—or the structure of the brain?

As the proverb says, quite correctly: "An empty belly is deaf to learning." But this hardly means that, when you have eaten the brain of an intelligent person, you will acquire that intelligence yourself. Yet the basic tenet of historical materialism does remind one of the savage's naïve belief that the food he eats will act directly on his brain. It is interesting to note that this belief is based not on experience but on outwardly plausible "general considerations." And the same thing applies to historical materialism. There are no facts—only "general considerations."

The influence of economics on politics and ideology—an influence dear to the hearts of Marxists—does of course exist. It may be plain to see or it may be hidden; and to discover this influence is an important task of historians and sociologists. But to raise it to the status of the principle of social development is possible only if one dogmatically refutes the obvious facts.

We eat in order to live; we do not live in order to eat. We know that economic factors impose certain limitations on us. But we also know that we have other—and higher—goals. And we are able to correlate economic goals with them.

"These are pure illusions," the Marxists tell us. "*Really*, all your higher goals are just clever disguises for the interest of the class you belong to."

What a marvelous word is "really"! When someone points to something white and says that "really" it is black and only seems white to you, there is no way you can object. All you can do is try to understand *why*, or *for what purpose*, you are told such a thing. With respect to Marx, the chief question is "why?" With respect to today's Marxist totalitarianism, it is "for what purpose?"

Why

> He was impractical in trivial matters, but practical in great undertakings. Although completely helpless in trying to cope with

> his own little household, Marx was able
> with incomparable talent to recruit and lead
> the army which was to carry out a
> revolution in the world.
>
> Franz Mehring[25]

Marx's basic animus was against the capitalist system of his day. And indeed, there is nothing just or reasonable about a society in which a small element of rich people control the production of material wealth with virtually no checks on their activity, while millions of poor people must sell themselves to the former as manpower, and at the same time lead a life of semi-starvation. Such a society requires a radical overhauling. The means of production, which by Marx's time had taken on a distinctly social character (and were tremendously costly) should be put under the effective control of society. Capitalism should yield to socialism.

But Marx was not the first socialist; nor was he the first revolutionary. He was not the only one to realize that the destitute industrial workers—the proletariat—whose numbers were then constantly growing, constituted a powder keg for revolution. Being "practical in great undertakings," Marx was the first to set himself the task (in order, of course, to "recruit an army") of *proving the inevitability* of a victorious proletarian revolution—of making the proletariat into a people chosen for the mission of blazing a trail to the radiant future. In a famous letter to Joseph Weydemeyer, he writes:

> Now as to myself, no credit is due to me for discovering the existence of classes in modern society or the struggle between them. Long before me bourgeois historians had described the historical development of this class struggle and bourgeois economists, the economic autonomy of the classes. What I did that was new was to prove: (1) that the *existence of classes* is only bound up with *particular historical phases in the development of production,* (2) that the class struggle necessarily leads to

> the *dictatorship of the proletariat,* (3) that this dictatorship itself constitutes only the transition to the *abolition of all classes* and to a *classless society.*[26]

And what kind of proof was to be adduced? *Scientific* proof, needless to say, since no other kind would have been acceptable in the middle of the nineteenth century. But what does it mean to prove something *scientifically?* It means to find some objective law—a law independent of the will of consciousness of human beings, like the law of universal gravitation. And where was such a law to be sought? Why, in economics—to which field the science of Marx's day had just begun to apply its methods. Thus arose "historical materialism," which holds that material production develops in accordance with its own immanent laws, while the will and consciousness of human beings are only its blind instruments. And the development of production "inevitably" leads to (you guessed it) the classless society, where everyone is equal, everything is just, and man is a friend, comrade, and brother to his fellow man. (What wisdom on the part of steam engines, levers of the first and second type, and other hardware!)

Marx's idea is essentially historical determinism and not materialism. Moreover, it is a *nihilistic* determinism which denies that spiritual culture plays a leading role in history. Marx borrowed both of these aspects from the science of his day. But that still does not make Marxism a scientific world-view, since it rejects the most important thing in science: the critical scientific method. In terms of its style of thought, Marxism is a doctrine of the dogmatic religious type.

When one bases one's political activity on the principle which holds that "social existence determines consciousness," one must constantly try to convince oneself and others of the rightness of that principle. As a logical result of that effort, the principle is gradually transformed (in fact, if not in words) into "economics is everything, spiritual culture is nothing." And one becomes a nihilist—an enemy of spiritual culture, and hence of culture in general.

Marxist Nihilism

Many adherents of Marxism are attracted to it because of its positive aspects: the socialist ideals and the determination to find effective methods to realize them. But the nihilistic aspect of Marxism is its most important trait—the one that determines the fate of Marxist political movements. It was this trait that Lenin took as a basis when he transplanted that Western doctrine to Eastern soil. Much was lost during the transplantation, but the Marxist nihilism remained. It yielded monstrous sprouts on the new soil; and it led the Leninist Party to the massive extermination of human beings, and then to its own self-destruction. This matter has been well studied by Russian philosophers who witnessed the rise and development of Russian Marxism: e.g., Nikolai Berdyayev and Simon Frank.

According to Marxist theory, the basis of the entire doctrine is dialectical materialism. From the latter is derived historical materialism, and from it, social and political goals. In the development of Marxism, however, the actual movement was in the opposite direction: from the political goal of a proletarian revolution toward the general principles of historical materialism, and from there to dialectical materialism as a philosophy of nature.

The tenet that matter is primary and consciousness secondary has, *per se*, no precise meaning. Of course, speaking scientifically, there is no doubt that consciousness arises at a certain stage in the development of matter (i.e., of reality *in toto*); but in the usual Marxist interpretation, the tenet includes something more: it affirms that consciousness is passive, and that it does nothing other than to reflect reality. The notion of creativity, and of the relationship between that concept and the consciousness and will of the individual person (a notion which is typical of present-day European philosophy, and which apparently derives from Henri Bergson) is totally lacking in Marxism. Marx wrote that for him the process of thinking was only a reflection of the processes of reality transferred to the human brain. The tenet that "consciousness is secondary" has nihilistic connotations: it diminishes such concepts as consciousness and thought to the point where they are eliminated as being something inessential, or "secondary." Consider, for instance, how unequivocally (and with what rapture!) the Soviet Marxist Deborin writes about this:

> The historical task faced by Marx and Engels was to "stir up a rebellion against the supremacy of thought," as it is expressed in the draft Introduction to *The German Ideology*. These few words actually capsulize that huge revolution in philosophy, the science of history, and the worldview in general that was effected by Marxism. Marxism *stirred up a rebellion against the supremacy of thought, subordinating it to material reality.*[27]

A fine philosophy indeed! If Marxism decreed such a miserable fate for thought, what is in store for kindness, tolerance, and love?

Marxism's transposition of the two highest levels in the hierarchy of behavior plans destroys values common to all humanity. The reversal created a real paradise for the revolutionary bent on destruction: Human beings as such no longer exist; they are only members of different classes. Class interest is the highest interest, and anyone claiming to be thinking of interests that transcend class and are common to us all is a deceiver. Society falls to pieces. There are no rules when dealing with "class enemies." Such is the conclusion to which Marxism leads—a conclusion for whose sake its entire philosophical component exists.

From this angle of vision, it is interesting to compare Marx and Engels with Feuerbach, who reinterpreted the Hegelian dialectic in the spirit of materialism, thereby contributing the only really valuable idea in dialectical materialism. And he interpreted religion—Christianity in particular—in the same materialistic, positivistic way. In reading

The Essence of Christianity, one is often amazed at how modern this work is in its approach and method, and how many of its ideas are still valid today.

Marx and Engels did not approve of Feuerbach's social philosophy, as it was based on a concept of *man* and *values common to all mankind*. Therefore, Marxism recognizes Feuerbach as a materialist in general, but labels him an idealist in the sphere of history. In a letter to Marx dated August 19, 1846, Engels gives the following account of *The Essence of Christianity,* which had just been published. "Apart from a few subtle comments, he is altogether stuck in the same old rut. . . . He's still talking about the 'essence,' 'man,' etc."

Engels was especially exasperated whenever love was mentioned in a sociological or philosophical context. In his essay on Feuerbach, he wrote:

> But what we must not forget is that it was precisely these two weaknesses of Feuerbach that "true socialism," which had been spreading like a plague in "educated" Germany since 1844, took as its starting point, putting literary phrases in the place of scientific knowledge, the liberation of mankind by means of "love" in place of the emancipation of the proletariat through the economic transformation of production. . . .[28]

That was written in 1888. One suspects that thirty or forty years earlier, instead of "through the economic transformation of production" Engels would have written "through the victorious proletarian revolution," or some such thing. As he grew older, however, he became less militant. Yet his revulsion toward the word "love" remained in full force. At several points in that essay, in order to convince the reader that the word was inappropriate, he modified it with the adjective "sexual," thereby twisting Feuerbach's meaning and committing a kind of forgery in discussing Feuerbach's doctrine. Engels writes: "Thus, finally, with Feuerbach, sexual love becomes one of the highest forms, if not the highest form, of the practice of his new religion."[29] Yet on that same page he quotes a passage in which Feuerbach says that "the heart is the essence of religion." The heart—not the sex organs.

Marxism differs from other socialist doctrines in that it consistently leans on hatred—class hatred. Whoever rejects hatred is regarded by Marxism as an enemy—just as dangerous as a class enemy. Hence Engels' bilious feelings toward "love." He returns to the subject again and again:

> But love! Yes, with Feuerbach love is everywhere and at all times the wonder-working god who should help to surmount all difficulties of practical life—and at that in a society which is split into classes with diametrically opposite interests. At this point the last relic of its revolutionary character disappears from his philosophy, leaving only the old cant: Love one another—fall into each other's arms regardless of distinctions of sex or estate—a universal orgy of reconciliation![30]

The practicality of Marx and Marxists in great undertakings is at the very least dubious. One must pay a price for the rejection of universals. At first, members of the "enemy class" only are outlawed. But *"l'appétit vient en mangeant."* Lenin says:

> One must not write about Party comrades in a tone that systematically fills the workers with hatred, revulsion, contempt, etc., toward those who disagree with them. But one *can and must* write in that tone about splinter groups.

But the "splinter groups" belong to the same class! He goes on:

> One must fill the masses with hatred, revulsion, and contempt toward those people who have *ceased* to be members of the single Party; who have become political enemies; who have tripped up our social democratic organization in its electoral campaign. Toward such politi-

> cal enemies I have always waged—and if the schism happens again, or is broadened, I shall always wage—a war of *annihilation.*[31]

The systematic spreading of hatred, and the waging of a war of annihilation, are key concepts in Leninism. The citation testifies that this arsenal was being used not against the enemy class but against rival fractions of the Party. Subsequently, a wave of hatred and annihilation, which rolled over the whole country, wiped out the divisions between classes, parties, and factions.

Predatory animals, although equipped to kill, have a system of instincts which prevents them from killing those of their own species on a mass scale. Humans have no such instincts; but they do possess death-dealing instruments, and much more terrible ones. In lieu of instincts, we have culture, which includes rules that serve the same function. So long as culture was tribal, those rules applied only to the tribe; when culture became global, they became universal. When those rules are rejected, we become something much worse than animals. Engels' theoretical peevishness towards "the old cant: love one another" becomes in practice the concentration camps of Solovki and Magadan.

For What Purpose?

> "How miserable," Marx exclaims, "is a society that knows no better means of defense than the executioner!" But in Marx's day the executioner had not yet become a philosopher [. . . . and at least made no pretense of universal philanthropy.]
>
> Albert Camus[32]

But if the nihilism toward the universal values of spiritual culture that is derived from the principle that "social existence determines consciousness" proves to have a destructive effect on society, for what purpose is this principle needed by the established totalitarian society?

The answer is simple. The destruction of spiritual culture is dangerous for a society in which that culture is the basis of stability, or even an essential element of stability. But for a totalitarian society based ultimately on the fear of physical violence, the destruction of spiritual culture is indispensable to stability. Thus while poisonous substances can kill organic matter, they do not harm an inorganic metallic structure but only clean it of excrescences. Therefore, one and the same system of ideas, the same language and style of thought, can be used successfully by totalitarian Marxism both to destroy a society before seizing power and to cement it afterward. But that cementing is a forcible, mechanical fastening together of the parts—a kind of fettering.

Here I must point out that in every sociopolitical doctrine—and especially in Marxism—there are usually several strata and seams. There are Marxists who advocate a pluralistic democracy; there are Marxists who are prepared to accept a positivistic philosophy of nature; and there are Marxists who accept Lenin (although with some reservations) but activly oppose totalitarianism. And all of them quote Marx and Engels, just as the faithful adepts of Soviet Marxism-Leninism do, finding in their works an expression of their own views, and regarding themselves as their followers. I realize that some of these honest and thoughtful people who regard themselves as Marxists will accuse me (some in fact already have) of distorting Marx's concepts—of oversimplifying them and taking a one-sided approach to them. I have already been told (and shall be again) that what I am combatting is not "real" Marxism but the vulgar Soviet version of it, which is far removed from the views of the founders.

To a considerable extent, this is true. I am in fact talking about official Soviet Marxism-Leninism; and I have very good reason to do so. It is precisely this Marxism—the real Marxism under whose aegis millions of people are living—which has transformed the world, and continues (alas!) to transform it. I have not set myself the task of making a comprehensive analysis of the relationship of Marx's and Engels' views to Soviet Marxism. Certainly Marx and Engels did not preach totalitarianism. On the contrary, to the very ends of their lives they plainly saw the threat of a totalitarian, "barracks-type" socialism, and issued several warnings against it. But that does not change matters. Marxism became a tremendous world force in its totalitarian form. This cannot be denied, and it cannot be ascribed to accident.

Marxism contains traits and elements that I not only welcome but in which I see the only hope for the salvation of mankind. These elements, however, are not specific to Marxism: they are widely scattered throughout the European culture of the nineteenth and twentieth centuries. The elements which are specific to Marxism are precisely those which in their aggregate have led—and will always lead—to totalitarianism. These elements are simple and primitive. They cannot be vulgarized because they already are vulgar in the extreme. "Everything is simple," as Mikhail Bulgakov says somewhere.

After the Marxists' seizure of power, the principle that "social existence determines consciousness" changes its sign (to use the language of mathematics), owing to a simple procedure which one must credit with even a certain degree of logical elegance. The new society is declared to be classless. Or at any rate, virtually so, in the sense that if classes do remain, the contradictions between them are declared to be "nonantagonistic." All the arguments that were used to break down the state are used now to strengthen it. Simple, and a stroke of genius. Indeed, there is no state in the world stronger than the Marxist State. True, Marx taught that under socialism the state would wither away; but for some reason Marxists remember this only until power is seized, at which point they promptly forget it. The dictatorship of the proletariat (meaning in practice, of course, the dictatorship of the Party bureaucracy), which in theory is regarded as a transitional stage, becomes the final stage—the goal of the transformation. This is not surprising: actually the Marxist doctrine of the withering-away of the state is pure rubbish—mere romantic prating. The state cannot wither away; and the people who have come to power know that very well. According to Marxist theory, socialization of the means of production should solve all the basic problems of society. Actually, of course, nothing of the sort takes place. The new chiefs are faced with the same problems as their predecessors. But they believe only in economic transformations, in the necessity for close unity, in a leading role for the Party, and in the doctrine that social existence determines consciousness. They believe in anything you like except the leading role of the spiritual principle, and the necessity for tolerance and love. Moreover, that belief is not merely a matter of practice: it is a matter of theory, of principle. What kind of state other than a totalitarian one could such people found?

Economic Fetishism

"Historical materialism." "Social existence determines consciousness." What do Soviet citizens understand these things to mean?

Philosophical categories and definitions cannot be equated with scientific statements, which can be verified and used to predict events, plan actions, etc. Philosophy contains elements of both science and art. Like science, it makes use of abstract concepts. Like art, it makes use of a language that is profoundly unformalized and perhaps cannot be formalized. Again, it operates on the level of intuition, creating a certain atmosphere or style of thought and a system of images, propositions, and judgments whose existence is not distinctly apprehended. These images and judgments exert a most decisive influence on human behavior—a stronger influence, as a rule, than do logical discourse and exact calculations. With respect to the images and atmosphere of philosophy, it is senseless to enter into disputes about particular assertions and counterassertions. In philosophical texts, as in literature or the holy books of different peoples, you can always find enough material to draw the formal conclusion you want, or to reject the one you don't want. For example, Soviet philosophers, after enthusiastically proving at length that social existence determines consciousness, must promptly make a reservation (as did Marx and Engels) about the "relative autonomy of consciousness." Lord only knows what that means. But clearly the reason for the reservation is that the philosophers cannot be accused of simply ruling out and denying the role of consciousness. This reservation, however, for all practical purposes changes nothing: neither the general atmosphere nor the general style of historical materialism. The ethos of a philosophy consists of something much more than a series of formal answers to one question or another.

In the tenet that "social existence determines consciousness," Soviet man understands "social existence" as a kind of force sufficient in itself and having nothing to do with him as an individual. First of all, it is material production, which develops in accordance with its own immanent, deterministic laws. Determinism is in general very typical of the Soviet style of thinking. Modern science, of course, has reached the firm conclusion that the laws of nature are essentially only *restrictions.* They do not so much determine the course of events as exclude certain possibilities. But Soviets are in every way protected against such notions: it is impressed upon them that the notions are "idealistic and unscientific." Soviets live in an atmosphere of nineteenth-century determinism, and are inclined toward fatalism.

I wish to reemphasize that historical and philosophical materialism have nothing in common. Historical materialism merely asserts that the material phenomena associated with the production of material wealth are decisive for historical development, whereas the material phenomena in the human brain associated with thought and spiritual culture, are something derivative and secondary—a "reflection" of the first group of phenomena. In any case, it is in this sense that the tenet is understood by millions of people. This is not materialism but obscurantism—a primitive kind of consumerist philosophy. It provides the theoretical basis for regression and dehumanization.

In a textbook on historical materialism, we read:

> As a system of knowledge about the world, science necessarily developed from practice and from the practical needs of mankind. But modern bourgeois ideologies regard science as purely a creation of human reason. They claim that all the most important events in the history of science took place thanks to the enthusiasm and thirst for knowledge of some gifted individuals. But this account leaves unexplained the origin of that enthusiasm, that thirst for knowledge, and that interest on the part of those gifted individuals.[33]

It never even occurred to the Soviet author that a thirst for knowledge might be an immanent trait of the human personality. What a paradox! In his theory, Marx took as a point of departure the struggle against commodity fetishism (consumerism), charging that fetishism was the *private* religion of the citizens. Yet Marx's followers have elevated that same economic fetishism to the rank of a compulsory *state religion*.

The Individual[34] and Society

One of the favorite words in Soviet propaganda and textbooks is "the people."[35] "The people is the creator of history." "The people is the decisive force in historical development." But for Soviet man, "the people" is just as much of an abstraction, just as much of an extremely impersonal force, as "social existence." In order to establish a link between the concepts "I" and "the people," one must ascertain how an act of my free will can affect the people as a whole. If these informational links are analyzed concretely, we inevitably arrive at concepts of the individual's basic rights. But that is precisely what Soviet ideology strives to prevent at any cost. By using the term "the people," the role played by the individual personality is minimized. "What am I?" asks a Soviet citizen. "I'm just like everybody else."

And how does Marxism interpret the concept of the human personality?

Let us look into the latest edition of the *Philosophical Dictionary,*[36] a book which, by the way, has its own prehistory. The 1940s and 1950s witnessed the publication of several editions of the *Short Philosophical Dictionary,* which reflected very accurately the belligerent spirit of that era. That dictionary became famous for the fact that one of its editions contained the newly coined word "cybernetics," which was defined more or less as follows: "A reactionary pseudoscience created by the lackeys of imperialism in order to distract the toilers from the class struggle." This definition became a laughingstock, and caused much trouble to Soviet philosophers. It became necessary to acknowledge that the definition was erroneous. Then, in the relatively liberal 1960s, a new dictionary of philosophical concepts was prepared. Among those called in to work on the project were philosophers reputed to be freethinkers. (Later, many of them were not allowed to publish at all, and some of them even emigrated.) The new dictionary differed strikingly from the old one. The abusive language had vanished; and one could discern a desire to provide at least some information on that part of the world not under Soviet domination.

Let us now open that liberal dictionary to the entry under "Person," where we read:

> A human being, with his socially conditioned and individually expressed traits: intellectual, emotional, volitional. The scientific concept of the Person is based on the Marxist definition of man as an aggregate of social

> relations. From this it follows that those traits proper to the Person cannot be inborn but, in the final analysis, are determined by the historically given social system. . . .

"Wait just a minute" we say, rubbing our eyes. "A person without inborn traits? That's too much even for Marxists! It can't be. Something's wrong here."

And indeed, when we look more closely, we see that there is a second definition:

> In psychology, each individual human being, with his inherent, individual traits of character, intellect, and affect. A Person's psychological traits include. . . .

So for Marxists there turn out to be two different concepts of the person. In history and sociology, the individual is an aggregate of social relations. Individuals are not living people with innate and acquired characteristics, but walking aspects of social relations—their personification, as it were. These zombies, who subordinte themselves to objective laws (objective indeed: they *are* objects!), determine the dynamics of human development. In psychology, on the other hand, an individual is precisely what a person is usually understood to be; but that concept has not the slightest relevance to history or social problems. It is relevant only to one's personal life—when, say, one quarrels with one's spouse; or when one goes to a psychotherapist for treatment.

It would be difficult to express more clearly the essence of the totalitarian philosophy.

Marxism does not deny the role of the outstanding individual in history; but reduces that individual's role to that of a mere "objective necessity," although the need for such an individual can be very pressing when the occasion demands one. The idea that the future is open to us, that it is a result of our free (individual and collective) choice, is completely alien to the Soviet style of thought. When the mentors of our society look backward and explain to us what has happened, they find that each change in the course of events was an objective necessity—something not hard to do with hindsight. When they look ahead, each future decision of the authorities is likewise declared to be an objective necessity. A creative act, a discovery, an invention—all such things turn out to be forms of objective necessity. According to Marxism an inventor does not invent; he "satisfies an objective need for the invention."

Like any other species of determinism or fetishism, Soviet Marxism has its share of mysticism. It is only by virtue of their form that the words "objective necessity" sound scientific; in content they are the equivalent of the ancient Greeks' "Fate" or the Christians' "Will of God." And just as the Christian monarchs derived their authority from God, the chieftains of the Marxist society derive their authority from "objective necessity." The obliging sacrificial priests interpret that phrase in whatever way they are ordered to at the moment. The ordinary Soviet citizen, like a person in the Middle Ages, takes the priests' prophecy with a grain of salt. But he has no doubts as to the legitimacy of the priesthood or its basic principles and approach. Historical materialism is served up to the ordinary Soviet citizen as a "science"; and science is something in which the citizen trusts and for which he has great respect. For the citizen, science is as indisputable as God was for the people of the Middle Ages.

The similarity between the Soviet and medieval style of thinking is by no means superficial. To the contrary, the similarity runs quite deep, whereas the outer symbols differ very much. We are dealing here with the same social outlook, the same conception of the individual and society, and of the individual and history.

The medieval style of thought and the medieval style of life support each other. It is said that if it is repeatedly suggested to you that you are a thief, you will become one. When it is constantly drummed into your head that social existence determines consciousness, then it will ultimately begin to determine your consciousness. The essence of your personality will be eroded, and you will become the slave of circumstance. And when you see all around you people just as impaired, and living according to the same laws, your belief in the correctness of historical materialism's basic tenet will become unshakable, and your behavior will be affected accordingly.

Things have come full circle; one can no longer tell whether the Soviet citizen is so docile because he believes in historical materialism, or whether he believes in historical materialism because that makes it more convenient for him to behave docilely.

But what about the leaders? Are they free? Do they feel themselves to be the creators of history?

Hardly. In order to create history, it is not enough simply to occupy high office: one must also *be able to create*. But everything we know about Soviet "chieftains" strongly indicates that they are incapable of this; by lacking such ability—by lacking a profound understanding of the world and insight into the future—people remain the slaves of circumstance. They live amid the hustle and bustle of immediate problems; they merely react, doing only what is necessary to preserve their station. Under these conditions, politics is reduced to intrigue. The movement of Soviet society is not controlled by the human creative will. It occurs blindly, spontaneously.

Jean Jaurès has a different view of Marxism:

> Marx said that until now human society has been governed by fatality and the blind movement of economic forces; that institutions and ideas are not the conscious work of free men, but the reflection in the human brain of man's life in society. We are still in the stage of pre-history. Human history will truly begin only when man, escaping from the tyranny of unconscious forces, will be able to control production itself by his reason and his will.[37]

I can understand such an approach, although I cannot agree with this extremely categorical judgment of mankind's past history. History does, after all, include some brilliant breakthroughs caused by genius; they may perhaps be the essence of history. Nonetheless, I welcome wholeheartedly the goal set here. Unfortunately, today in the Soviet Union we are farther from that goal than we have ever been.

At the level of policy, the Marxist-Leninist philosophy is refracted, in a quite natural way, into a total absence of the concept of individual rights. For instance, a book titled *The Fundamental Principles of Political Knowledge* (Moscow, 1974) contains the following headings and sub-headings:

> Human Society and Its Development . . . Social Formations . . . Production and Its Development . . . Why the Working Class Needs the Party . . . What the Party Requires of a Communist . . . The Forms and Methods of Party Leadership . . . The Economics of the Developed Socialist Society . . . Strengthening the Soviet State . . . The Development of Socialist Democracy . . .

Wait a minute! Isn't there something here about the rights of the individual? No.

> The Soviets of Workers' Deputies . . . The Tasks of the Trade Unions . . . Marxism-Leninism on the Forming of the New Man . . . Developing the Consciousness of the Masses . . . Socialist Competition . . .

The concept of the human rights is not included in the *Fundamental Principles of Political Knowledge* in the Land of Victorious Socialism!

Totalitarianism and Economics

In destroying the individual personality, the totalitarian society has deprived itself of the source of creativity. In rigidly restricting the exchange of information and ideas, it is blocking its own access to normal development, and in particular to the development of the national economy. I quote an excerpt from a joint letter that Andrei Sakharov, Roy Medvedev, and I sent to the leaders of the Soviet Union in the spring of 1970.

> In the course of the past decade, threatening signs of breakdown and stagnation have been observed in the national economy of our country, although the roots of these difficulties originated in a much earlier period and bear a very profound character. The growth rate of the national income is steadily dropping. There is a widening gap between the requirements for normal development and the real returns from new industrial production. Numerous facts point to errors in determining technical and economic policy in industry and agriculture, as does impermissible red tape in the decision of urgent problems. Defects in the system of planning, accounting, and incentives often lead to a contradiction between local and institutional interests on the one hand and public and state interests on the other. As a result, necessary reserves for the development of production are not available, or are not utilized, and technical progress is sharply impeded.
>
> Because of these factors, the natural wealth of the country is frequently destroyed without control and with impunity: forests are cut down; water reservoirs are polluted; valuable agricultural lands are despoiled; soil is eroded and rendered unfit for cultivation; and so forth. It is common knowledge that there is a chronically grave situation in agriculture, especially in livestock. Real income of the population in recent years has hardly risen; nourishment, medical services, and everyday services

improve very slowly and unequally between regions. The items of goods in short supply grow. There are obvious signs of inflation. Especially alarming for the future of our country is a slow-down in the development of education. Factually, our general expenditures on education of all types are less than in the United States and are growing more slowly. There is a tragic growth in alcoholism, and narcotics addiction is beginning to make itself felt. In many regions of the country crime is rising systematically, including crime among teenagers and youth. Bureaucracy, compartmentalization, casual attitudes toward jobs, and lack of initiative are growing in the work of scientific and technological organizations.

A decisive factor in the comparison of economic systems is labor productivity. Here the situation is worst of all. Productivity of labor as before remains many times lower than in the developed capitalist countries, and its growth is slowing down. This situation is particularly grave if you compare it with the situation in leading capitalist countries and, in particular, the United States.

By introducing into the economy of the country elements of state regulation and planning these countries have rid themselves of the destructive crises that earlier tore capitalist economies apart. The widespread introduction of automation and computer technology into the economy insures a rapid growth of the productivity of labor, which in turn enables the partial overcoming of severe social difficulties and contradictions (as, for example, ways of establishing unemployment benefits, the shortening of the working day, etc.). Comparing our economy with the economy of the United States, we see that our economy lags not only in quantitative but also—which is saddest of all—in qualitative respects.

The newer and more revolutionary the section of the economy the greater the contrast between the United States and us. We have exceeded America in coal production but lag in extraction of oil, are ten times behind in natural gas and production of electric power, hopelessly behind in the chemical field, and immeasurably behind in computer technology. The last is especially essential, for the introduction of the computer into the economy is a factor of decisive importance, radically changing the character of the system of production and all culture. The phenomenon is justly called the second industrial revolution. Yet the capacity of our computers is hundreds of times less than that of the United States, and as regards utilizing computers in the economy the disparity is so great that it is impossible even to measure it. We simply live in a different epoch.

The situation is no better in the field of scientific and engineering discoveries. Here there is no feeling of a growing vitality in our role. On the contrary, at the end of the 1950s our country was the first in the world to launch Sputniks and send a man into space. At the end of the 1960s we lost our leadership and the first men to land on the moon were American.

This fact is just one of the external evidences of actual and growing disparity, on a wide front, of the scientific and technical level of our country and that of the developed countries of the West. In the 1920s and 1930s the capitalist world suffered a period of crises and depression. At that time we were creating industry at an unbelievable pace, by employing the enthusiasm of the nation that was a result of the revolution. At that time our motto was: "Catch up with America and overtake it." And we actually were doing this for several decades. Then the situation changed. The second industrial revolution began. And now, at the beginning of the 1970s, we can see that we did not catch up with America; we fell behind her more and more.

What is the matter? Why didn't we become the trailblazers of the second industrial revolution? Why couldn't we at least stay even with the most developed capitalist countries? Is it really true that the socialist system provides poorer possibilities than the capitalist for the development of productive forces and that in economic competition socialism can't beat capitalism?

Of course not! The source of all our difficulties is not in the socialist system. On the contrary, it lies in those qualities and conditions of our life that run counter to socialism and are hostile to it. Their cause—anti-democratic traditions and norms of public life—arose during the Stalin era and has not been completely liquidated to this day. Economic constraints, limitations on the exchange of information, restrictions of intellectual freedom, and other anti-democratic distortions of socialism that took place in Stalin's time are still accepted as a kind of necessary cost of the process of industrialization.

It is supposed that these distortions did not affect seriously the country's economy, although they had extremely serious consequences in the political and military fields, for the fate of wide strata of the population and whole nationalities. We are leaving aside the problem of how far this point of view may have been justified regarding the early stages of development of a socialist economy, but the reduced rate of industrial development in the prewar years testifies to the contrary. There is no doubt that with the beginning of the second industrial revolution these phenomena have become the decisive economic factor and the basic obstacle to the development of the country's productive forces.

Due to the increase in the size and complexity of economic systems, problems of organization and management have taken first place. These problems cannot be solved by one individual or even several individuals who possess power and who "know all." They demand the creative participation of millions of people on all levels of the economic system. They demand a wide exchange of information, and this is what distinguishes contemporary economics from, say, the economics of the countries of the ancient East. But in the process of exchanging information and ideas in our country we face insurmountable difficulties. Negative phenomena and real information about our faults are kept secret because they might be "used for hostile propaganda."

The exchange of information with foreign countries is haunted by the fear of "penetration of hostile ideology." Theoretical conceptions and practical proposals that seem somehow too bold are suppressed instantly without discussion, out of fear that they may "destroy the foundations."

One can see clear distrust of creative thinkers, critics, and active personalities. Under these conditions, those who advance on the career ladder are not those distinguished by high professional qualities and principles but those who by their words display dedication to the cause of the Party, but who in deeds are distinguished only by dedication to their own narrow personal interests or by passive performance.

Restrictions on freedom of information not only make difficult any control over the leadership, not only frustrate the people's initiative, but also deprive even those heading middle-level administrations of both rights and information, transforming them into passive bureaucrats. Our leaders receive incomplete and edited information and cannot use their power effectively. The economic reforms of 1965 were extremely useful and an important beginning, calling for the solution of important questions in our economic life. But we are convinced that simple economic measures alone are insufficient for the fulfilling of all these tasks. Moreover, these economic measures cannot be fully undertaken without reforms in the sphere of administration, information, and public knowledge. The same is true of such often-promised initiatives as establishing complex industrial organizations with a high degree of independence in administrative, fiscal, and personnel questions.

It may be concluded that the solution of all economic problems requires a scientific answer to such general and theoretical questions of socialist economics as forms of management feedback, pricing decisions in the absence of a free market, general planning principles, etc.

We are talking a lot now about the necessity of the scientific approach to problems of organization and administration. This, of course, is correct. Only a scientific approach can help overcome difficulties and realize all the possibilities for the direction of the economy and for the technological progress which the absence of capitalist ownership ought to make possible. But the scientific approach requires full information, impartial thinking, and creative freedom. Until these conditions are met (not just for some individuals, but for the masses) the talk about scientific management will remain empty words.

Our economy can be compared with the movement of traffic through an intersection. When there were few cars, traffic police could handle it quite easily and movement was normal. But the number of cars steadily increased. A traffic jam developed. What can be done? The drivers can be fined or the policemen changed. But this will not save the situation. The only way out is to widen the intersection.

The obstacles that prevent the development of our economy can be found outside it, in the political and public area, and all measures that do not eliminate these obstacles will be ineffective.

The consequences of the Stalin era are still negatively affecting the economy, not only directly because of the impossibility of a scientific approach to the problems of administration and management, but also in no less degree indirectly through the general lowering of the creative potential of representatives of all professions.

But it is creative labor that is becoming more and more important for the economy under the conditions of the second industrial revolution. In this connection it is impossible not to speak of the problem of the relationship between the State and the intelligentsia.

Freedom of information and creativity are essential for the intelligentsia because of the nature of its activities and its social function. The desire of the intelligentsia for greater freedom is legitimate and natural. The State, however, suppresses this desire through all kinds of restrictions—administrative pressure, dismissals from work, and even trials. This brings about mutual distrust and profound mutual misunderstanding, which make most difficult any fruitful cooperation between the Party-State structure and the most active—that is, the most socially valuable—strata of the intelligentsia. In conditions of contemporary industrial society, where the role of the intelligentsia is growing continuously, this gap can only be termed suicidal.[38]

Science and Chess

> Long live the Party of Lenin and Stalin,
> which made Michurin known to the world,
> and created in our country all conditions for
> the flowering of advanced materialist
> biology!
>
> T. D. Lysenko, 1948

What is the best way to evaluate the Soviet Union's contribution to world science? One way is to take as a criterion the Nobel Prizes awarded in the natural sciences. Every year, three Nobel Prizes are awarded for the most important discoveries in three leading natural sciences: physics, chemistry, and physiology or medicine. That these prizes are awarded objectively is acknowledged by the entire world. The Nobel Prize is the highest international award a scientist can receive, and the number of Nobel Prizes received by a nation's citizens can be taken as a rough indication of that country's contribution to world science. (The applied sciences and engineering are not taken into account.)

Let's look at a list of the Nobel Prizes awarded from 1945 through 1974. When a prize is awarded simultaneously to two or three scientists, let us consider that each one has received one-half or one-third or a prize accordingly. We find that during the period in question citizens of twenty nations received Nobel Prizes. If we total up the number of prizes received by the citizens of each nation, we shall see that the first six places are shared among six nations:

Table 1. Distribution of Nobel Prizewinners

Country	*Number of Prizes*
U.S.	42 2/3 prizes
England	18 2/3
Germany	5 5/6
USSR	3 1/6
Sweden	3 1/6
France	2 1/2

Thus we see that Soviet contribution to world science cannot be compared to that of the U.S. and England, which together received more than sixty of the ninety prizes awarded in the past thirty years.

To roughly evaluate the effectiveness of our system as regards scientific productivity, let us calculate for all countries the number of Nobel Prizes per 10 million inhabitants (the equivalent of a "small country"). If we do, we obtain the results shown in table 2.

Table 2. Number of Nobel Prizes per 10 Million Inhabitants, Ranked by Country

Country	*Population in Millions (1968)*	*Total Number of Prizes in 1945–74*	*Proportionate Number of Prizes*
1. Sweden	7.9	3 1/6	4.0
2. England	55.3	18 2/3	3.4
3. Switzerland	6.1	1 5/6	3.0
4. Norway	3.8	5/6	2.19
5. U.S.	200.0	42 2/3	2.135
6. Finland	4.7	1	2.128
7. Ireland	2.9	1/2	1.55
8. Holland	12.8	1 1/3	1.04
9. Germany (FRG & GDR)	74.0	5 5/6	0.79
10. Czechoslovakia	14.4	1	0.69
11. Australia	12.2	5/6	0.67
12. Argentina	23.6	1 1/3	0.56
13. Portugal	9.5	1/2	0.53
14. France	50.3	2 1/2	0.50
15. Canada	20.8	1	0.48
16. Austria	7.3	1/3	0.35
17. Belgium	9.6	1/3	0.35
18. Italy	52.8	1 1/2	0.28
19. Japan	101.4	1 2/3	0.16
20. USSR	237.8	3 1/6	0.13

Needless to say, the order in which countries appear in this table cannot be taken as an accurate reflection of their scientific effectiveness, owing to the great relative fluctuation of the index in the case of nations whose citizens have received a Nobel Prize once or twice. Yet in the aggregate, the figures enable us to draw qualitative conclusions. Thus we see that in terms of the proportionate number of Nobel Prizes, the Soviet Union ranks twentieth out of twenty, thus outranking only those nations which received no Nobel Prize at all during the period studied. If, among the latter, we consider those with a population of more than 40 million, we can state fearlessly that Soviet science is better developed than that of China, India, Pakistan, Bangladesh, Indonesia, Brazil, Nigeria, and Mexico.

Intellectually gifted people see the falseness and poverty of the Soviet ideological and political system better than others do. In the case of such a person, esthetic feelings alone—quite apart from moral factors—militate against his becoming part of the system. When he does so, it is only at the cost of crippling himself. Therefore gifted people are not only repelled by the system but strive to distance themselves from it. They tend to seek the most theoretical fields of activity, involving themselves in areas least connected with the system, and where they can achieve results in isolation. This process is also favored by the weakness of Soviet mass technology, and its organizational muddle. The consequences produced by these factors can easily be seen in the relative successes in different aspects of Soviet culture. By world standards, its position in mathematics is better than in physics; and in science generally, it is better than in industrial technology. But the best thing to be in the Soviet Union is a chess player!

A person playing chess makes his moves *himself,* at his own risk. No one gives him orders, and no one interferes with him. The rules of the game are strictly defined, unchanging, and *international.* This, it would seem, is an isolated instance of a rather touching unanimity among members of all classes and parties. Morality is a partisan morality. Art is a partisan art. Science is a partisan science. Only chess is non-partisan. How wonderful! And it has never occurred to anyone—not even in the "best" days of the Stalin era—to divide chess openings into "materialist" and "idealistic" moves. Finally, the state loves chess players; and it supports them with a view to winning prestige in the international arena. As a result, the USSR is indisputably the world's greatest chess power.

Sometimes it seems to me that the nation's best intellectual resources have been thrown away on chess.

Art

One particular literary work, together with the context of its genesis, serves for me as a symbol of Soviet art as the Party leadership wants it to be viewed. This symbol is a caricature, but one not conceived by a splenetic satirist. Instead, it is taken from life.

In the summer of 1954, as a recent university graduate, I was working in the town of Obninsk, 100 kilometers from Moscow, at the same institution through whose efforts the nation's first atomic electric power plant was put into operation. That event occurred in late June. On July 1, all the big newspapers carried a press release from the USSR Council of Ministers on the event. It was also carried by *Literaturnaya gazeta*, the organ of the Soviet Writers' Union. Alongside the press release, on the front page of that paper, was printed a poem by Sergei Mikhalkov titled "A Priceless Contribution." Mikhalkov was already a famous man, having co-written the words of the Soviet National Anthem. (Today he is a Very Important Person in the Writers' Union—chairman of the Moscow Section.) Every reader of *Literaturnaya gazeta* had an opportunity to compare the press release from the Council of Ministers with Mikhalkov's poetic masterpiece:

USSR Council of Ministers:	*Sergei Mikhalkov:*
In the Soviet Union, through the efforts of Soviet Scientists and engineers, work has now been completed on the designing and building of the first industrial power plant using atomic energy, with a useful output of 5,000 kilowatts.	Our Soviet scientists Put into operation (Thus doing their bit for science) A 5,000-kilowatt station.

USSR Council of Ministers:

On June 27, 1954, the atomic power plant was put into operation, and provided electric current for the industry and agriculture of adjacent regions.

For the first time, an industrial turbine is operating not by burning coal or other kinds of fuel but by splitting the nucleus of an atom of uranium.

With the actuating of the power station, a real step has been made toward the peaceful utilization of atomic energy.

Sergei Mikhalkov:

For the happiness of the nation,
Of the workers and peasants, too,
In a cause that is worthy and noble.
Uranium has been used.

There stands the new power station:
Mighty and puissant is she!
As fuel for her operation
She uses atomic energy.

There stands the new power station,
An example showing clearly that we
Who live in the Soviet Union
Are engaged in peaceful activity.

Here, everything is manifested: the task that the poet set for himself, his way of working, and the finished product . . . But there was a flaw. The press release from the Council of Ministers contained one more paragraph which, for some reason, was not reflected in Mikhalkov's poem. It strikes me as unlikely that Mikhalkov could have failed to write the fifth stanza merely because of an oversight. Perhaps the reason was technical: lack of space on the page, or something of the sort. In any case, I promptly decided to correct the mistake and wrote the missing verse, which I herewith present, along with the last paragraph of the press release:

Soviet scientists and engineers are now doing the preliminary work for building industrial atomic power plants with an output of 50,000 to 100,000 kilowatts.

Our Soviet scientists
Are preparing new contributions:
They're engaged now in drawing up blueprints
For 100,000-kilowatt stations!

The ending I provided for Mikhalkov's unfinished poem was fully approved by my associates—the very people who were designing the new stations.

In the textbook on historical materialism that I quoted above, we read:

> In bourgeois society, the toilers have foisted upon them, in lieu of high art, the products of so-called mass culture: the "creations" of hacks, primitive in form and anti-humanistic in content. Only a socialist revolution gives the people access to genuine, high art, and enables every person with artistic taste to become a creator of art.[39]

For the Docile Ones

Are Soviet citizens happy? In comparing the subjective worldview of a person living in Soviet society with that of people living in more open and freer societies, it is very important to take age into account. As we know, ontogeny (the development of the individual) to a certain degree repeats philogeny (the development of the species). And something similar happens in cultural development. The traits of totalitarianism belong to the highest levels of the social organization and culture. Therefore, one does not directly feel the fetters of totalitarianism until one has assimilated the preceding levels of culture. Children are everywhere children, and children in different countries have more in common with each other than they do with adults in their own countries. Adults may see how totalitarianism cripples the mentality of children from their very early years—how it makes them into totalitarian persons. But the children either do not perceive this at all, or else they apprehend it as something secondary. And indeed the child's inner world is so dynamic and vivid, and the process of cognizing reality so engages his entire being, that the specific traits of that reality recede into the background. The same thing applies to adolescence. The spectacle of a pair of young lovers, is equally touching under whatever social system. So is that of a young mother with her child. Everywhere, people love in the same way. (At any rate it is true when the Soviet Union is compared with the countries of the West, since the cultural segments in question roughly coincide.)

But the period of growth comes to an end, and the period of maturity sets in. Now the subjective feeling of gratification depends upon the extent to which a person *fulfills himself.* It depends, that is, upon the degree to which his actual contribution to culture, to life on this planet, corresponds with what he wants to, and can, contribute. Among human beings the need for self-fulfillment varies widely. There are people who have no such need and are quite content with nothing more than a comfortable life. But this, I think, may be regarded as an anomaly. For the normal person, self-fulfillment is a prerequisite to subjective gratification—to happiness.

Here the totalitarian society imposes rigid limits on a person. And the more strikingly manifest are one's creative impulses, the more galling are the restrictions. One begins to feel them in adolescence; but it is at about age thirty that one sees that there is no more room to move, as if you hit your head against the ceiling. Then one becomes a sort of oldster for whom the best in life is already far behind. In effect, he dies, since after thirty life without self-fulfillment has no meaning. Professional advancement bought at the price of violence to one's conscience does not yield gratification; the feeling that "this is not what I want" remains. And it is these living corpses—these zombies—these personified social relationships—who, as the Soviet press reports, invariably "vote for," "unanimously approve," and "wholeheartedly support" whatever is suggested by the superiors.

But what can be said about the things of everyday life—about the standard of living, for example? It is well known that the living standard of ordinary Soviet citizens is much lower than their Western counterparts. During the first thirty years after the war, it did improve constantly, although very slowly. Rapid improvement occurred only in the first few years after the death of Stalin. (In the last years of the Stalin era, the living standard in rural areas had been horribly low.) In recent years, people have begun to dress markedly better. On the other hand, there is still an acute shortage of basic foodstuffs, especially meat. The variety of foodstuffs available is very limited, and the consumer is constantly faced with the question. "Where can I get it?" A Frenchman who had lived in Moscow for a year, summarized his impressions as follows: "A Soviet citizen goes to the store as primitive man went hunting." And what would he have said if he had lived in the provinces rather than in Moscow?

Recently, a woman I know went to Mordovia to visit a political prisoner. The day she arrived, the settlement near the labor camp was humming with activity: some codfish had been delivered to a store. People told one another the news; and the wives of the soldiers and MVD officers guarding the prisoners were standing in line. One MVD officer was telling another on the phone: "They've just brought in some codfish. I ordered some for you, too!"

The situation is especially bad with respect to fruits and vegetables, so that the Soviet citizen's diet is completely unsatisfactory from the viewpoint of modern nutrition. In state stores, vegetables are of low quality, and are available—if at all—only in a very limited variety. On the market, vegetables are very expensive. Fruit is expensive both on the market and in the state stores. At state prices, it would take everything my wife earned in a day (and she has a higher education plus considerable seniority) to buy two kilograms of apples.[40]

Without a free press, Soviet citizens lack the only effective means of combatting abuses by the authorities, and other irregularities that affect their lives. The newspapers do print stories about shortcomings and abuses, but only when they do not involve highly placed officials and are not of general significance. Otherwise, they would be a "smear on Soviet reality." Statistics on crime, epidemics, or natural disasters are officially declared secret, and there are even more data that are unofficially secret.

Medical care in the USSR is at a frightfully low level. Doctors are badly overworked; there are waiting lines in the polyclinics; and the hospitals are crowded beyond belief. Also, everyone can cite cases when patients have died because of mistakes by doctors. It is well known, furthermore, that in the Soviet Union it is virtually impossible to obtain modern, effective drugs, and doctors are even prohibited from prescribing drugs that are in short supply; otherwise their patients would complain that these drugs were not available at the pharmacy. But not even this problem can be posed openly, and there is no way of demanding that the government take effective steps. As for medical care for the higher Party and State officials, it is handled by a special department: the Fourth Department of the Ministry of Public Health, where there is no lack of modern drugs (they are imported); nor do the patients queue up, or lie in the corridors of hospitals.

A problem is also presented by the pollution of the environment. On the site of the Podolsk Nonferrous Metallurgical Plant, where dormitories and other dwellings are located, the air pollution is eighty times greater than the allowable norm. This problem was raised during the All-Russian Campaign To Protect the Environment, and was discussed by the local District Executive Committee in September 1974. The heavy pollution had been going on for over a year, and the plant's chief power specialist stated at the meeting that he could foresee no solution for another two or three years. It seems that air-purifiers were both very expensive and very hard to come by.

Podolsk is but forty kilometers from Moscow. It may be assumed that in outlying areas, such cases are equally common. But how could even rough figures be obtained? Even if some specialist dared to write an objective, unvarnished report on the situation, he would have no hope of publishing it. The chief function of the Soviet press is to "educate," not to inform. Information is allowed only to the extent that it does not interfere with the "educating."

Here is how Candidate of Geological Sciences K. A. Muravyova treats the problem of air pollution in a pamphlet published by the Znaniye Society for the mass reader:

> The problem of the pollution of the air, as of the rest of man's environment, is a social problem. At first glance it may seem that the pollution of the environment is typical of socialist and capitalist societies in equal degree, since industry is everywhere developed, and pollution is an unavoidable consequence of technological progress. But that is only at first glance. Actually, the chief difference consists in the attitude of the given social system toward nature; in the system's ability to eliminate pollution and restore an environment that is both viable and pleasant to man. The capitalist corporations refuse to bear responsibility for the pollution of the environment that they have caused, and try in every way to conceal their guilt. They agree to half-measures, and then only if it does not affect their profits. . . .
>
> Socialism has eliminated the basic defects of the capitalist society. . . . In a socialist society, conservation of the environment is a social necessity, since it is important to the people's general welfare and health, and corresponds to the interests of the entire society. In a socialist society, too, there is pollution of the environment. But it is on a much smaller scale, and is due to other causes: in part, to the fact that the socialist society inherited from capitalism an environment that was already polluted and damaged to a considerable degree.[41]

So it turns out that the cause of the trouble is the pollution produced back in the days of tsarist Russia! That is a very interesting explanation, especially if we take into account the following facts communicated to me by a knowledgeable biologist.

Owing to the pollution of the water by industrial wastes, there has been a sharp drop in the number of fish in the rivers and lakes of the Soviet Union. In 1900, the annual catch of salmon [*losos'*] from Lake Ladoga was 200,000 kilograms. Today, it is 5,000 kilograms, or forty times less. In Lake Ladoga and the rivers in its vicinity, the catch of salmon [*losos'* and *sëmga*] has declined tenfold. The construction of plants on the shores of Lake Baikal resulted in immediate pollution of the water and a decline in the catch of fish. According to data for 1968, the volume of polluted water was about 75 cubic kilometers, or 2,500 times higher than the projected figure. Between 1953 and 1967, the annual catch of the valuable Baikal omul fish (*Coregonus autumnalis*) dropped more than sixfold. In the Sea of Azov, the annual overall catch has declined more than elevenfold in merely the past twenty years.

Soviet society lives in ignorance of itself. There is an old Russian saying which cautions that one should not "carry the garbage out of the hut."[42] I have always been amazed at its foolishness. After all, it is perfectly plain that if you *don't* take the garbage out of the hut, the hut will become unfit to live in. Yet that saying and that principle constantly figure in quasi-official propaganda. The argument runs as follows: in exposing our own defects, we give our enemies occasion to rejoice, and put a weapon into their hands. And for some reason the saying works: it sets people against those who criticize the society and expose its defects; it appeals to a superficial, vulgar vanity for whose sake it demands that elementary cleanliness be sacrificed. It is amazing that such a saying ever came into usage; and it is even more amazing that it is still in existence.

A person living in the Soviet Union is completely at the mercy of a monstrous bureaucratic machine. This applies both to so-called common people and to those holding high positions in the bureaucratic hierarchy. The only difference lies in the kind of cogs they turn, and the kind of cogs that turn them.[43] The subordination to the bureaucratic machine—the acceptance of its absolute authority over every form in which life manifests itself—is the same for everyone except the heretics-dissidents; it makes everyone similar and equal. Today, this machine is not so senseless as it was in the past: it does not destroy those who submit to it; but it remains a machine—a thing without a soul. Its levers and wheels are those meaningless phrases, repeated from one year to the next, which replace normal, logical thought: automatic, unanimous voting; acknowledging *a priori* that each and every decision by higher authority is correct; blocking information channels; juggling with facts, total surveillance; eliminating any show of individuality; demagogy and mass stupefaction. The totalitarian state machine is in no way affected by the human soul or by reason. It follows its own inhuman laws; and the shadow of those laws lies across every human face.

For Those Who Are Not Docile

Repent now, wretched, erring one,
And all will be forgiven:
Tenderly, to the sound of singing,
You'll be brought back to your true home.

But if you balk, saying "I will
Never yield! . . . Not *that* again!"
Out of the darkness will come men
On cat's feet, who know how to kill.

Vl. Lifshits[44]

For all the importance of the massive brainwashing and the erection of barriers to the flow of information, direct physical suppression of dissent remains the basic essential component of steady-state totalitarianism. It is the axle around which revolves the flywheel of the totalitarian State machine. The percentage of people upon whom force must be used is small; but that force is employed to its fullest.

Let us look at the *Chronicle of Current Events*. This periodical reports on the kind of political repressions that are becoming known to the world at large. In reading the *Chronicle,* one is amazed at the harshness of the punishment meted out for exercising an elementary human right: the right to exchange information and ideas. Here is a brief rundown on some typical cases.

> Cronid Lubarsky, astronomer, Candidate of Physical and Mathematical Sciences: in October 1972 in Noginsk, Moscow Oblast, charged with duplicating and circulating *samizdat.* Sentence: five years in a strict-regimen labor camp.
>
> Semyon Gluzman, psychiatrist: in October 1972, in Kiev, charged with anti-Soviet agitation and propaganda—an indictment based entirely on the testimony of witnesses, since a search at his home turned up nothing. Gluzman was accused of the "ideological degradation" of the co-defendant, Lyubov Serednyak. One of the witnesses, a colleague of Gluzman's, testified that when he asked Gluzman why he was working in Zhitomir instead of Kiev, Gluzman had replied: "Because I'm a Jew." This sufficed for the court to charge him with Zionist propaganda. The real reason for Gluzman's arrest was probably the KGB's suspicion that he had co-authored the document known as "An *In-Absentia* Psychiatric Examination in the Case of P. G. Grigorenko." Sentence: seven years in a strict-regimen labor camp, and three years of internal exile.
>
> Stefaniya Shabatura, a graphics artist whose works are mentioned in volume 6 of the *History of Ukrainian Art:* in 1970 a group of writers and artists from Lvov, including Shabatura, requested permission to attend the trial of Valentin Moroz. Sentence: five years in a labor camp, and three years of internal exile.
>
> Igor and Irina Kalynets/Stasiv: in Lvov, in 1972, they were put on trial for having, like Shabatura, requested permission to attend the trial of Valentin Moroz. Details of indictment unknown. Sentence: six years in a strict-regimen labor camp, and three years of internal exile.

> G. V. Davydov, geologist, father of three children: tried in Leningrad in 1973 on a charge of preparing and circulating *samizdat.* Sentence: five years in a strict-regimen labor camp, and three years of internal exile.
>
> V. V. Petrov, blue-collar worker: same case. Sentence: three years in a strict-regimen labor camp, and two years of internal exile.
>
> Evgeny Sverstyuk: tried in Kiev in April 1973 on a charge of having written works of literary criticism published in the West and in *samizdat,* and with having had "anti-Soviet" conversations with neighbors and acquaintances. Sentence: seven years in a strict-regimen labor camp, and five years of internal exile.
>
> Alexander Bolonkin, aeronautical engineer, Doctor of Technical Sciences, author of about forty scientific articles: tried in Moscow in November 1973 on a charge of preparing and circulating *samizdat.* Sentence: four years in a labor camp, and two years of internal exile.
>
> Vasily Lisovoi, Evgeny Pronyuk, and I. Semanyuk: tried in Kiev on November 1973. When Pronyuk was arrested (on the street) his briefcase was found to contain many typed copies of a letter to the Central Committee and "prominent persons of the Soviet Union": academicians, writers, officials of the state, etc. The letter had been co-written by Lisovoi, a Candidate of Philosophical Sciences and a member of the Communist Party of the Soviet Union, and Pronyuk, who like Lisovoi was on the staff of the Ukrainian Academy of Sciences' Institute of Philosophy. In the letter, the authors called the attention of the Central Committee to several unlawful trials recently held in the Ukraine for political reasons. Sentences: Lisovoi—seven years in a strict-regimen labor camp, and three years of internal exile; Pronyuk—seven years in a strict-regimen labor camp and five years of internal exile; Semanyuk—four years in a strict-regimen labor camp.

And so on, endlessly . . .

It is not easy to get hold of the full text of an indictment in a political case. When this has been managed, the lack of proof in the indictment, and its arbitrary nature, show very plainly in the awkward bureaucratic language. Here, for example, is the indictment brought against three Crimean Tatars in a trial held in Zaporozhye in the Ukraine. (The Crimean Tatars are trying to exercise the right to live in their homeland, the Crimea, from which each and every one of them was "resettled" in 1944.)

> Indictment in the criminal proceedings brought against Eskander Kurtumerov, Evazer Khalikov, and Regat Ramazanov under Article 187–1 of the UkSSR Criminal Code.
>
> The pretrial investigation established the following:
>
> The defendants Kurtumerov, Khalikov, and Ramazanov, after having been warned by organs of the State not to circulate fabrications known to be false which defamed the Soviet State and social system, did not draw the appropriate conclusions and continued their criminal activities systematically.
>
> Thus on March 18, 1973, at 29 Tsiolkovsky St. in Melitopol, they took an active part in a meeting of young people where, in the presence of twenty-five persons, they circulated fabrications known to be false and defaming the Soviet State and social systems, thereby distorting the national-minorities policy of the USSR.
>
> On March 18, at another gathering of young people, at 36 Tsuryupa St. in Melitopol, which was attended by twenty persons, Kurtumerov, Khalikov, and Ramazanov again slandered Soviet reality in their speeches.
>
> Moreover, the defendant Kurtumerov wrote articles titled "History," "The Crimea," etc., which contained fabrications known to be false that defamed the Soviet State and social system; and he made patently libelous notes on copies of two pamphlets, T. I. Oizerman's "The Marxist-Leninist Concept of Freedom" and A. Kulagin's "A Generation of Optimists," and on the journal *Problems of History*.
>
> The defendant Khalikov drafted several manuscripts, such as "A Note to the Chairman of the USSR Supreme

> Soviet's Council of Nationalities," "A Protest," "The Criminals Triumph," etc., which libel the Soviet State and social system.
>
> The defendant Ramazanov also prepared several MS texts (e.g., "To People of Good Will") addressed to various Party-Soviet organs which libel the policy of the CPSU and the State and social system.[45]

The indictment goes on to repeat the same charges against each of the three separately, without any attempt even to specify what were those false and libelous assertions of the defendants, still less to prove that they were false.

Sentences: Kurtumerov—two years; Khalikov and Ramazanov—two and one-half years in a labor camp.

The Chronicle #33 contains a report on the conditions under which political prisoners are held in labor camps and prisons. In a letter which he managed to smuggle out, one prisoner, V. P. Azernikov, a physician, describes conditions in the strict-regimen camps in Mordovia.

The prisoners exist in a state "of latent hunger." The caloric content of the diet is far below that required for the hard labor they do. The food contains virtually no animal proteins or vitamins. Cases of food poisoning are frequent. The air in the workshops is polluted with sawdust, abrasive dust, and the fumes from acetone and acids. This makes it easy to contract pulmonary diseases such as silicosis. Treatment is begun only when the disease has reached a critical stage, and even then it is limited to relieving the symptoms. Chronic diseases (gastrointestinal, cardiovascular, ophthalmic, fungus infections, periodontosis, etc.) are not treated at all, even though they are widespread in the camps. A prisoner is excused from work only if his temperature is above 100 degrees. Cases when prisoners are excused from work because of an illness not accompanied by a fever are very rare. The doctor cannot exceed the so-called norm for exemptions (1.7 percent of all prisoners), even during a flu epidemic. Some camps have no doctors, doctor's assistants [*fel'dsher*], or nurses. Medical specialists visit the camps only once or twice a year, or even less often. Physicians who are prisoners are not allowed to treat their fellow-prisoners: it is prohibited by a special order. The camp doctors have available only the simplest kind of drugs, and sometimes their shelf life has long since elapsed. The dirt road leading from the camps to the hospital is so bad, and the prison trucks so poorly equipped to transport patients, that the trip may endanger the patient's life. There have been cases where extremities have been fractured, and injuries to the spinal column have occurred, as a result of the trip. For heart patients, the trip along that road is quite unbearable. Frequently, persons who are in perfect mental health when they come to the camp are mentally ill by the end of their term.

On November 2, 1972, Yuri Timofeyevich Galanskov died in one of the Mordovian camps.[46] He had been arrested in January 1967 and sentenced to seven years in a strict-regimen camp for his work in defense of human rights. An ulcer which had been giving him serious trouble even before his arrest made his life in the labor camp very difficult. Relatives and friends, together with his fellow-inmates, asked the authorities to see that he was given adequate medical care. In particular, they asked that he be put on a special diet and given a thorough examination at the Ministry of Internal Affairs at the special hospital in Leningrad. In the autumn of 1972, owing to the aggravation of his condition, he was taken to the Dubrovlag hospital compound in the settlement of Barashevo. After undergoing surgery, he developed peritonitis and died.

The situation is no better in other camps, as witness the following incident, which took place in one of the Perm camps.[47] During an inspection by a medical board, its chairman, Lieutenant Colonel T. P. Kuznetsov declared that his purpose in coming to the camp was not to excuse prisoners from work because of illness but rather to compel them to work. Many prisoners who for many years had been classified as disabled, were reclassified as able-bodied. One of them, a Lithuanian named Kurkis who had an ulcer, had not worked for years. After the board's finding that he was able-bodied, he was assigned to heavy work—spading up the "off-limits zone." Perforation of his ulcer occurred the very first day. The superintendent of Camp #35 telephoned Lieutenant Colonel Kuznetsov, the surgeon for that camp, but he refused to come and see the patient. Kurkis died . . .

Other communications tell what happens to fighters for civil rights who have been given repeated long sentences; e.g., Vladimir Bukovsky and Valentin Moroz. Moroz was put in Vladimir Prison, in the same cell with regular criminals. They tormented him, and kept him from sleeping at night. One of them, using a spoon-handle sharpened like a knife, slit open his stomach. Moroz had to be sent to the hospital, where the wound was stitched up. Following that incident, he was placed in solitary confinement at the request of both himself and his wife.

After serving more than three years in prison, Moroz requested transfer to a labor camp. According to current legislation, when a prisoner has served half of a prison term, he may be transferred to a camp, provided he has not violated prison regulations. Moroz had no record of violations except for one thing: during a visit from his wife, he had talked with her in Ukrainian, and had refused to switch to Russian—for doing which he was deprived of what was left of the visit. On those grounds, he was denied transfer to a camp. On July 1, 1974, he declared a hunger strike.

In an appeal to "all kind-hearted and humane people on this earth," his wife Raisa Moroz wrote:

> On November 5 my husband Valentin Moroz, a political prisoner in Vladimir Prison, received a visit from his family. It was the 128th day of his hunger strike. . . .
>
> Valentin is terribly thin (114 pounds, with a height of five feet, eight inches). His face is swollen, and he has bags under his eyes. He complains of heart pains. But what has caused him the most pain is the tube through which he has been force-fed since the twelfth day of his hunger strike. The tube cuts into the sides of his throat

> and esophagus. When they pull it out, it is all bloody. He still feels the kind of pain he felt with the very first feedings. Between feedings, he is in an almost-continuous state of unconsciousness. But from time to time he forces himself to get up on his feet, because he fears that otherwise his legs might atrophy. . . .

One of the most inhumane inventions of the Soviet penal system is the confinement of dissenters in psychiatric hospitals for compulsory treatment with drugs which depress the consciousness and will. This method symbolizes the role of totalitarianism on the historical plane. Thus physicians at the Dnepropetrovsk Special Psychiatric Hospital, where Leonid Plyushch was confined, prescribed large doses of haloperidol for him, in tablet form. When his wife visited him in October 1973, she found him depressed, apathetic, and sleepy. In August and September, before the "treatment," he had written her many long, informative letters. But afterward he had virtually stopped writing, and could not even read. In January 1974 his condition was as before: he was sleeping most of the time; he could not read or write; and he did not want to go out for walks in the prison yard, because it was too cold for him. When L. A. Chasovskikh, the attending physician, was asked by Plyushch's wife what symptoms of his illness indicated the necessity for continuing the treatment, she replied: "His views and convictions." And she refused to answer any more questions about diagnosis and treatment.

In April 1974 they had stopped giving Plyushch any drugs whatsoever, because he had developed pains in the abdomen, and the doctors had become alarmed. After the drugs had been discontinued, his condition began to improve: the swellings started to go down, and the pains went away. He was transferred to another ward, where there were fewer patients and it was quieter. He began to read again. But then they resumed the injections of insulin in increasing doses. He developed an allergic rash and itching, but the injections were continued. After each injection, Plyushch was tied to the bed for four hours . . .

Autumn 1974: the trial of Mikhail Kheifets, a teacher of Russian language and literature in Leningrad. The main charge brought against him in the indictment was that he had written an article, "Joseph Brodsky and Our Generation," which he had shown to a few acquaintances. Sentence: four years in a strict-regimen camp, two years of exile.

In Armenia, several trials of Armenians took place in 1974. They were charged with nationalism, specifically with having joined the "National United Party of Armenia," whose aim is the secession of Armenia from the USSR. Fourteen persons were convicted. They received sentences of up to seven years in strict-regimen camps.

January–April 1974: in Kazakhstan, a series of trials of Soviet Germans who were seeking to emigrate to West Germany. Sentences: Abel, Tissen, Verner, Fertig—three years of incarceration; The Valentin brothers and Viktor Klinny—two years. August: several Germans convicted in Estonia.

Vilnius, December 1974: five persons convicted. Maximum sentence: eight years in a strict-regimen camp (Petras Plumpa).

All such events take place against a background of many searches, interrogations, detentions, and extrajudicial repressions (dismissals from employment, etc.). At any moment in time, new trials are being prepared. Vladimir Osipov was arrested in October 1974, and Sergei Kovalev in December. Andrei Tverdokhlebov, Secretary of the Soviet Group of Amnesty International, was arrested in April 1975. At the same time, three other moves were made against members of that group. In Kiev, the writer Mikola Rudenko was arrested. He was released two days later, after having signed an understanding not to leave the city. In Moscow, searches were made at the home of Vladimir Albrekht, and at my home. For twelve hours, persons representing the Procuracy and the KGB lorded it over me in my own apartment. The inventory of confiscated materials (including rough MSS, letters, etc.) consisted of 212 items. During the month of June I was interrogated six times—technically as a witness in the Tverdokhlebov case, but actually (of course) because I myself was being investigated. This was evident from the questions they asked me. For example: "What part have you taken in helping the children of political prisoners?" Or: "Where did you get your information about the Svetlichny case in the Ukraine?" Etc., etc.[48]

Part II
Socialism

Pessimism and Optimism

> True optimism has nothing to do with any sort of lenient judgment. It consists in contemplating and willing the ideal in the light of a deep and self-consistent affirmation of life and the world. Because the spirit which is so directed proceeds with clear vision and impartial judgment in the valuing of all that is given, it wears to ordinary people the appearance of pessimism. . . .
>
> Albert Schweitzer[1]

The picture of Soviet society painted in part I may give the reader the idea that the author is a pessimist. Such is by no means the case. To bring out unpleasant truths is as much the duty of the optimist as it is of the pessimist. A pessimist is a person who claims to see nothing good in the future. Hence he does not work toward it, since in his view that would be senseless. An optimist is a person who does not attempt to predict the future, but instead works for it. He reasons that the future is unpredictable: it depends upon how we view it and how we plan for it. Optimism is, in this view, much less complacent than pessimism. The optimist by no means affirms that Good will triumph; he merely allows that it might do so. And he refuses to believe that Evil must inevitably triumph.

In that sense, I am an optimist. My optimism has two foundations. The first is a conception of history which, in contrast to the Marxists' Historical Materialism, might be called "Historical Idealism." This conception has just as little in common with philosophical Idealism as Marx's Historical

Materialism has with philosophical Materialism. It merely affirms that in the relationship between social existence and social consciousness, the latter is the governing factor, determining the development of society as a whole. If that is so, we human beings are free to choose our own fate. And if we do not want totalitarianism, we have the capacity to reject it.

The stabilization of totalitarianism described in part I is currently directly observable. However, other events are taking place beneath these surface phenomena. The fight for civil liberties has had its consequences. And the same thing applies to the many private conversations, discussions, and actions which are known to only a limited number of people but are taking place throughout the USSR. Societal life consists of both underground and above-ground currents; and at certain moments the underground currents come to the surface. What is going on now is a process of ripening: the gradual transformation of views toward life in general, and of approaches to specific problems.

What directions can this underground transformation take? Is it capable of engendering a social consciousness that can oppose totalitarianism and achieve social reforms?

We are living in an age of science and industry. Today, the scientific worldview provides the basis for social consciousness, while industrial production determines the forms and conditions under which social consciousness develops. The rise of totalitarianism is unquestionably part and parcel of the scientific-industrial era—the fruit of that era. From this fact, it is sometimes concluded that a social consciousness whose cornerstone is science rather than Christian faith (as was the case in the Europe of pre-totalitarian times) leads to totalitarianism—or, in any case, cannot lead us out of it. So the only hope for change is to go back to a Christian consciousness. Otherwise, there is no source from which one can get the strength, the spiritual energy, to combat Evil. Such is the viewpoint of Alexander Solzhenitsyn; and it is shared by some (although not a great many) members of the Soviet intelligentsia. *From Under the Rubble* was written for the most part, from that viewpoint.

For me, a return to the Christian fundamentalism is impossible; and I am deeply convinced that it is impossible for the great majority of our contemporaries. Thus if I shared Solzhenitsyn's point of view, I would be a confirmed pessimist. But I do not share it. I maintain instead that the ideological prerequisites of totalitarianism are associated with the scientific (and pseudo-scientific) ideas of the nineteenth century. I maintain that in our time orderly construction of a worldview on the basis of the scientific philosophy of nature and the critical scientific method engenders a life-affirming and antitotalitarian consciousness capable of vigorous social action. And this is the second foundation-stone of my optimism.

I shall link the social consciousness I have in mind with the word "socialism." That word, however, is used in many different contexts and with extremely varied meanings.

What Is Socialism?

I shall begin my discussion of this question with a few quotations from Igor Shafarevich's article "Socialism" in *From Under the Rubble.* Shafarevich is a confirmed opponent of socialism, and I do not agree with his interpretation of the causes and essence of that phenomenon. It is nevertheless remarkable that whereas many (perhaps most) of its adherents regard socialism as simply a political system, one of its enemies should call upon us to see in it a worldwide historical phenomenon—one that extends far beyond the sphere of politics and is based on the deepest strata in human nature. On that point, I agree with him entirely.

After quoting several excerpts from Lenin's article "Three Sources and Three Components of Marxism," along with excerpts from Dudu Tiam, an ideologue of "African socialism" ("African societies have always lived by an empirical, natural socialism which can be termed instinctive") and Jamad ed-Din al-Afghani, an ideologue of Islamic socialism ("Socialism is a part of the religion of Islam"), Shafarevich writes:

> What kind of peculiar phenomenon is this that it can evoke such different judgments? Is it a collection of unconnected movements which for some incomprehensible reason insist on sharing one name? Or do they really have something in common beneath their external variety?
>
> The most basic and obvious questions about socialism do not seem to have been answered at all; other questions, as will be seen later, have not even been asked. This ability to repel rational consideration seems itself to be yet one more enigmatic characteristic of this enigmatic phenomenon.[2]

As examples of ancient socialist societies, Shafarevich cites Ur (2200–2000 B.C.) and the empire of the Incas. He also includes Plato's doctrine and certain medieval heresies among the socialist doctrines. This is a very broad interpretation of the concept of socialism, and very few people will agree with it. Yet I find it rather sound. The resemblance between the Soviet Union or the People's Republic of China and the empire of the Incas is simply too profound and significant. And after all, it is not only the leaders of those countries but the enlightened Westerners, too, who call them socialist.

Shafarevich goes on to say:

> if socialism is characteristic of almost all historical eras and civilizations, its origin cannot be ascribed to any causes associated with the traits of any specific period of culture: not to the conflict between productive forces and production relations, and not to the psychological traits of the African or Arab peoples. Attempts at this kind of interpretation distort the perspective hopelessly, squeezing that tremendous phenomenon of world

> history into an ill-fitting framework of particular economic, historical, and racial categories. Later we shall try to approach this problem from a diametrically opposite viewpoint, recognizing that socialism is one of the most basic and universal forces acting throughout the course of history.[3]

And further:

> an ideology like socialism, capable of inspiring great popular movements and of creating its own saints and martyrs, cannot be based on falsification: it must be imbued with a profound internal unity.[4]

I agree. But what I disagree with is Shafarevich's view that a basic and primordial trait of socialism is "the elimination of private property, the destruction of religion, and the ruin of the family." He feels that socialism's ultimate goal is to wipe out man's individuality: to establish a worldwide utopia of the kind preached by Shigalev [Shigalyov] in Dostoyevsky's *The Possessed*, and a totalitarian state of the Huxley-Orwell variety. From that premise, Shafarevich draws the conclusion that the triumph of socialism will mean the actual destruction of humanity, and most likely will lead to its literal, physical death. Then he draws his next conclusion. It is quite a fantastic one: that the death wish is the motivating force of socialism:

> but the closer you become acquainted with socialist philosophy, the clearer it becomes that there is no error here, no aberration. The organic connection between socialism and death is subconsciously or half-consciously felt by its followers without in the least frightening them at all. On the contrary, this is what gives the socialist movements their attraction and their motive force. This cannot of course be proved logically, it can be verified only by checking it against socialist literature and the psychology of socialist movements. And here we are obliged to limit ourselves to a few heterogeneous examples.[5]

Shafarevich's examples do not convince one of the correctness of his thesis. He finds in socialists a readiness to sacrifice themselves for the sake of the higher goal that has been proclaimed, and sometimes a kind of fascination with that readiness. The trait in question is altogether human, however, and characteristic of others besides socialists. But for some reason, Shafarevich feels that in socialists it is a manifestation of the death wish and of the "pathos of perishing." Even in quoting Engels' remark on the inevitable cooling down of the earth, Shafarevich does not see it as one of the "fruits of scholarly minds forced to bow to the truth, however drastic it might appear to be," but as a manifestation of the death wish. And into that same pot he puts Mao's statement that "the death of half of the world's population would not be too high a price to pay for the victory of socialism throughout the world." Next he enlists the aid of Freud's theory that the death wish is one of the basic drives determining man's psychic life. From that point on, his logic runs as follows:

> And socialism, which captures and subordinates millions of people to its will in a movement whose ideal aim is the death of mankind, cannot of course be understood without the assumption that those same ideas are equally applicable to social phenomena; that is, *that among the basic forces influencing historical development, is the urge to self-destruction, the human death instinct.*[6]

I am convinced, however, that the death wish—even if it does exist—plays no role in all this. For me, those destructive and totalitarian aspects of socialism that we see in history are not the nucleus of the phenomenon but rather its shell, which must be removed if one is to understand its origin.

What, then, is the nature of socialism's nucleus? I maintain that it has the same nature as do all the great religions which have given rise to the civilizations of the past and present. Socialism is the religion of the future global civilization—that civilization which is right now in the throes of birth.

In itself, there is nothing new in likening socialism to religion; the resemblance between them is too striking not to be noticed. But for over a hundred years, that resemblance has been viewed as a detraction by both socialists and religious people. The Christians have gone no further than to link the *ideological basis* of Christianity with a moderate socialist *political program*—something that only stresses the opposition between socialism and religion. As for the socialists, they fly into a rage whenever the resemblance between socialism and religion is pointed out to them. But I consider that resemblance an asset.

The Religious Emotion

I have already mentioned the hierarchy of goals in the behavior of higher animals and humans. From the viewpoint of the external observer, the achievement by animals of the various goals constituting that hierarchy is indispensable to their continued existence and reproduction; i.e., in the final analysis, to the survival of the species. But from a subjective viewpoint, the process of achieving goals is associated with *emotions*. The details of the cybernetics of emotions are not known. We know only that when it is impossible to reach a goal that in some way figures in the hierarchy or plan, a negative emotion results; when such a goal is reached, a positive emotion results. Different emotions arise in achieving different goals (satiety, satisfaction of the sex instinct, victory over an enemy, etc.). Because emotions are stimulated by goals on different levels, and because of the pervasiveness of the emotions (as well as from what we have learned about the structure of the nervous system), the conclusion must be reached that the emotions are very ancient and very common phenomena. One would probably not be mistaken in saying that there is a particular emotion corresponding to each goal, and that the variety of the emotions reflects the variety of goals.

Let us now recall the difference between humans and animals as regards the mechanism for forming a hierarchy of goals. For an animal, the highest level of the hierarchy (the supreme goal) is an aggregate of basic instincts. To these instincts correspond the most basic emotions. In humans, we find a capacity for the socially conditioned construction of the highest level in the hierarchy of goals. Now let us ask ourselves the following question: If the mechanism of emotion is lodged deep within the structure of the central nervous system, should we not expect that in the process of the metasystem transition which transformed an animal into man, the appearance of the new goal-setting apparatus would be accompanied, on the subjective plane, by the appearance of a new class of emotions?

I believe the answer is yes, and I offer the following definition: The religious emotion is that which corresponds to the movement toward the supreme goal, which transcend biological instincts.

In its negative form, this emotion is manifested as unaccountable yearning when it is clear that something very important is lacking, but one does not understand what it is. (This is one of the first profoundly human feelings.) In its positive form, this emotion is called by various names: mystical feeling, illumination, grace, sensing the presence of God, for example.

Let us try to analyze the concepts associated with the religious emotion. The first of these is the concept of the meaning of life. Religiousness is first of all understood as filling life with a significance which makes meaningful even the details of daily living. In the light of my definition of the religious feeling, and of the relationship between the higher and lower goals in the hierarchy, this aspect of religiousness is understandable in and of itself. Another aspect of the religious emotion—the fact that it is always described as something "higher"—is likewise an obvious corollary of our definition.

Also, the concepts of infinity, eternity, and immortality are closely associated with the religious emotion. Many, if not all, mystics use the phrase "communing with eternity" to describe their experience. This aspect is associated with our realization of our own mortality, and with the *suprapersonal* nature of the supreme goal. The reproductive instinct that we find in animals has already set out "suprapersonal" (if we may so speak of animals) goals for the individual. But the animal's instinct is not something the creature realizes. In humans, the elaboration of the supreme goal takes place in a consciousness which reflects not only all of the goals already fixed (including those conditioned by instinct) but also the finiteness in time of one's personal existence. It is clear that such a consciousness can be satisfied only by a suprapersonal supreme goal. The awareness of one's own mortality is one of the chief factors in humanization. It demands some kind of communication with the eternal, the immortal. And for a mortal being, the only way to meet that demand is to fix a suprapersonal supreme goal expressed in terms of the eternal—or, at any rate, in terms of something that goes so far beyond the limits of human life that the imagination does not distinguish it from the eternal.

One other important characteristic of the religious emotion is that, like other properly human emotions (for example, the sense of the beautiful and the sense of the funny, whose connection with the process of humanization I analyze in *The Phenomenon of Science*), it is *culturally*—and not just biologically—conditioned. Biologically, humans are endowed only with a potentiality for the religious emotion. In order for that potentiality to be realized, the religious emotion must be *developed,* just as we develop our imagination, our appreciation of beauty, our sense of humor. If it is not developed, it may persist only in the form of vague, unrealized impulses which play no significant role in life.

The logical concept of the supreme goal is involved in the religious emotion, but it by no means engenders the latter automatically. There is of course a profound link between the world of ideas and the world of the emotions: this is evidenced, for example, by the excitement one feels upon getting a good idea. It would be ludicrous, however, to think that the religious emotion can be imposed by a simple decree of the supreme goal expressed in some verbal formulation.

The development of the religious emotion is usually a long process requiring the assimilation not only of certain logical concepts but also of certain *images;* also, of personal example and direct impact on the emotional sphere. Therefore, the entire culture of the society as a whole takes part in the development of the religious emotion. (At any rate, this is true of the great majority of people: certain individuals may have an inner life that does not resemble that of other people.) The aggregate of the methods for developing the religious emotion (including, of course, verbal formulations of the supreme goal) forms a society's *religion.*

There is no doubt as to the reality and strength of the religious emotion. When a person undergoes deprivation and hardships, and even sacrifices his life for the sake of certain higher goals, it is the religious emotion which supports him, compensating for other emotions.

On the Question of Terminology

When we use old terms in a new context, and hence modify the corresponding concepts, we are taking the liberty of asserting that certain aspects of those concepts are "essential," so that we retain them, while others are "nonessential" and can be dealt with at our discretion. What is essential in the use of the word "religion" in a historical or social context is the affirmation of a suprapersonal supreme goal (or, what is the same thing, of suprapersonal supreme values), and the existence of a system for inculcating the emotions corresponding to that goal. The existence of these traits suffices for us to speak of religion and the religious emotion. I dare-say that the other characteristics of the religions known to us, including such common ones as a belief in "the other world" expressed in one form or another, must be regarded as nonessential or secondary, for the formation of the supreme goal is precisely that component of religion which endows it with its historical role—motivating masses of people. Therefore, I shall use the word religion to designate any system for the elaboration of the supreme goal, regardless of that system's relationship to traditional religious doctrines. The word's etymology does not hinder this expansion of the meaning; it favors it. Religion probably derives from the Latin verb *religare,* "to bind fast"; i.e., to bind up the lower, earthly human being with what is higher, eternal, divine. Modernizing this meaning just a bit, we can reformulate it as "binding up the personal with the suprapersonal supreme goal."

But why do all of the world's traditional religions cling so stubbornly to the otherwordly element? Or, to use the language of philosophy, "the transcendental"? Because transcendental concepts give them a basis for the supreme goal. They legitimize it as uniquely "true." They bring man to an acceptance of the supreme goal.

One tendency in human culture that has been well studied from a positivistic viewpoint is the tendency to *objectify* phenomena in the human sphere—to rethink them as universals external to man. I do not know who was the first to clearly point out that tendency, but in Feuerbach's *Essence of Christianity* the idea is already formulated, and serves to underpin the entire work. In the history of culture, objectification appears in various forms. The objectification of the connection between name and meaning engenders the magic of primitive peoples. The objectification of abstract concepts engendered Plato's Theory of Ideas, and other kinds of philosophical idealism later on. The transcendental element in religion is an objectification of the supreme goal's transcending nature. Indeed, the supreme goal cannot be deduced from any other goal, because it is the highest. It cannot be found or discovered, because it is a goal. It can only be established by an act of the will: "created from nothing," from "the transfinite." In its objectified form, the existence of the supreme goal is perceived as the existence of a supreme reality beyond the range of our senses and cognition.

The concept of God masks the genesis of the supreme goal. The emphasis shifts to the question of the *existence* of God, and the supreme goal is declared to be only one of His aspects—it is derived from God's existence. The question of the *will* is thus transformed into the question of *knowledge* or *belief*. (There is, at base, no difference between these two concepts.) An act which is basically volitional appears as an act of discovery—unveiling the real. When that act has been performed and the religious emotion becomes, for a person, an indisputable and self-evident fact of one's inner life, it is apprehended as irrefutable evidence of God's existence. The circle has been closed.

Marxist Man and Dostoyevskian Man

In his historical theory, Marx regarded man as an *economic being*. But the success of his theory, despite its impotence in predicting events, proves a truth that is just the opposite: man is not an economic being. Marxism has become tremendously influential because, and only because, it has turned out to be a successful way of eliciting and intensifying the religious emotion in the guise of a theory of political science. For man is a *religious being*.

It was not just Marx but Positivism—and no doubt the entire culture of the nineteenth century—that underrated the importance of the religious element. "Love and hunger rule the world" was one of the most popular aphorisms. But love and hunger can already be found in the animal kingdom. Can one really say that the difference between humans and animals is so slight, so superficial, that the same factors which are the most important in the animal kingdom, and determine its development, determine the development of man's world?

Within the framework of my definition of religion, and of the religious emotion, the assertion that man is a religious being becomes almost tautological. For the fact is that in the hierarchy of goals and behavior plans, religious plans form the highest level. Hence they determine those aspects of behavior which are most common and most enduring. Yet this formal answer is not too convincing, because the question still remains: To what degree, and how intensively, does the religious level influence the life of each person? And how does it influence the development of society as a whole?

The salience of the religious element, the intensity of the religious emotion, and its role in the fate of a human being are highly individual matters which vary within broad limits. Dostoyevsky has given us vivid characterizations of persons with a very highly developed religious emotion. Dostoyevskian man is religious man *par excellence*. The religious substance—the problem of the supreme goal and the meaning of life—permeates him entirely, and determines his thoughts and acts in each detail. Dostoyevskian man is a person in whom the religious element has luxuriated to an overwhelming degree and engulfed all the other levels of the hierarchy. He has none of those "simple and natural" human sentiments which bind us to the maternal womb of biological, natural harmony: he sees and feels through the prism of the higher values. And his instincts, no matter how strong they may be, are refracted through that same prism. Essentially, each of his feelings is religious, with its characteristic contradictions, insatiability, and tragic coloration. Dostoyevsky's great contribution to world culture was that he created a new type—a new biological species, if you will—of man: religious man in his pure, extreme state. This new type created by Dostoyevsky has had a profound influence on twentieth-century culture.

Marx's economic man is the good-hearted old chap of

the nineteenth century. Without philosophizing, he goes to the market to exchange one frock coat for fifteen yards of cloth. He bends every effort to make the highest profit on the capital he has invested. He acts only out of considerations of personal gain, out of calculation, out of the urge to satisfy his *needs.* The last-named is a key word in understanding his essence. Economic man may be defined as a being striving for the maximum satisfaction of his needs.

(At this point, I cannot refrain from quoting yet another sentence from Engels' essay on Ludwig Feuerbach: man "requires preoccupation with the outside world, means to satisfy his needs, that is to say, food, an individual of the opposite sex, books, conversation, argument, activities."[7] The touching simplicity with which Engels lists "an individual of the opposite sex" among the means of satisfying one's needs would no doubt be impossible to attain in our time.)

Economic man is altogether a legal abstraction. His behavior is relatively simple, and more or less predictable. He can serve as a modular substitute for a human being in solving certain particular problems; for example, those having to do with the functioning of the market or the circulation of capital. But to build on this foundation a universal conception of human history—and that with pretensions to specific prediction (O the boundless presumption of the 19th century!)—is like explaining the work of an electric motor by analogy with a steam engine, without the slightest reference to the notions of electric current and magnetic field.

Dostoyevskian man and Marxist man are two opposite poles of human nature. While Marxist man is devoid of an essential part of human nature, Dostoyevskian man, dominated to an extreme degree by the ever-present and ever-tormenting religious-ethical element, is not a norm either. But what role does the religious level play in the lives of ordinary, normal people? What is the mechanism of its influence?

Historical Idealism

> . . . Every age lives in the consciousness of what has been provided for it by the thinkers under whose influence it stands.
>
> Plato was wrong in holding that the philosophers of the State should also be its governors. Their supremacy is a different and a higher one than that which consists in framing and issuing laws and ordinances and giving effect to official authority. They are the officers of the general staff who sit in the background thinking out, with more or less clearness of vision, the details of the battle which is to be fought. Those who play their part in the public eye are the subordinate officers who, for their variously sized units, convert the general directions of the staff into orders of the day: namely, that the forces will start at such and such a time, move in this or that direction, and occupy this or that point. Kant and Hegel have commanded millions who had never read a line of their writings, and who did not even know that they were obeying their orders.
>
> Albert Schweitzer[8]

I have mentioned briefly the relationship between the higher and lower levels in the hierarchy of behavior plans. Let us now consider the matter in greater detail.

When we observe complex cybernetic systems constructed on the basis of a multi-level control hierarchy, we discover *cycles* nested in one another (I define cycle as a sequence of roughly identical situations, actions, etc.). A long cycle consists of a certain number of repetitions of a shorter cycle, and may itself be a component of an even longer cycle. If, for example, a worker at a plant is driving rivets into a certain part, the minimum cycle will consist of raising the hammer and bringing it down on the rivet. A certain number of these cycles, together with certain repetitive actions, make up a longer cycle: hammering in the rivet. If we assume that twenty rivets must be driven into each part, that gives us the next cycle. The cycles involved in the manufacture of particular parts, and the implied presence of many workers and a diversity of tools, combine to make the production cycle for one article. An even larger-scale cycle is that involved in the production and sale of a batch of articles, together with the corresponding elements of buying raw materials, etc. Finally, the largest-scale cycle is associated with putting new articles into production, adopting a new technology or economic policy, or a change in top management, etc.

This way of structuring operations is typical of all organized systems. It is by no means random but instead is a result of the fact that organized systems are formed phylogenetically (if not ontogenetically) by means of sequential metasystem transitions: the integration of existing components with the creation of a new level of control. Each structural element has a definite time frame: the length of the work cycle. The newly created control level does not replace the existing control apparatus in each of the elements integrated but merely coordinates their functions, and perhaps modifies them. Therefore, the typical functional unit of the higher level comprises a certain aggregate of the units on a lower level. A *cycle of cycles* is formed.

In the behavior of animals and humans, we can distinguish three obviously different kinds of cycles:

1) The cycles associated with movement. For a human being, a typical cycle of this kind is one step. The typical length of the cycle is about one second.

2) The cycles associated with digestion. In a human being, this cycle takes several hours; i.e., about 20,000 movement cycles.

3) The cycles associated with sexual reproduction. Here one cycle may be equated with the period of time required to produce offspring and rear them to the age of sexual maturity. For a human being, this cycle may be figured at fifteen years, which again equals about 20,000 cycles on the preceding level.

Of course there is far more to the hierarchical structure of behavior than is indicated by this breakdown. Each of these levels has its own intricate structure, its own sublevels, and its own intermediate cycles. But all of these cycles, which have a common biological origin, also have another trait in common: they do not extend beyond the limits of the individual's life. Only the suprapersonal supreme goal established by religion (in the broad sense in which I am using that word) can create norms of behavior which function over many generations. The source of these norms is the society's culture and not human biological nature. Religious behavior plans assure a link between generations; only they can have a greater duration than that of an individual life. They do not (if we disregard distortions) abolish, replace, or contravene the behavior plans of the lower (i.e., the biological) levels: they control them—as best they can, because control, first, is not the same thing as absolute power, and, second, necessarily involves some random error.

If we walk through a factory, we shall see workers, machine tools, and conveyor belts. But we shall learn nothing of the economic aspect of the plant's operation (the demand for the product, its relative quality, cost, etc.). Yet it is precisely that aspect which is chiefly responsible for the fate of the plant as a whole. And the same thing applies to a society. We are constantly going through cycles nested in cycles. And the reality closest to us—the reality directly presented to us—is the reality of the innermost (i.e., the shortest) cycles. We are constantly in the power of the forces moving us through those cycles. They are very great forces, and we see their effect everywhere around us. Then we say, "Love and hunger rule the world."

But when we have moved through the entire cycle, we

shall have returned to our starting point. All our cycles have a lowest common denominator—the cycle of human life. We are born; we experience hunger and satiety, love and hatred; then we die. This alone tells us that, on the historical plane, what we should regard as decisive are not the obvious powerful forces that propel us through the cycles but those which, although not evident at first glance, function constantly and effect a divergence between our starting and finishing points. The circle (in Hegel's figure) turns into a spiral. For that matter, this phenomenon occurs even in the short term. We are constantly setting goals for ourselves, and achieving them; the circle is then closed. Then we set ourselves a new goal; but the cycle it engenders will not exactly coincide with the previous one. The difference between these cycles will be determined by factors external to them—factors from the next higher level of the hierarchy.

If we view society as a multilevel cybernetic system, we arrive at the conception I call *historical idealism*, in contrast to the Marxist conception. Historical idealism affirms that it is precisely *ideas* which dominate society and, in the final analysis, determine its development—its destiny. In the interaction between the way of life (including the production system) and the way of thinking, the dynamic, revolutionary element is the way of thinking and not the way of life. For a cybernetician, this is almost an obvious corollary of the most general laws of nature. A human being rarely thinks about why he lives and how he should live. And when he does, he usually gets confused. The behavior plans of the highest level, which dominate his society, are something he takes for granted; and he is not inclined to notice their influence on his own life. It seems to him that thinking about "all sorts of supreme goals," and the meaning of life is idle philosophizing that has no bearing on real life, with its real problems. But over long intervals of time, the behavior plans of the highest level prove decisive: they determine the transformation, in time, of the inner cycles. They do not eliminate the goals of the lower level, but they determine the methods of attaining them. There are many ways of appeasing hunger;

and it is *not* the sensation of hunger that determines which of those ways will be chosen. The imaginary Marxist man, given a choice between a job that pays 150 rubles a month and one that pays 151 rubles, will choose the latter, regardless of any "higher considerations." But in fact, as studies by sociologists have shown, when a young worker is choosing a job, the prestige is at least as important as the wage—usually it is more important. As for the concept of the prestige attached to various kinds of work, it is a direct reflection, in the mass consciousness, of the supreme goal, which (consciously or unconsciously) is present in the culture of the society.

In wars, revolutions, mass movements, and individual actions demanding great exertion of spiritual strength—in all those events in which history is, as it were, condensed—the religious element takes on decisive significance. In such situations, passion—not calculation—motivates people. The Marxist man hides under the bed, while the Dostoyevskian man—with both his darker side and his sunny aspect—rises to his full height.

In constructing their theory, Marx and Engels drew only upon the history of Europe. Noting a parallel in the development of the economy and ideology, they declared that economics—material production—was primary, while spiritual culture—ideology—was secondary. This conclusion was arbitrary, since one cannot, on the basis of an isolated phenomenon, draw conclusions as to cause-and-effect relationships. For Marx, the cultural background of Western Europe remained a constant factor whose role could not be clarified because he had no alternatives. Since his time, however, we have had many proofs of the decisive influence of cultural factors over economic ones. The end of the nineteenth century witnessed the rapid penetration of European technology and ideology into many countries, both independent and colonial. Let us compare, for instance, the economic development of Japan and Turkey. Neither country was ever a colony. Both, it would seem, had the same opportunity for utilizing modern production methods. Then why do we see such a sharp difference between them as regards the level and pace of development? Plainly, those differences which enabled Japan to set out on its specific path of development (and to achieve amazing economic results) are to be sought in the cultural sphere. Another comparison is no less instructive. The writings of Max Weber showed the close link between Protestantism—a cultural factor which at first glance has nothing in common with economics—and the development of capitalism in Europe. The European colonization of America offers a striking example of that link. Here we have what is almost a pure experiment. Settlers from both Protestant and Catholic countries came to the new continent. Life began from scratch, and the conditions for everything were more or less equal. Protestant America, the U.S. and Canada, became the world's leading industrial powers. But Catholic Latin America is still rated as "developing."

Socialism Defined

Socialism is a religion which proclaims the integration of mankind as its supreme goal. In offering this definition, as in defining religion, I am taking the liberty of asserting that in the many doctrines and movements called socialism, it is precisely this trait that is essential. I assert that this is what gives socialist movements their strength—a strength that comes from the religious emotion. Of course in defining socialism, one might take as an alternative the aspiration toward universal equality and justice. But it seems to me that these traits of socialism derive from the idea of integration. In socialist doctrine, justice is usually understood as equality; and equality serves as a means for establishing universal brotherhood. Humanity must merge into a single, united family: such is the dream of the socialists. The idea of equality *per se* can hardly appeal to the religious emotion. The destruction of private property and the family advocated in certain socialist doctrines—something that Shafarevich takes to be one of the chief traits of socialism—is a secondary derivative from the idea of equality.

The specific content of the concept of integration may vary in different socialist doctrines; but they, unlike traditional religions, all share the "earthly" or "this worldly" interpretation of that concept. Aspiration toward communion with something infinite and eternal is an organic part of the religious emotion. Socialism rejects—or at any rate is not satisfied with—the transcendental interpretation of integration. For it, the concept of the supreme goal is indivisible from human society, and is unthinkable without it. Hence the word "socialism." However concretized the concept of the Good, for all socialists the highest goal that the individual can and should have, is the good for the society as a whole.

There can be little doubt that the idea of integrating individuals touches certain strings deep in the human soul and elicits very strong emotions. The effect of integration appears sometimes as positive and sometimes as negative. In the latter case it is described in such phrases as "the effect of the crowd" or "mass psychosis." We also rate as a negative such aspects of integration as the elimination of personal responsibility, the ecstasy of submission, and relinquishing the burden of freedom. Intoxication with power is also apparently based on the phenomenon of integration. When describing the effect of integration in a positive way, people speak of "the feeling of fellowship," the "joy of being a member of the collective," etc. Individualized personal relationships, such as friendship and love, based on a close spiritual affinity, also belong among the effects of integration, which are rated as positive.

From this list of the various aspects of integration, one may conclude that socialist movements, too, can lead to both positive and negative results. And this is the case. It is only adherence to the idea of integration which, quite unconditionally, engenders all socialist movements, since it is the source of their vigor and has the greatest stability of all of socialism's practical and theoretical traits. This is especially plain in the history of the Soviet state. The ideas of freedom, equality, and democracy were present in the original doctrine, along with the idea of social integration ("Workers of the world, unite!"). But these ideas got lost along the way. All that remained was integration. Given the definition of socialism that I have offered, the present-day Communist state must be counted as one of its forms: the totalitarian form. In this barbaric, monstrous form of socialism, the integration of individuals is achieved only at the price of such violence to them that they lose their human essence. First they lose the opportunity, then the capacity, for creativity—for an authentic spiritual life.

Russia, China, Cuba: We have seen how socialist revolutions have invariably led to a totalitarian system. On the other hand, when socialist parties come to power in the countries of northern Europe by peaceful, parliamentary means, they are in no hurry to call their countries socialist. So that up to now, the kind of socialism that calls itself socialism, exists only in the form of totalitarianism. This compels us to ask the question: Is a nontotalitarian socialism possible?

It is by Marxist socialism that the present-day totalitarian systems were fathered. Therefore, in seeking an approach to nontotalitarian socialism, we must return to our analysis of Marxism, in order to scrutinize both the causes of its success and the roots of totalitarian-socialist barbarism.

Scientific Socialism

More than a hundred years have passed since the birth of Marxism, and it is still the most vigorous form of socialism and no doubt the most widespread—even if we exclude those totalitarian-socialist countries where it is imposed by force.

But what particular traits of Marxism have secured this position for it? And, since it is generally acknowledged that not a single one of Marx's predictions has come true, why do so many people insist on calling themselves Marxists?

The answer to the second question, it seems to me, lies in the fact that the Marxists themselves (although they do not acknowledge it) treat Marxism as a religious doctrine and not as a scientific theory. If all (or at any rate many) of a theory's predictions fail, nothing is left of it. At that point, people are not usually inclined to continue honoring the founder's name. More likely, they are eager to disown it—to emphasize that now they have worked out, or are working out, a new theory which, unlike the old one, will yield correct predictions. But things are quite the other way around when the basic value system of a religion is involved. Then, people tend to associate it with the names of the most ancient of its founders. For a religion, longevity is an advantage: it shows that its value system is characteristic of human nature and plays a role in the history of mankind. Time sanctifies the supreme goal and makes it traditional. The continuity of a religion from generation to generation carries within it the idea of integration—integration in time.

To turn to the first question, plainly, Marxism has had a tremendous influence on history precisely because it effected a synthesis—and a very successful one for its time—of the religious element with the political and scientific elements.

The synthesis of a socialist religion with a political revolutionary movement was achieved with the concept of the proletariat as a class whose historic mission was to establish socialism through the revolutionary overthrow of the existing order. In Lenin's words:

> The chief contribution of Marx and Engels was in steering socialism toward a confluence with the labor movement. They created a theory of revolution which explained the necessity for that confluence, and gave the socialists the task of organizing the class struggle of the proletariat.[9]

Marxist socialism's founders, leaders, and activists were not workers: they were not fighting for their own liberation from capitalism, or for a crust of bread for their families. They were animated by a religious drive—by an aspiration toward the socialist ideal. And they felt that the most reliable—indeed, the only—way to attain that ideal was to use as leverage the wrath of the downtrodden—their revolutionary potential. Lenin taught that it was the task of the socialist intellectuals to inculcate the working masses with the revolutionary socialist ideology ("socialist consciousness").

Marx synthesized religion and science by developing the concept of *scientific socialism.* A realization of the tremendous role played by science and technological progress, and their influence on society, was of course nothing new in Marx's time. The idea of progress was the favorite offspring of the Enlightenment. Herder, Condorcet, and others were enthralled by the idea of progress; for them it took on a religious character. The era of the French Revolution witnessed the confluence of philosophical rationalism and traditional attributes of religion, including religious feeling. People began to elaborate rational religions. The Jacobins preached the Cult of Reason. Robespierre spoke at a festival honoring the "Supreme Being." Auguste Comte (1798–1857) preached a positivist religion of Mankind. In pre-Marxist French socialism, the development of science and industry was one of the pillars of doctrine. In the writings of Saint-Simon we find "The foundation of freedom is industry." Moreover, Saint-Simon proclaimed that one must approach the history of society from a scientific position, and that such an approach would lead one to the conclusion that a new social order had to be established. Thus it is Saint-Simon, not Marx, who should be regarded as the founder of scientific socialism. As things turned out, however, it was Marx's concept that prevailed, with many of his contemporaries, as being the most closely linked to scientific thought; and the terms "Marxism" and "scientific socialism" became synonymous. This development was of course helped along by Marx's and Engels' constant emphasis on the scientific character of their dogma, calling it nothing less than a scientific theory or a scientific discovery. In an essay titled "Socialism: Utopian and Scientific," Engels wrote:

> These two great discoveries, the materialistic conception of history and the revelation of the secret of capitalistic production through surplus value, we owe to *Marx*. With these discoveries, socialism became a science. The next thing was to work out all its details and relations . . .[10]

Finally, it must be acknowledged that Marx and Engels were themselves scientists in the sense that they specialized in the science of society; and they had a fairly good knowledge of the natural sciences. Both the strong and the weak points of their doctrine reflected the spirit of science in their day.

What is "scientific socialism"? If socialism is a religion, is not this phrase self-contradictory and meaningless?

The supreme goal cannot be deduced from anything—not even from science. However much we work at science, however much we study the structure of the world, we shall never learn what we *should* strive for. Nonetheless, our knowledge of the world, the concepts we use, and the language we speak have a very direct bearing on the formation and expression of the supreme goal. The scientific method and the scientific picture of the world do not determine religious values—the religious supreme goal—in a unique way. But they do set limits; they make some versions of religion more acceptable than others, and they provide ways of expressing religious values. The volitional component—the assertion of the supreme goal—is the nucleus of religon. But this nucleus does not float in isolation; it is closely bound up with culture as a whole. If this is borne in mind, the concept of a scientific socialism is completely natural. And in an age of science, socialism must be scientific in order to have a chance of success.

If we look at Marx's scientific socialism in the light of

these considerations, we can separate its real significance from its seeming significance, and in the contradictions between the two we can detect one of the causes of its deterioration.

From the outset, Marxism was represented as a scientific theory. And in fact it did contain as an element, one specific scientific theory: that of capitalist production. Like many other theories in social sciences, it was vastly oversimplified and inexact (one may even say dubious), so that it became obsolete very rapidly. But Marxism's real significance was that it was a religion buttressed by the science of its day—a religion expressed and preached in scientific terms. It really was a scientific socialism; and as such, it made an irresistible impression on its founder's contemporaries. (It still is making that kind of impression.) In the nineteenth century, it was necessary to fill in the vacuum left by the decline of Christianity; in the twentieth century that need has become even more pressing.

Marxism is deficient not because it is a form of religion (that is one of its virtues), but because it does not want to admit openly that it is a religion, and because it is based on a stage in scientific thought that has been superseded.

The Present Century versus the Last One

As I noted in part I, the logic of Marxism's development was that of a political pragmatism whose aim was to make a socialist revolution as quickly as possible and at whatever cost. But the content of Marxism, and its success, are something quite different from the logic of its development. Political pragmatism may be characteristic of the leaders of movements, but the rank and file do not become involved in movements out of shrewd calculation. They are influenced by emotional and intellectual factors which go deeper and are often unconscious. Marxism is the nineteenth-century socialism. Marxist nihilism, the ideological basis of totalitarianism, cannot be explained merely by pragmatism: it has its roots in the scientific worldview of that era.

The picture of the world that Marx and Engels got from the science of their age was broadly as follows: Very small particles of matter move about in virtually empty three-dimensional space. (According to some theories space was completely empty; according to others it was filled with "ether.") These particles act on one another with forces which are uniquely determined by their velocity and arrangement relative to one another. The forces of interaction, in their turn, uniquely determine, in accordance with Newton's laws, the subsequent movement of the particles. Thus each subsequent state of the world is determined, in a unique way, by its preceding state. Determinism was a typical feature of the scientific worldview of that time.

In such a world there is no room for freedom: it is illusory. Humans, themselves merely aggregates of particles, have as much freedom as a wound-up watch mechanism. In general, the human personality and spiritual life are illusory concepts.

Of course philosophers have always understood the relativistic nature of any picture of the world. The fact that our knowledge of the world is a product of our sensory perceptions was central to all European philsophy. The founder of Critical Philosophy, Immanuel Kant, anticipating twentieth-century science, even refused to recognize space, time, and causality—the holy of holies of the mechanistic worldview—as "things-in-themselves." Instead, he declared, they were forms of our perception of reality. But it was precisely Critical Philosophy to which the Materialist philosophers of that time were the least sensitive. Along with the unsophisticated "common man," they upheld a Naïve Realism which simply dismissed Critical Philosophy, not knowing what to do with it. Apparently, the majority of natural scientists also upheld naïve realism—and that was only to be expected. At the time, science did not yet need Critical Philosophy. In a certain sense, it was even more "correct" for a scientist to be a naïve realist than a Critical Philosopher: this motivated one to work within the framework of the mechanistic conception, which at that time was very fruitful.

Nineteenth-century socialism arose on the basis of a Materialist philosophy of naïve realism. Marx and Engels were trained as Hegelians; i.e., in a spirit that was extremely uncritical, even anticritical. When they switched to Materialism, they merely made (as mathematicians say) "certain alterations in notation." As for Lenin, he was so much the political pragmatist that it is not clear whether he had any views which could be distinguished from his purposes. But those purposes, needless to say, agreed perfectly with the naïve realism of the "common man." Passionately, Lenin defended the latter against the rise of critical scientific philosophy in the early twentieth century.

Thus the founders of Marxist socialism, and the first generation of their followers, had a nineteenth-century mechanistic picture of the world as a background for their actions. The structures they erected fitted into that landscape very well. It is no wonder, however, that they are uncomfortable for anyone dwelling in them: in this scheme of things, the foundations of society (like those of the world as a whole) consist of soulless, abstract essences (productive forces, production relations, classes). And they are ruthlessly transformed by equally soulless and impersonal forces.

Even the most zealous proponent of a scientific worldview (and I count myself as such) must acknowledge that in nineteenth-century socialism there was only as much humaneness as was left in it by the Christian (i.e., prescientific) worldview. For Marx and Engels, the concepts of the individual (the person) and freedom were something taken for granted. They used those concepts rather often, and saw no harm in the fact that the concepts in no way figured in the *foundation* of their system (they probably never noticed). But such was the fact, and it was and is very important. At best, the concepts of the individual and of freedom, could have been tacked onto the system as a heritage from the previous era—

thus moderating the "socialisticalness" of socialism. This kind of thing did happen in those countries where that heritage was firmly rooted in social tradition. Where it was not, the Marxist system of views functioned in the pure state and brought about the natural result: a totalitarian society.

In the twentieth century the scientific worldview has undergone radical changes, incorporating Critical Philosophy as an integral component. This has occurred from necessity, and not without resistance from scientists accustomed to the views of naïve realism. It has turned out that subatomic physics cannot be understood within the framework of Naïve Realism but must be dealt with from the viewpoint of critical philosophy. Thus along with the twentieth-century's specific discoveries in the physics of the microworld, we must regard the *inevitability of Critical Philosophy* as a scientific discovery—one of the greatest of the twentieth century.

Accepting the viewpoint of Critical Philosophy means that the purpose and aims of scientific theories lie not in discovering the essence of "things as they are, independently of the observer," but merely in ordering our sensations and (partially) predicting them. We have become a great deal more modest than were the scientists of the last century. And the world has become a great deal more mysterious. It has turned out that the subject and the object of cognition are indivisible; and because of that, in any attempt to go beyond a certain point in studying "things-in-themselves," we encounter various impossibilities and paradoxes.

We now know that the notion that the world is "really" space in which small particles move along definite trajectories, is illusory: it is contradicted by the experimental facts. The picture of the world provided by modern science does not go beyond the framework of our sensations. The metaphysical "really" has been rejected once and for all time. But that is not all. When "really" fell, so did its constant satellite, determinism: the conviction that all phenomena "really" have their own causes, and are uniquely determined by them. And this rejection is not merely an abstract result of the acceptance of Critical Philosophy but a basic trait of modern physical theory that has been repeatedly confirmed by experiment. We now know that there are phenomena which do not, and cannot, have causes.

The advent of Critical Philosophy and the collapse of determinism means that we can no longer label our spiritual life (and free will in particular) an "illusion" which "really" does not exist. For spiritual life is just as much a fact of existence as the data from our five senses. The collapse of determinism not only gives room for personal freedom in the modern scientific picture of the world: I should say (although of course at this point, science leaves off and philosophy begins) that it *leaves an empty place which must be filled*. In the new, mysterious world of twentieth-century science, concepts of the individual person and freedom are an organic part of scientific thought. The mechanistic model of the world as a clock no longer exerts its blindfold effect on us.

Engels once listed the three scientific discoveries of the nineteenth century which were of fundamental importance to the Marxist worldview: the Law of the Conservation of Energy, the cellular structure of organic matter, and Darwin's theory of Evolution. I should like to list the three discoveries (actually groups of discoveries) of the twentieth century which are of fundamental importance to the scientific worldview of our day.

1. *The new physics:* the Theory of Relativity and quantum mechanics. These discoveries compelled us to revise our notions of space, time, and causality.

2. *The new mathematics:* mathematics and the Theory of Algorithms. Here the most important discoveries are Goedel's famous theorem, and the existence of algorithmically unsolvable problems. They dealt yet another blow to the complacency of scientists—a complacency which had already been shaken by the discoveries of the new physics. The new mathematics investigates so-called *sign systems* which have a dual significance. First, they can be imagined as idealized material structures—mechanical ones. These structures are relatively simple, and may exist in distinctly different

states. The idealization consists in the fact that they can function without wear for as long as one wants, and can have an unlimited number of memory (storage) units; e.g., tapes with small magnetized areas where a spot can be recorded or erased. The second significance of a sign system lies in the fact that all of our theories (including our theories about sign systems) are sign systems. And it turns out that even in this idealized world of sign systems where there are no inaccuracies of measurement or random errors, there are a tremendous number of impossibilities which limit our capacity to make predictions. Even in so simple a system as arithmetic there exists no finite set of axioms from which one can deduce all of the true arithmetical statements. And here is another impossibility: if we take a sign system in a certain initial state and set it in motion, there is no algorithm (general method) which will always determine, on the basis of the initial state, whether or not the sign system will ultimately stop!

3. *Cybernetics,* the new discipline, with concepts and approaches applicable to any kind of object, including living organisms and human society. (We shall discuss cybernetics in a special later section of this book.)

What conception of society will the modern scientific worldview lead us to? What will be the nature of late-twentieth and twenty-first-century socialism? How will it coincide with, or differ from, nineteenth-century socialism? Or is socialism necessary at all? And what are the alternatives?

I shall structure the analysis of these problems as follows. First, drawing on the history of the socialist movement, we shall consider two general problems important to ethico-religious doctrines: the role of the transcendental and the relationship between knowledge and will. Next, again using Marxism as a point of departure, we shall go on to the concept of evolution as the link between a description of reality and the Supreme Goal. Finally, I shall formulate my own idea of a twentieth-century scientific socialism, and proceed to consider certain of its specific traits in comparison with nineteenth-century socialism.

Transcendentalism and Idolatry

Socialism differs from traditional religions in that it lacks the concept of the transcendental. It is a religion based only on man and his reason, and not on the favor bestowed by some "higher powers" beyond the grasp of our senses and understanding. Its sources are in the Age of Enlightenment. Auguste Comte, a pupil of Saint-Simon, made the first attempt at systematically building both a "religion of mankind" and a social order based on the achievements of science and a "positive philosophy. (The term "positivism" is of his coinage.) Comte's motives were the very best: he wanted to show mankind the way to prosperity and happiness. But the system he built makes one shudder in horror: it is wretched, gloomy totalitarianism.

I believe that in the early nineteenth century, nothing else could have been expected; and I have already explained why. But there is another view which holds that the very idea of a religion of mankind—or, more accurately, a religion without transcendentalism—is faulty. In particular, this is the view of Albert Camus. He was one of the few who, as early as the 1940s, had the courage—despite the current intellectual fashion in the West—to grasp the essence of the totalitarian Marxist socialism, and oppose it. In *L'Homme révolté* (*The Rebel*), he has this to say:

> Comte's conclusions are curiously like those finally accepted by scientific socialism. Positivism demonstrates with considerable clarity the repercussions of the ideological revolution of the nineteenth century, of which Marx is one of the representatives, and which consisted in relegating to the end of history the Garden of Eden and the Revelation, which tradition had always placed at the beginning. The positivist era, which was bound to follow the metaphysical era and the theological era, was to mark the advent of a religion of humanity. Henri Gouhier gives an exact definition of Comte's en-

terprise when he says that his concern was to discover a man without any traces of God. Comte's primary aim, which was to substitute everywhere the relative for the absolute, was quickly transformed, by force of circumstances, into the deification of the relative and into preaching a religion that is both universal and without transcendence. Comte saw in the Jacobin cult of Reason an anticipation of positivism and considered himself, with perfect justification, as the real successor of the revolutionaries of 1789. He continued and enlarged the scope of this revolution by suppressing the transcendence of principles and by systematically founding the religion of the species. His formula: "Set aside God in the name of religion," meant nothing else but this. Inaugurating a mania that has since enjoyed a great vogue, he wanted to be the Saint Paul of this new religion and replace the Catholicism of Rome by the Catholicism of Paris. We know that he wanted to see in all the cathedrals "the statue of deified humanity on the former altar of God." He calculated with considerable accuracy that positivism would be preached in Notre-Dame before 1860. This calculation was not so ridiculous as it seems. Notre-Dame, in a state of siege, still resists: but the religion of humanity was effectively preached toward the end of the nineteenth century, and Marx, despite the fact that he had not read Comte, was one of its prophets. Marx only understood that a religion which did not embrace transcendence should properly be called politics. Comte knew it too, after all, or at least he understood that his religion was primarily a form of social idolatry and that it implied political realism, the negation of individual rights, and the establishment of despotism. A society whose experts would be priests, two thousand bankers and technicians ruling over a Europe of one hundred and twenty million inhabitants where private life would be absolutely identified with public life, where absolute obedience "of action, of thought, and of feeling" would be given to the high priest who would reign over everything, such was Comte's Utopia, which announces what might be called the horizontal religions of our times. It is true that it is Utopian because, convinced of the enlight-

> ening powers of science, Comte forgot to provide a police force. Others will be more practical; the religion of humanity will be effectively founded on the blood and suffering of humanity.[11]

For a scientist, the dogmatic, categorical proclamation of the existence of anything at all is unacceptable. Modern Positivism, unlike its earlier versions, is ready to accept any linguistic constructions, provided they help to organize sensory and spiritual experience. For example, if a four-dimensional model of the world explains facts deduced from scientific experiments, we can say that the fourth dimension *exists* just as we say that the Newtonian Law of Gravitation exists. And if we were in possession of certain facts which would be convenient to describe as a continuation of the soul's existence after the decay of the body, we could say the soul was immortal. But in traditional religions, the transcendental concepts are introduced dogmatically; and the existence of the otherworldly is treated in a purely metaphysical manner, without any analysis. It "really" exists; and this is known to us through "revelation." A scientist cannot regard such an "existence" as anything but pure self-deception; as a result all the emotional aspects of the transcendental disappear for him: they wither and die under the harsh breath of skepticism.

Likewise, on the intellectual plane, one cannot build anything worthy of respect on this basis. Christian theology amazes me with its melancholy sterility. In its time, of course, it was an important form of intellectual life; but I believe that today it cannot be regarded as anything but an anachronism.

Nonetheless, I quoted the excerpt from Camus's book not so much in order to quarrel with him as to agree on his main point: setting off the transcendental religions against various forms of idolatry. I want, however, to analyze that opposition not in the traditional (for religion) metaphysical terms but from an operationalist viewpoint. The question we shall be concerned with is: In precisely what *observed manifestations* do idolatry and transcendental religion differ? Having put the question in that way, we arrive at the following definition: idolatry links religious emotions with *concrete objects,* while a transcendental religion links them with *extremely abstract concepts.*

With respect to evolutionary possibilities, the difference between these two types of religion is very great. Idolatry invariably leads to restrictions on creative freedom—to the stagnation and ossification of society. A transcendental religion at least *allows for* infinite development, because the content of abstract concepts changes as the culture evolves. The goals formulated in extremely abstract concepts are transcendental and unattainable, as benefits supreme goals. Idolatry directs a person toward an idol, while a transcendental religion directs him toward God; i.e., toward a vaguely surmised infinity. The observed difference consists precisely in the abstract nature of the supreme goal, and not in the fact of a metaphysical transcendentalism. The great monotheistic religions became possible only after a certain level of abstract thought had been reached. The God of those religions is an abstract idea.

Of course in its concrete social embodiment, no transcendental religion is entirely free of idolatry—as the principle of Papal Infallibility shows. In the process by which abstract ideas are concretized, specific goals and objects become their embodiments. And when these things overshadow the fundamental abstractions, idolatry has set in. In such cases the struggle against idolatry is a struggle to regenerate and renew the authentic transcendental religion. The Protestant Reformation offers a striking example of this. Idolatry is one of the barbarous forms of transcendental religion. And if we find it in Christianity, it is not surprising that we should find it in socialism. The cult of the "chieftain," the cult of class, and the cult of race are all different forms of socialist barbarism. The cult of the nation, which in the twentieth century became a universal calamity, is also a barbaric form of socialism. Present-day nationalism is potent and frightful because it has a religious coloration: Dostoyevskian man, not Marxist man, is in action.

Finally, the cult of humanity as a whole is also that of idolatry and barbarism. No particular persons, either individually or collectively, should stand on the top rung of the hierarchy of values and plans. At best, the cult of humanity is only vulgar narcissism and self-praise, needed only by those who do not feel in their hearts the greatness of "the phenomenon of man." One feels ashamed when one sees in the USSR the thousands of posters reading: "Glory to the CPSU!" "Long Live the Communist Party of the Soviet Union!" "The Party is the Brain, Honor, and Conscience of Our Era!" This kind of thing is found on posters put up all over the country, on the initiative (and under the observation) of the same Communist Party. It would be sad indeed if this way of praising oneself (which is essentially symptomatic of an inferiority complex) were to spread throughout all mankind.

In defining socialism as a religion of integration, I am taking a descriptivist position, not a normative one. I am merely trying to identify the common source giving rise to the various kinds of socialism, and endowing them with life. But that does not mean that I have no intention of taking a normative position; i.e., of expressing my views as to what socialism should be. Indeed, I intend to do precisely that. It might even be said that I intend to preach a definite religion—or a definite form of religion. That religion will be indivisible from science, just as the monotheistic religions are indivisible from a language containing abstract concepts. Camus's irony—with respect to both the "Saint Paul" and "the enlightening power of science"—does not affect me. I see no reason why the preaching of a new religion should be regarded as any more presumptuous than the proclamation of a new scientific theory. In the final analysis, there are as many religions as there are people. A person trying to answer the question why he is living reaches conclusions that may be at least as interesting to others as conclusions about the movement of the planets or the structure of insects' bodies.

That his conclusions are of a normative kind does not indicate a lack of modesty; for the subject of religion is of that kind. And science really does possess a tremendous power to enlighten although it has never aspired to replace the police.

Thus, I draw this conclusion: a religion must be founded on extremely abstract formulations associated with the supreme goal. My descriptive definition of socialism is based on a concept of the integration of humanity that is in no way concretized, and that consequently meets that requirement. It is very broad, and includes, among other things, the barbarous forms of socialism. I shall construct my norm by narrowing that definition. But narrowing is not total concretization. The core of the religion must contain an extremely abstract formulation, which is expressed in concepts taken from science and is reinterpreted as science develops. Such a religion may be called transcendental. It is a natural extension or continuation of the metaphysically transcendental religions in a society that has accepted a critical, scientific worldview. To use Camus's metaphor, such a religion is not "horizontal" but "vertical," aspiring upward. Its ideals, which elicit the religious sense, lie not in the sphere of the phenomena immediately around us but in the abstractions on a higher level. The replacement of metaphysical transcendentalism by a transcendental abstractness susceptible of critical analysis is the inevitable result of religion's having been invaded by the philosophy of the modern scientist.

Knowledge and Will

Herewith another quotation from Camus. In comparing the reality of Stalin's empire with the predictions of Marxism, he writes:

> How could a so-called scientific socialism conflict to such a point with facts? The answer is easy: it was not

> scientific. On the contrary, its defeat resulted from a method ambiguous enough to wish to be simultaneously determinist and prophetic, dialectic and dogmatic. If the mind is only the reflection of events, it cannot anticipate their progress, except by hypothesis. If Marxist theory is determined by economics, it can describe the past history of production, not its future, which remains in the realms of probability. The task of historical materialism can only be to establish a method of criticism of contemporary society; it is only capable of making suppositions, unless it abandons its scientific attitude, about the society of the future. Moreover, is it not for this reason that its most important work is called *Capital* and not *Revolution?* Marx and the Marxists allowed themselves to prophesy the future and the triumph of communism to the detriment of their postulates and of scientific method. . . .
>
> Marxism is not scientific; at the best, it has scientific prejudices. It brought out into the open the profound difference between scientific reasoning, that fruitful instrument of research, of thought, and even of rebellion, and historical reasoning, which German ideology invented by its negation of all principles. Historical reasoning is not a type of reasoning that, within the framework of its own functions, can pass judgment on the world. While pretending to judge it, it really tries to determine its course. Essentially a part of events, it directs them and is simultaneously pedagogic and all-conquering. . . . The pseudo-reasoning ends by identifying itself with cunning and strategy, while waiting to culminate in the ideological Empire. What part could science play in this concept? Nothing is less determined on conquest than reason. History is not made with scientific scruples; we are even condemned to not making history from the moment when we claim to act with scientific objectivity. Reason does not preach, or if it does, it is no longer reason.[12]

While I agree with Camus on the contradiction between the prophetic and scientific components of Marxism, I emphatically disagree with him on the role of reason in science and in history. In my view, he does not properly separate those elements which should be separated. For him, German ideological reasoning is an absolute evil—one that he sets off against scientific reasoning. But the components that should actually be separated out and set off against each other—components that differ profoundly in both their nature and their function—are those of knowledge and will. Scientific reasoning may be equated with the first component, taken in its pure form. Scientific investigation must be dispassionate and unprejudiced: if the investigator sets out with the intention of reaching certain conclusions, his research will be worthless. The second component is unadulterated will, based on nothing and justified by nothing. This element may be called irrational: it does not come within the sphere of reason—of logical discourse.

Thus we shall distinguish between the two components: knowledge and will. Now, it would be unjust to say that the "historical reasoning" of German ideology (best expressed, of course, by Hegel) is directly opposed to the scientific method, since that reasoning also contains a cognitive element. Yet of course it also contains, in abundance, a volitional element—one that is purposeful and judgmental. This explains its active historical role. The trouble is not that the German ideology tried to combine the volitional and cognitive elements but that, in it, will masqueraded as knowledge. From Hegel, this masquerade of will as knowledge migrated into Marx. The sad result of this sleight-of-hand was that the cognitive, scientific component ended up in a hopeless situation: having lost its impartiality, science became the servant of politics. Will masquerading as knowledge was a wolf in sheep's clothing. The prophetic-political element in Marxism—the volitional element—gobbled up the scientific component.

But the volitional and cognitive elements are hardly mutually exclusive in history. We all know from personal experience that in our own lives, these two elements manage somehow to combine, so why shouldn't they do so in history? They don't merely have to masquerade as each other.

After European culture had been badly shaken by World War I, irrationalism and antirationalism became fashionable. More and more people began to talk about "disenchantment with the power of reason," "reason's inability to determine the course of history," etc. And the horrors of Hitlerism and Stalinism were taken to be a confirmation of these views (to which, by the way, Camus subscribed). But for some reason, the antirationalists overlooked the fact that the tragic events of the twentieth century have resulted not from an excess of reason but from a lack of it. Those tragic events did not represent a conflict between the academies of science of the nations involved. The demagogy that resulted in the wars took its nourishment from the psychology of *mass man*.

Mass psychology, not a power struggle among the military aristocracy, determined the foreign and domestic policy of European nations. And for all the charges that can be brought against the mass psychology of this century one cannot accuse it of an excess of reason and logic. Reason was relegated to the background; and so far it has not gained the position it should have.

In representing his religion as a political system based on science, Marx committed what was essentially an act of deceit. (Comte was more honest: he called his religion a religion.) And deceit can never be practiced with impunity: Marxism paid for it by being made into a dogma. Although it did so reluctantly, and in a covert manner, Marxism had to resort to dogmatic belief, the very means of combining knowledge and will that had been repeatedly criticized during the development of European science. Dogma is a cornerstone of the Christian religion. Knowledge and will are merged into the concept of God. The specific aspects of God are reflected in a number of dogmas and sacred texts that are supposed to be accepted as the highest truths—those not subject to doubt or examination. Since the dogmas contain the concepts of Good and Evil, they are in fact directions which guide our will. For we call good those things we are supposed to strive after, and evil those things which should not be permitted.

For a religion of the scientific age, dogmatic belief is not acceptable. The combination of knowledge and will is asserted, but they must not be merged into a solid, unsegmented mass. They must be combined in a system such that there is a clear distinction between them. And here, as everywhere else, progress is achieved by means of the metasystem transition. In this case, our capacity always to draw the line between knowledge and will is a metasystem element with respect to the systems of knowledge and will.

Thus we can draw the following conclusion about the difference between the logical basis of earlier religions and that of religion in the era of critical thought:

> In lieu of a dogmatic belief that "one must because it is good," a modern religion proposes that a person perform an individual act of the will in setting a supreme goal; that he make a free choice, and realize his freedom in that choice.

In addition to its philosophical aspect, the trend toward a synthesis of knowledge and will has a social aspect as well. Each individual must be guaranteed the free exchange of information and ideas. Unless society recognizes this principle, unless it penetrates deeply into the consciousness of each person, the political will inevitably will blind itself and take us into tragic dead ends like those in which Soviet society finds itself today. The ability to maintain objectivity in research and in theorizing, independently of one's aims and emotions, must become a part of human culture. In society, the division between knowledge and will may to a certain extent be expressed in the division of labor between scientists and politicians. But only to a certain extent. The synthesis is effective only when it is achieved in the thinking of each and every person.

The Great Evolution

Marx's conception has some features that are attractive from the viewpoint of a scientist. The chief one of these is the idea that the universe is evolving, changing irreversibly, in accordance with some general law.

On the plane of methodology and epistemology, Dialectical Materialism is a typical example of what Comte called "metaphysical philosophy";—the objectifying of abstract concepts into a few essences. The critical positivistic analysis which underlies modern scientific philosophy has never affected Dialectical Materialism—at least not in its Soviet form. But if we do not regard Dialectical Materialism as an all-embracing philosophical system which includes "the only scientific and progressive epistemology" (as the Soviet textbooks would have it; actually, it is anti-scientific and reactionary), then that philosophy appears much more attractive.

First of all, we see that Dialectical Materialism occupies a natural and quite legitimate place in Marx's religious system. What does a religion need from science? A general picture of the world on which, in a natural and convincing manner, one can inscribe the supreme goal. That is what the founders of Marxism sought in the science of their day. The idea that the world was evolving in accordance with definite laws was generally accepted. But merely to postulate evolution was not enough. Some general considerations, some general laws of development which would lead us to the supreme goal, were very much to be desired. Marx found them in Hegel's dialectic and, in his own words, "turned them upside down," declaring that the new laws, previously unknown to science, were laws of nature.

An arbitrary act? Perhaps! From the viewpoint of a rigorous-minded scientist, this was the greatest insolence. The new "laws of nature" were not laws at all, but the same kind of metaphysical speculation that Hegel had indulged in. They could not be expressed in scientific language; experimentally, they could be neither confirmed nor disproven; and they could not be used to predict events. From the viewpoint of Comte's Positivism, these "laws" should have been rejected as pseudo-science and pseudo-philosophy.

But the contemporary Positivism is very different from Comte's stern variety. Comte had rejected all concepts that did not find direct expression in the sphere of experience, and also every theory based on such concepts—even if it agreed perfectly with observed data and enabled prediction. In particular, he rejected the wave theory of light because it involved the concept of the ether. Comte believed that a scientist was entitled to accept only the kind of hypothesis which does not simply tally with experience but necessarily follows from it. To reject such a hypothesis would actually be to *contradict* experience. We now know that there are no logical grounds for such restrictions, and that if they were imposed, one would have to abandon many powerful theories. We regard scientific theories (along with works of art, philosophy, and literature) as free creations of our mind. They serve a unique purpose: as *models* of reality which help us to orient ourselves with respect to events, and to predict them. These models make up an entire spectrum in terms of how completely *formalized* they are; i.e., how well they are separated from that part of our subjective experience which cannot be externalized. At one end of the spectrum we find fully formalized theories (e.g., arithmetic). When we apply such theories (in our case, when we perform arithmetical operations), we disengage ourselves from the nature of the object to which the theory is applied and function in a purely formal manner, according to rules that are strict, fully determining, and clear (so much so that these rules can be entrusted to a machine: to a calculator or computer). The interpretation of a formalized theory—that is, establishing a link between its concepts and the phenomena of reality (in our case, counting objects)—must likewise be something that everyone without exception can understand and perform. And in principle, it must be within the competence of a machine. Thus a formalized theory separates itself from the human brain that created it, and becomes an autonomous ("objective") model of the external world.

At the other end of the spectrum of models we find works of literature and art. We are confronted with synthetic artistic images which address themselves to our individual experience. Such images may have a potent effect on one's perception of reality, and on one's behavior. But this takes place subconsciously, at the level of intuition; and the mechanism of that effect is not apparent. In the subconscious, calculation and proof do not come into play.

Completely formalized theories are an ideal of science, but they cannot arise from thin air. The concepts on which they are based pre-exist, in a nonformalized state, in the language and day-to-day activity of human beings. Often they find expression in philosophy and literature. Critical analysis of the concepts, plus experimentation, leads to the creation of formalized theories. Therefore, the entire spectrum of our models of reality, from Dostoyevsky's novels to arithmetic textbooks, plays a role in the evolution of human knowledge. We cannot separate pure science from pure art. Nor can we draw a line between science and philosophy, or philosophy and art. If we do, we block science's advance toward the building of new theories. All models have a right to existence—provided, of course, that we bear in mind the necessity of a critical approach to each of them.

In Marx's interpretation, the concepts and laws of the Hegelian dialectic may be called "scientific-artistic" images of the world, reflecting its development, evolution. They are necessary to religion in that they form a link between the formalized, technical element of the scientific picture of the world, and those factors (usually not known to us, or not realized by us) which prompt us to accept the supreme goal, and to feel that it is ours. If these images are arbitrary, it is only in the sense that any and every scientific theory is arbitrary. But they unquestionably do the job of organizing our experience. We see in them a kind of truth—a kind of correspondence to observed phenomena. Obviously, the influence that Hegelian dialectic had on people's minds was due to the fact that it caught in some form (although a rather vague one) some important traits of development. And people sensed this intuitively. The idea of development, of evolution, is closely tied to the idea of a goal. The notion of evolution creates an anisotropy of time, a nonequivalence between past and future, and thereby leads to the formation of a goal. The idea of evolution is a link between science and religion. This no doubt explains why the Hegelian system exerted such a powerful influence on people's minds and stirred a rapture which, plainly, was in part religious. Marx channeled that rapture into politics. German idealism created an artistic image of the world—a world which, in its very foundation and essence, contains the idea of evolution and is almost identical with it. Marx fitted the necessity of a proletarian revolution to that picture.

In describing evolution in terms of metasystem transitions, and in declaring that the metasystem transition is the universal quantum of evolution, I am following in the footsteps of Hegel and Marx. Here we have a typical example of the gradual movement of concepts toward precision and formalization. My definition of the metasystem transition already fully meets the standards for a scientific definition.[13]

The basic law of Hegel's dialectics—thesis, antithesis, and synthesis—is closely related to the concept of the metasystem transition. The Hegelian triad may be regarded as one particular case, or a simplified description, of the metasystem transition. When we take two elements which stand toward each other in a relationship of contradiction and combine them in a metasystem, we effect their synthesis. On this synthesis the contradictions between the components do not disappear. Rather, they are suspended (to use the terminology of Hegel and Marx) owing to the mechanism of control. This is one case of the metasystem transition. In the general case, there is an integration of many subsystems which do not necessarily stand in a relationship of contradiction to one another. But even in this case the dialectic can use its own terminology, declaring the existence of many integrated subsystems to be the negation of uniqueness, which negation is then replaced again by a single system—the metasystem. The appearance of a new quality in the process of development always takes place by means of a metasystem transition. As a rule, the formation of the metasystem is preceded by a quantitative accumulation of subsystems. Thus the metasystem transition can be regarded as a transition from quantity to quality.

Evolution, Social Integration, and Freedom

In *The Phenomenon of Science*, viewing evolution in terms of metasystem transitions, I reached certain conclusions regarding the prospects for human evolution, the role of science in that process, and the ethico-religious conception which, in a natural manner, is included in the scientific worldview. To summarize those conclusions:

1. The structure of the biosphere indicates three large-scale, genuinely revolutionary metasystem transitions: the integration of macromolecules to the formation of cells, the integration of cells to the formation of the multicellular organism; and social integration—the formation of human society.

2. Of the multicellular organisms, only man represents the kind of component whose integration is a revolutionary metasystem transition creating a qualitatively new level in the organization of matter. Communities of animals may be regarded as the first (unsuccessful) attempts to carry out that revolution. What sets man apart is his language-making capacity, which itself is a result of a definite metasystem transition in the structure of the human brain, as compared to those of the higher animals. Language serves two functions: communication among people, and the modelling of reality.

These two functions are, on the level of social integration, analogues to those of the nervous system on the level in which cells are integrated into a multicellular organism. Language is, as it were, an extension of the human brain. Using the material of language, people make models of reality (sign systems) such as never existed in the brains of animals.

Moreover, language is a unitary common extension of the brains of all members of society. It is a collective model of reality that all members of society labor to improve, and one that preserves the experience of preceding generations.

3. Society can be viewed as a single super-being. Its "body" is the bodies of all people, plus the objects made by them: clothing, dwellings, machines, books, etc. Its "physiology" is the physiology of all people, plus the *culture* of society; that is, a certain way of controlling the physical component of the social body and the way people think. The emergence of human being and social integration mark the appearance of a new mechanism of Universal Evolution. Before human emergence, the development and improvement of the highest level of organization—the structure of the brain—occurred as a result of the struggle for existence and Natural Selection. This was a slow process requiring many generations. In human society, the development of language and culture is a result of the creative efforts of all its members. That selection of variants necessary to increase the complexity of the organization of matter by the trial-and-error method now takes place for the most part in the human brain: it becomes indivisible from the willed act of the individual person. The human being becomes a point of concentration of Cosmic Creativity. The rate of evolution has speeded up manyfold.

4. The evolution of human society's culture takes place via metasystem transitions in its structure. Modern science is the highest stage that has so far been reached in the sequences of metasystem transitions. Moreover, having mastered the principle of the metasystem transition, science has become a self-developing system. If culture is the physiology of the "super-being," and language is its nervous system, then science is its brain. Science is the highest level of the hierarchy in the organization of organic matter. It is the terminal bud of a growing tree—the focal point of the Great Evolution. This accounts for the significance of the cosmic phenomenon of science as part of the phenomenon of man.

5. Science represents the organization of human knowl-

edge but not of will. It answers such questions as: "What exists?" "What will happen if . . . ?" "What must be done in order to . . . ?" But it cannot, by definition answer, without any "ifs" or "in-order-tos," the question, "What must be done?" The problem of the supreme goal remains outside the domain of science; its solution requires an act of the will. In the final analysis, it is the result of a free choice.

But this in no sense means that science has no influence over how we go about solving the problem of the supreme goal. Science provides a definite representation of the world, and of our possible role in it. Depending upon the nature of that representation, acts of the will are more or less feasible. Even more important, science gives us a language in which to describe reality, and hence in some degree to predict it. In particular, any goals that we can set must be expressed in that language.

6. The concept of evolution is the central idea of modern science. Evolution has led to the emergence of intelligent life on earth. And even though we realize how slight is our sphere of influence in the Cosmos, we are still entitled to regard ourselves as a phenomenon of cosmic significance. Our experience in investigating developing systems has shown that a new quality at first appears in small volume; but in time, owing to its potential, it takes over a maximum of living space and builds a bridgehead to a new and even higher level of organization. The prospects for the "hominization"[14] of the Universe strike us as a real possibility. No one can affirm that this will inevitably take place: we may perish or cease to develop. But on the other hand, no one can deny the existence of that possibility.

The science of the twentieth century assigns a much more honorable place to the volitional act of the individual person than did nineteenth-century science. Evolution is not a predetermined process. The laws of nature do not uniquely determine each subsequent state of the world; they merely impose restrictions, leaving a vast area of indeterminacy. Evolution means the elimination, at all times and in all places, of that indeterminacy. Collisions of elementary particles and decisions taken by human beings are both examples of the elimination of indeterminacy. The second of these events has an incomparably larger scope in both space and time; and in proportion as the Universe is "hominized," that scope will increase. That act is familiar to us, inwardly, as a manifestation of our own free will. A willed act is a thread in the fabric of the Great Evolution. In a large, closely bonded system like human society, it is possible, owing to the presence of trigger mechanisms, that any individual act, although minute on the overall scale, will lead to great changes. In the course of time, the creative achievements of individuals influence the entire history of mankind. And the effect of decisions made by statesmen is obvious to everyone. A no less important role, however, is played by the cause-and-effect chains leading from obscure events to great ones. If one thread is broken, the entire fabric may be destroyed. And any willed act performed by an individual person can have tremendous significance.

7. No one can act against the laws of Nature. Ethical teachings that run counter to the general trend of evolution—i.e., which set goals that are incompatible with it—cannot bring about a constructive contribution to evolution by those who follow such teachings. This means that the former, in the final analysis, will be erased from the world's memory. Such is the nature of development: that which corresponds to its general, abstract plan is eternalized in the structure of the developing world; that which runs counter to it, is overcome and perishes.

The foregoing gives rise to the following conclusion as regards social integration. If humanity sets itself goals which are incompatible with social integration, or which in some way restrict that process, the result will be an evolutionary dead end: further creative development and the engendering of new qualities will become impossible. In such a case, we shall perish sooner or later, and the task of spiritualizing the Universe will be taken on by other branches of the Great Evolution. In the developing world there is no repose: all that does not develop perishes.

8. But there is another path in addition to that of rejecting integration, whereby mankind may end up in an evolutionary cul-de-sac; namely, if en route to integration, people's freedom is sacrificed for the sake of uniting them. The process of social integration has never gone on so furiously, and in such plain view, as today. Modern science and engineering have put every person within the sphere of influence of every other person. Modern culture is global. Modern nations are huge mechanisms, with a tendency to regulate the behavior of everyone ever more rigidly; to foist upon him, from outside, his needs, tastes, and opinions. Hence today we can see, better than ever before, the contradiction that social integration entails. It is a contradiction between two necessities: that of including the human being in the system—in the whole which is consolidating itself; and that of preserving him as a free, creative individual. This poses a fundamental problem: How can this contradiction be resolved? How can movement toward integration be combined with movement toward freedom? Our future—if we are to have any—depends upon how successfully this problem is solved.

We have no grounds for assuming, *a priori*, that the contradiction between integration and freedom is an unsolvable one. The personal, creative principle is the essence of the human being—the prime mover of evolution in an age of reason. If it is suppressed by social integration, movement will stop. On the other hand, social integration is also indispensable. Without it, there can be no further development of culture, and no increase in the power of the human spirit over Nature. It is the essence of the new level in the organization of matter.

But why must we assume that social integration and personal freedom are incompatible? After all, integration has been successfully effected on other levels of the organization. When cells combine into a multicellular organism, they continue to perform their biological functions—metabolism and fission. The new quality—the life of the organism—does not appear *despite* the biological functions of the individual cells but *because* of them. The creative act of a free will is the "biological function" of the human being. In the integrated society, it must be preserved as an inviolable foundation, and the new qualities must appear through it and because of it.

9. It is hardly likely that at present anyone would undertake to predict how far the integration of individuals will go, and what forms it will take. There is, however, no doubt that the direct exchange of information among the nervous systems of individual people, and their physical integration, will become possible. It is probable that physical integration will give rise to higher and qualitatively new forms of a suprapersonal consciousness; and that will be a process that could be described as merging the souls of individual people into an Over-Soul (to use Emerson's coinage). The "pan-human" Over-Soul will in principle be immortal, just as humanity is in principle immortal. One can only guess as to the relationship between the individual consciousness and the pan-human consciousness; but it seems quite possible that the physical integration of individuals will solve the age-old contradiction between reason and death.

10. So long as that contradiction is not solved, the only kind of immortality we can consider seriously is the immortality of our contribution to the Great Evolution of the Universe. A will to immortality in that sense has always been a motivating force in the creativity of people whose worldview is basically scientific.

The awareness that we are mortal is one of the starting points in the process of becoming human. For a rational being, the thought that death is inevitable creates an agonizing situation from which he seeks a way out. Rebellion against death, against the disintegration of one's own person, is common to all people. It is the source from which, in the final analysis, all religious doctrines get the volitional component essential to them. It is the will to immortality.

Christianity takes as a point of departure an absolute belief in the immortality of the soul. The rebellion against death is utilized as a force prompting people to accept Christian doctrine (after all, from the outset it promises immortality). But under the potent action of critical intelligence, notions of the soul's immortality and life beyond the grave—which once were very clear and concrete—have become ever more opaque and abstract, and are losing their emotional force of persuasion. Accordingly, the old religious systems are losing their influence. If a person is raised on the ideas and images of modern science, the will to immortality can lead him to only one goal: to make his own personal contribution to the Great Evolution; to eternalize his personality in all subsequent acts of the world drama. In order for that contribution to be eternal, it must be constructive. Such is the supreme goal that a human being sets for himself. Its concretization depends on the state of our knowledge—on our notions about evolution. One remarkable feature of that goal is the organic synthesis of the personal and the universal. It engenders a feeling of responsibility for the common cause—for the process of evolution. For everything that threatens that process—in particular the stupid selfishness of the Philistine—threatens each person's contribution; it threatens to make his life meaningless.

In considering all these things, we must bear in mind that the difference between knowledge and will remains; it cannot be eliminated. If a person cannot, or will not, perform the requisite act of will, then no science or logic will make him accept the supreme goal and feel his responsibility for the Great Evolution. The Philistine who has firmly decided to live as a slave of circumstance and rest content with his wretched private ideal, will not be elevated by anything, and will pass from the stage without a trace. He who does not want immortality will not get it. Just as the animal deprived of its instinct for reproduction will not perform its animal function, so a human being deprived of the will to immortality will not perform his human functions; he will betray his destiny.

From Traditional Religions to Socialism

Taking the foregoing into account, I call socialism (the socialism that I accept and am ready to preach) an ethico-religious doctrine which proclaims humanity's supreme goal to be unlimited social integration combined with guarantees for, and the development of, the creative freedom of the individual. This is scientific socialism: first, because the idea and emotional persuasiveness of the doctrine depend upon "scientific-philosophical" and "scientific-artistic" images; second, because science is proclaimed as the instrument of integration.

This concept of socialism would appear to resemble the "ethical socialism" of German Social Democracy more closely than it does any other kind. And if I had to use one of the existing labels to designate my views, I would probably choose that one. But I consider it extremely important to stress the religious—not merely the ethical—character of socialism. Religion includes ethics, but is more than ethics. Thus it includes a certain notion of the real—a notion which does not simply recommend that we accept certain aims and norms of behavior but engenders a definite emotion: the religious emotion. Traditionally, what we mean by "ethics" is something impassive derived from considerations of expedience or postulated as an *a priori* logical principle, like the axioms of mathematics. Religion, however, addresses itself to feelings, and cultivates them. And feelings, emotions, are direct forces that stir masses of people. One of the most effective ways for reason to influence history is by cultivating feelings. The history of socialism shows quite plainly the role played by emotions in that movement. Socialism's enemies see in it only the action of destructive emotions. But lacking a detailed analysis of a phenomenon's essence, one should not judge it by its first stages. And it is quite inadmissible simply to ignore a part of socialism, as Shafarevich does in his article when he passes over the reformist currents in Social Democracy. In his exposé of socialism, he unmasks only the barbarous variety. One might even say that from barbarous socialism he takes only the barbarity while ignoring the socialist element. Shafarevich's position is that of a Christian. But after all, Christianity has had its barbarous forms, too. It was Christians who tore Hypatia to pieces in 415 A.D. Shafarevich's arguments against socialism are those of a Roman patrician against Christianity.

If we disregard all the simplifications and vulgarizations, we find that the emotion embodied in the concept of social integration is constructive. It touches strings deep in the human soul. The idea of immortality is inseparable from the idea of integrating individual persons (provided, of course, that we rule out the naïve notions of a life after death which differs hardly at all from life on this earth). In the traditional religions, the idea of integration is invested with the robes of (philosophical) spiritualism, and presented as union with God. Like the scientific approach, spiritualism entails a certain method of organizing our spiritual and emotional experience. It would be wrong simply to disregard everything that humanity has done in direct and close connection with the spiritualistic (or idealistic) approach. The question is, however, what approach should serve as a basis for one's worldview, and in particular for dealing with integration? If we take spiritualism as a basis, we block the way to any forward movement. The most we can count on here is to give each person an opportunity for certain experiences—perhaps very exotic ones. That is not very much, especially if we bear in mind that when it comes to creating exotic experiences, even crude chemical techniques of altering brain functions—not to mention the potential of feasible biological procedures—can compete very handily. In taking as our basis the critical scientific method and a materialistic approach to integration, we open up prospects which are fantastic (and, it must be admitted, a bit weird).

The transition from spiritualism to the scientific method is a metasystem transition, since the latter comprises a critical analysis of all linguistic usages and all forms of the organization of experience, including Spiritualist forms. This transition is consequently a step along the path of evolution; and it is irreversible. Socialism is the direct heir of all the great religions of the past—the only great religion possible in an age of science.

In scientific socialism, the spiritual transcendency of the earlier religions is replaced by a combination of extreme abstraction in the formulation of the supreme goal, and concreteness in the derivative goals at all stages of development. But what new element does this replacement bring to the religious emotion? And does it not have a destructive effect on it?

I should say that it doesn't. After all, human nature remains the same. If there is something in it that elicits the religious emotion, the latter won't vanish. Only the conceptual, verbal aspect of the spiritual life will undergo transformation. As I have said, moreover, the basic concepts on the borderline of the religious-emotional sphere—such concepts as the mysterious nature of the Universe, the meaning of life, the integration of individual persons, immortality, and transcendency—will not fall by the way. But they *will be rethought.* This rethinking consists, basically, in updating the borderline conceptual stratum, and bringing it into line with the realities of our language and thought in this age of science and industry. Thus on the basis of general considerations, the transformation will more likely help to cultivate the religious emotion, than suppress it.

Meditations on the meaning of life in the context of the idea of evolution, creativity, and the primordial freedom of the personal act of volition, will have a tremendous effect on a person's psyche, and on his whole life. As for myself, personally, I know very positively that it was the ideas I expressed in *The Phenomenon of Science* and in the earlier version of this book which changed my system of values and made me a dissenter. My profession (physics plus cybernetics) played a decisive role in the development of those ideas.

Incidentally, a disproportionately large number of Soviet dissenters are scientists; and among the latter, a disproportionately large number are physicists. There are probably many reasons why this is so, but my guess is that the most important of them is the concept of the Great Evolution, which is an integral part of the thinking done by a scientist—especially a physicist, a biologist, or a cybernetician. Either consciously or unconsciously, that concept serves as a basis for forming one's own moral criteria—criteria which do not coincide with those foisted upon one by a cynical totalitarian society.

The Relativism of General Principles

As we have seen, what chiefly differentiates present-day science from that of the last century is that today's science incorporates much more organically the idea of the individual's freedom. That idea figures not only in the formulation of the supreme goal but also in the viewpoint toward the structure of the world and the mechanism of evolution. From this angle of vision, totalitarian socialism of the Soviet type may be regarded not merely as a barbarous species of socialism but as not being socialism at all.

Other traits of modern scientific thought have also left their imprint on sociopolitical thinking. I should like to single out two of them. There is one difference between the modern scientist's style of thinking and that of scientists in earlier times which often passes unnoticed but which, it seems to me, has very tangible social consequences. It concerns the scientist's attitude toward the content of his work. Previously, scientists thought only in terms of *discoveries*—that the laws of Nature were lying ready and that the scientist's job was merely to open the eyes of his contemporaries to their existence. But today, thanks chiefly to the new physics, the psychology of the scientist has changed markedly. Modern physicists have come to realize that science is only a certain way of organizing sensory experience. This has become essential to physicists, enabling them to understand the new physical theories. And when we accept this notion, we begin to realize that we are not so much discoverers as creators—creators of new models of reality which prove to be more or less useful in organizing experience. Of course the element of discovery has not entirely disappeared, but science is now more likely to take on the character of a successful *invention*.

In the scientific disciplines closer to sensory experience than the new physics, this factor does not play such an important role. Yet its influence has extended both to philosophy and to the methodology of science as a whole. The words "model" and "modeling" are now among the most common in scientific literature. A scientist prefers to say he has *built a model (or a theory)* rather than to say that he has *discovered a law*. The word "discovery" is used only with respect to directly observed phenomena. The idea of the relativism of all general principles and laws—their instrumental, practical character—has become firmly rooted in science.

But what bearing does this have on social problems and politics? The scientist's way of thinking spreads although slowly, through the entire society. The layman cannot master the technical details; but gradually (and often unconsciously) he assimilates the spirit of change—the new style in philosophy and methodology. This applies especially to those politicians who make a show of being in step with the times and summon up science as one of their allies. In the days when laws were being discovered it was natural for the politician to do as Marx did and "open the eyes" of his contemporaries to the objective laws of social development he had allegedly discovered; today, in order to be successful in a society where people's minds are influenced by the scientific worldview, the politician must express himself more or less as follows: "There are several competitive models which describe the problems of our society and, accordingly, indicate the way to solve them. The model in which I put the most trust is such-and-such. So let's base our decision-making on this model. I'm sure that we'll see pretty soon whether it's good or bad, and then we can draw the appropriate conclusions."

The psychology of the discovery of laws engenders an "all-or-nothing" mentality in politics. Either the law exists, or it doesn't. It is either a great truth or a regrettable delusion. In the consciousness of the masses to whom the politicians address themselves, this is interpreted as follows: society is either structured "correctly" (i.e., in accordance with the laws of Nature) or "incorrectly" (i.e., in contravention of them). In the latter case, society must be ruthlessly destroyed and then rebuilt. This trait of the earlier science makes it akin to the dogmatic religions, since a dogma is likewise either altogether true or altogether false. In terms of methodology, European science from its very beginnings was skeptical and critical: it demanded repeated experimental verification, and recognized the relativism of any announced truth. But in terms of ontology—its notion of the real—it was just as dogmatic as religion. The methodology of science was the professional affair of scientists, but the ontology lay at the basis of the worldview, and was transmitted to the broad strata of the population.

In all its aspects, modern science is striving to make us evolutionists, and gradualists in politics. The further its influence reaches, the more firmly will these traits become fixed in society. But this does not mean giving up revolutionism in thought and in deed, if by "revolutionism" we mean depth of transformation. The history of twentieth-century science offers striking examples of revolutionism, and teaches us to look for bold and unexpected solutions.

The critical scientific method is penetrating ever more deeply into people's minds. In particular, the penetration of this method into philosophy has rid it of that kind of thinking in "all-or-nothing" terms with respect to general laws and principles which was akin to classical religious dogmatism and served as a nutrient medium for fanaticism.

Cybernetic Thinking

The second kind of modern scientific thinking I should like to single out is called *cybernetic thinking.* It is of recent origin, and has not yet penetrated deeply enough into the consciousness of society. But that process is going on; and I consider it of very great—even decisive—importance in the development of scientific socialism.

Cybernetics is in vogue; and its well-publicized achievements are influencing industry—and even our daily lives—to the point of transforming them. But what bearing does that have on the sociopolitical views of the majority who are not cyberneticians, and on their way of thinking? Do I not perhaps have in mind an indirect influence via technological progress and changes in lifestyle?

On the contrary, what I have in mind is a direct, conceptual influence. In making our judgments and setting our goals, we start with the reality around us; and we describe that reality by means of some system of concepts and terms. Any system for describing reality is incomplete; it selectively emphasizes some aspects and plays down others. Such a system therefore has an essential influence on our own systems of values and goals. But that influence is not obvious: since we constantly use the same reference system, we are inclined to take it for granted, and to identify *our* description with "objective reality."

The most general and most frequently used concepts form what might be called a "background conception of reality." There is no fully-determining relationship between a background conception of reality and a system of values and goals. Some influence, however, is exerted: different background conceptions incline one toward different judgments and goals. Thus when there is a change in the dominant background conception, there is likewise a change in the dominant system of values.

In European culture before the twentieth century, the

background conception of reality was based on mechanics and chemistry. Its nucleus may be described as follows: the world is an aggregate of atoms possessing certain qualities. In that conception, the concepts of system, structure, and organization were ontologically secondary—derivative. By contrast, the cybernetic background conception of reality (which will probably be the dominant conception of the twenty-first century) puts these concepts in the foreground. A cybernetician thinks not in terms of the *quality* of components but in terms of the *relationships* among them.[15] In chemo-mechanistic thinking, the way things are organized is considered to manifest their "essence." In cybernetic thinking, the way things are organized is declared to *be* their essence.

As might be expected, the chemo-mechanical conception of reality inclines one toward an individualist conception, in which society is perceived as an aggregate of people-atoms. The human personality possesses, by its very nature, the attributes of wholeness, absoluteness, and indivisibility. It also possesses other attributes, and a capacity for self-improvement—for developing "good" qualities and suppressing "bad" ones. Society is necessary insofar as it enables the human personality to manifest its qualities and perfect them. Beyond that, society has no value: it is merely a form of "peaceful coexistence" among individuals.

In the cybernetic conception of reality, the human personality is one of the levels in a unitary cosmic organization. First, a person is regarded not as an atom but as a system with a complex hierarchical structure. Second, a person is viewed as a subsystem of an overall, encompassing system—human society. The cybernetic background conception of reality inclines one toward a socialist conception of society. When its concepts are concretized, in whatever manner, the meaning and value of a person's life must be deduced from the meaning of society's own existence. The common good is something more than the sum of individual goods.

The Inevitability of Integration

Individualism may be of various kinds, depending upon which attributes of the individual are considered "good" and which are regarded as "bad." Here we touch upon the sphere of religion. The individualist conception of society fits in well with a metaphysically transcendental religion. It combines with and supplements that religion to form a blend that can serve as a basis for a more or less viable social order. The concept of God constitutes a supreme level which unites the individuals and makes for social stability. The chief moral principles are derived from the idea of God, and those principles are of course such as to make it feasible for people to coexist.

Such was the situation in Europe so long as the Christian religion was the basis of society's spiritual life. Unity in Christ was the symbolic form of social integration, and the admonition to love one's neighbor was its instrument here on earth. To a certain extent, the Spiritualist transcendence of Christianity overcomes the limitations of individualism; or, more precisely, it serves as a form in which our inherent craving for integration can be manifested. At the same time, the notion of the divine spark implanted in the breast of every human being elevated (at least in theory) the human personality to a height unattainable by dogmatic or political considerations.

For these reasons, the Renaissance (the rebirth of classical individualism within the framework of the Christian religion) brought about a luxuriant flowering of culture in Europe. It effected that synthesis of integration and freedom which alone makes possible a constructive evolution. The chemo-mechanistic background conception of Nature occupied an important and naturally determined place in that synthesis.

The decline of the Christian religion is destroying the synthesis of integration and freedom achieved by many generations of Europeans. That destruction is not taking place all at once. For a certain length of time, the traditional concepts and norms of behavior (in those segments of society where they have existed at all) will continue to be transmitted to the next generation. But the ground has been cut from under their feet. Sooner or later, they will collapse.

Whereas integration without freedom leads to the ossification of society, or to the obscurantism of Church or Party, freedom without integration leads to society's breakdown. A society cannot be built on a basis of pure individualism. There do of course exist several sound principles which, within the framework of the individualist conception, help (as best they can) to make life bearable for a person (the most important of such principles is expressed in the admonition "do unto others as you would have them do unto you"). These principles address themselves to the reason and far-sightedness of society's members. Nor can it be said that they do so in vain: their influence on society is not at all negligible; and it grows as a society develops.

But such principles are not enough. Society demands certain sacrifices of a person—especially in times of crisis. From an individualist viewpoint, the only justification for such sacrifices is the calculation—in the spirit of Chernyshevsky's "enlightened self-interest"—that in the long run you (or at least a loved one) will be rewarded for making them. Society, however, demands sacrifices (little ones constantly, big ones on occasion) that are *not* rewarded in the lifetime of the individual or loved ones.

Of course the theory of enlightened self-interest may be modified by expanding the number of "loved ones" to include society as a whole. But in a nonreligious, mechanistic conception of society, there is no link between my person, my feelings, and the individual benefits conferred upon members of society whom I do not know. The common good turns out to be an artificial, abstract construct that cannot withstand testing by hardships, and breaks down into its component parts.

Finally, there is one question that proves fatal for the individualist society: Who is to make the sacrifice, and how much must he sacrifice? If the sacrifice is not a manifestation of a striving toward a religious supreme goal organically incorporated into the person's consciousness and emotional sphere, but rather a result of calculation, then the "equal" apportioning of sacrifices becomes important. But sacrifices cannot be apportioned "equally." Attempts to measure them, and the attendant quarreling, engender the kind of society for which nobody wants to sacrifice anything.

Humans are capable of social integration—and that alone makes integration inevitable. Those ideologies and associations of human beings which do not provide for the level of integration attainable under other circumstances are doomed to extinction. Social integration may be compared to the process of crystallization. There exists a mechanism which combines atoms into a crystal—a definite, ordered structure more stable than others. Sooner or later, individual atoms either regroup into a new crystal or are absorbed by existing crystals. The question now facing us all is not *whether* the process of social integration will take place but *how* it will take place. Will it result in a monstrous totalitarianism which secures integration by force, terror, and spiritual castration? Or will it lead to a genuine socialism whose motive force is the free human personality?

Mechanistic and Cybernetic Integration

In the chemo-mechanistic model of society, human beings are in a certain sense *elementary*, like Dalton's atoms. They are alike—hence egalitarianism; they are mutually impenetrable—hence individualism. Of course there is no direct logical connection here (people aren't atoms, for all that); but there is an expansion and diffusion of a certain conceptual schema taken from science. And the scientific-artistic images formed on the basis of that schema impart a definite direction to thought, although they are not always manifested in the form of clear-cut logical conclusions.

What does society look like when modeled mechanistically? In its general outlines, it reminds one of the conversion of a gas into a liquid or solid. In high school physics textbooks, this process is described as follows. When the distance between the centers of atoms is greater than the sum of their radiuses, the atoms are attracted to each other. When they come closer together, they begin strongly to repel each other. The force of attraction between atoms rapidily decreases with distance, so that in a rarefied gas the atoms seldom interact: they collide with one another only rarely. As the density of a substance increases, the atoms come within one another's sphere of attraction; and if the temperature is not too high, the substance goes into a condensed state in which the force of attraction, with no pressure from without, combines the atoms into a single substance. In a condensed state, the atoms are packed closely together (to put it crudely), so that the application of even strong external pressure results (in contrast to the case of a gas) in only a slight decrease in volume.

In the cybernetic model of social integration, the unit being integrated (a person) figures, first of all, as a complex *system* characterized by a multilevel control hierarchy. Social integration is a metasystem transition involving the emergence of a new level in the hierarchy—one that controls the highest level of organization of the subsystems being integrated, i.e., individuals. Control, as I have stressed more than once, does not mean that the functions of the object being controlled are taken over, but merely that these objects are put into certain conditions, as a result of which their activity is coordinated. It is the highest control level of the integrated subsystems that is first of all subject to control by the emerging metasystem. On the other, lower, levels of control, the integrated subsystems retain considerable—or even complete—independence. For instance, the formation of multicellular organisms did not alter the biochemical processes which are responsible for heredity, and the formation of human society did not restructure the nervous system of each individual.

We can now see that in a certain sense the mechanistic and cybernetic models of integration work in opposite directions. Mechanistic integration works from the outside in. When the atoms come closer together, their shells interact. First it is attraction, but when they come still closer, a strong repulsion arises. Social integration in the mechanistic manner is the forced collectivization of people into communes, kolkhozes, etc. on the confident assumption that they will naturally combine into an ideal social structure, just as carbon atoms form diamonds under high pressure.

The cybernetic integration of society works from the inside out. It begins as coordination and integration of the consciousness of individuals, i.e., on the highest level of the control of human behavior ("spiritual culture"). The integration on the lower levels—in the sphere of industry, everyday life, and people's physical actions—should be a consequence (an automatic result) of integration on the level of consciousness. Only this kind of integration has any chance of continued development—of constructive evolution.

In contrasting the mechanistic and cybernetic models of social integration, I have stirred up an ancient controversy as to how to go about establishing universal brotherhood on earth. Should we start with dividing all property equally and living together in communes? Or should we first educate ourselves and others in a spirit of love, tolerance, and forgiveness? In the popular consciousness, the first approach is associated with the concept of socialism, and the second with Christianity. But when we analyze the concept of socialism in the terms suggested by modern science, only the second approach is genuinely socialistic, while the first represents socialist barbarism. Christ's teachings show the way toward socialism.

Of course it is not enough merely to preach Christian moral principles. That is only a start. Christianity, with its separation of the spiritual and the corporeal (and its concern only for the spiritual) restricted the idea of integration to that of souls. From the viewpoint of cybernetics, it correctly indicated the point of departure for integration; but it did not provide a perspective—a look at the process as a whole. For a certain length of time, the famous dictum "Render unto Caesar the things which be Caesar's" played a beneficient role—one that perhaps even saved the situation. This was a concession—a bone thrown by the soul to the body—made in order to retain some degree of independence. By separating the spiritual from the corporeal, the transcendent Spiritualism of Christianity preserved Western Europe, in the process of integration, from all-consuming totalitarianism. But in our day the philosophical foundations of Christianity have become an obstacle to further progress. A socialist should regard Christianity as a forerunner. He feels gratitude toward it, and takes a good deal from it. But he takes only what he considers necessary; and he rethinks and recasts in his own way what he has taken.

The Battering Fist

The Party
is a million-fingered hand
clenched
into one
battering fist.

Vladimir Mayakovsky[16]

If one were to choose a single, brief phrase to characterize the barbarism of the Marxist-Leninist variety of socialism, one might say simply: "mechanistic social integration." This phrase reflects all the basic negative traits of Marxism-Leninism: Economic Determinism, belittlement of the role of spiritual culture, reliance on "revolutionary" force. These traits are the result of a hasty and clumsy application of certain aspects of nineteenth-century science. They are reminiscent of the phrenologist who tried to gauge a patient's psychic proclivities by smoothing out the bumps on one part of his skull and making bumps on others. Mechanistic integration cannot bring about any other society than a totalitarian one. It means forcibly squeezing human beings together, compressing them.

In the cybernetic model of integration, socialism is above all a *phenomenon of culture*. As it takes root and develops in people's consciousness through the agencies of philosophy, science, literature, and art, the socialist mentality makes it possible to elaborate new forms of relationships among people; to restructure social and governmental institutions on the one hand, and production systems on the other. Any attempt to effect the integration of organized systems from the lowest or middle level of the hierarchy (in particular, from the economic level in the case of social integration) rather than from the top is a cybernetic absurdity. It would be as if we took it into our heads to combine ten workers into one "big worker" by binding their hands together into one "big hand" and their feet into one "big foot." Another image—a very instructive one—was used by Mayakovsky in the lines of poetry (quoted above) that children learn by heart in the Soviet Union.

An example of cybernetic integration would be a human hand with its fingers unhampered by pressure from other fingers and controlled from a common center—the brain. This is the hand that can perform an operation or play a piano. The fist, however, is a symbol of mechanistic, totalitarian integration: it can only batter, destroy, annihilate. Totalitarianism is a million-fingered fist drawn back for a blow at humanity.

Structural-Functional Parallelism

The conflict between social integration and the free personality within the framework of a general, positivistic approach to the problems of society, is reflected in the following excerpt from an essay by Herbert Spencer in which he formulates his disagreements with Auguste Comte:

> M. Comte's ideal of society is one in which *government* is developed to the greatest extent—in which class-functions are far more under conscious public regulation than now—in which hierarchical organization with unquestioned authority shall guide everything—in which the individual life shall be subordinated in the greatest degree to the social life.
>
> That form of society towards which we are progressing, I hold to be one in which *government* will be reduced to the smallest amount possible, and *freedom* increased to the greatest amount possible—one in which human nature will have become so moulded by social discipline into fitness for the social state, that it will need little external restraint, but will be self-restrained—one in which the citizen will tolerate no interference with his freedom, save that which maintains the equal freedom of others—one in which the spontaneous co-operation which has developed our industrial system, and is now developing it with increasing rapidity, will produce agencies for the discharge of nearly all social functions, and will leave to the primary governmental agency nothing beyond the function of maintaining those conditions to free action, which make such spontaneous co-operation possible—one in which individual life will thus be pushed to the greatest extent consistent with social life; and in which social life will have no other end than to maintain the completest sphere for individual life.[17]

Here Spencer opposes his British liberalism to Comte's French *étatisme*. Yet the contrast between these two ideals of society is not so absolute as it seems to Spencer. The compatibility of liberalism and *étatisme* depends upon what we understand by "hierarchy" and "government"; or rather, upon what concrete forms they assume.

To begin with Spencer's position, it can be said that the spontaneous cooperation that he advocates in no way contradicts the idea of integration. Moreover, spontaneous cooperation does not obviate the necessity for a hierarchy: in a society with millions of members there will be so many spontaneous associations of citizens (associations of all kinds: cultural, economic, and those serving the needs of everyday life) that the representatives of these associations will have, in their turn, to join together in other associations. Otherwise society would simply fall to pieces. Yet even those associations (associations comprising representatives of the first level) will be no doubt too numerous, so they will have to set up yet another level in the hierarchy. And so it will go until they have formed a multilevel hierarchical system of representatives with, at the summit, a "countable" number of people capable of effective contact with one another. A hierarchy in one form or another is indispensable when large systems are being organized. This is a law of cybernetics, and there is no getting around it.

As for freedom, even Spencer admits that it cannot be absolute. He is compelled to bring in "social discipline" and the restrictions that societal life puts on the individual life, etc.

Now let us look at the question from Comte's angle of vision. The development of society is the development of a hierarchical system of government, meaning control. But what kind of control? To control a subsystem is not to strip it of all autonomy. In societal relationships, control can hardly be boiled down to subordination and coercion; that is merely the crudest, most imperfect kind of control—the mechanistic kind, one might say. If we imagine society as a huge watch mechanism, as Comte did, the hierarchy of cogwheels will indeed fully determine the movement of each part, to which it transmits the energy of the mainspring. But self-developing cybernetic systems have a different structure. They are built from the bottom up by means of sequential metasystem transitions in which each new level, instead of eliminating the functions of the preceding level, creates yet more functions of a different kind—a new kind of activity. In a well-designed cybernetic system there is a structural-functional parallelism: qualitatively different functions and kinds of activity correspond to different structural levels of organization. Also corresponding to the latter are the different concepts by which we describe the functioning of the level; so that in effect we have a "structural-functional-conceptual" parallelism.

For example: on the lowest organizational level of a computer, we have the electronic components: the ferrite cores, the transistors, the resistors, etc. Their functioning is described in terms of voltage and current, pulse duration, etc. From these components are built the basic units of the computer. One example is the arithmetic (data-processing) unit. In order to describe the way it is built and the way it functions, we need completely different concepts: the concept of a number in the binary system; the four operations of arithmetic; rounding-off; etc.

The sequence of operations performed in the arithmetic unit is determined by a program stored in the computer's memory unit. This is yet another level in the structure of our system; and to describe the functioning of that level we need still another set of concepts: transferring control, looping, memory allocation, and debugging. In the relationship between the levels, the largest structural-functional units of the preceding level become the smallest units of the next one. The programmer thinks in terms of arithmetic operations; but with rare exceptions, he is not concerned with how numbers are represented in the machine, or how the rounding-off is done. And never will he give a thought to the physics on which, in the final analysis, the functioning of the computer is based.

In a system which comprises only the computer, the program is the highest level of control. However, the computer performs a certain "service" function, being one subsystem of a bigger system, which includes human beings. A computer's program may, for example, be one for designing a nuclear reactor. In this case, it will be the result of the work done by people specializing in the physics of nuclear reactors—a kind of work characterized by its own specific concepts. This is yet another level of the hierarchy. Finally, we can distinguish still one more level: an educational system. Specialists in programming, and in the physics of nuclear reactors, must be trained. And this educational process also has its own specific traits and concepts, which are directly relevant to the work. Thus in the broad sense in which I use the concept of control, education is included.

Let us now consider a few examples of structural-functional parallelism in the sphere of social integration, starting with politics. Politics is the control of people's behavior. The simplest method of control is by direct command. A certain number of people are separated from the basic mass and form the level of commanders. These commanders issue orders to their subordinates in the same way as the latter issue orders to their own hands and feet: by an act of will. (I am thinking of the extreme case of the commander–subordinate relationship—the kind that exists, say, between a slavedriver and his slave.) Here we have no structural-functional parallelism: one and the same kind of control is used on the level of the individual persons, and on the level where a group of people is subordinated to one superior. This method is "anticybernetic."

By contrast, a society governed by *laws* and not *people* offers an example of structural-functional parallelism. Here control is, in the final analysis, exercised by those who interpret the law and enforce it. The functioning of this level is determined not by the will but by the concepts of *rights* and *duties.* This mode of control is more flexible, and is an improvement over the command method. Of course it is by no means an absolute, universal method of solving all problems of government or control in society. Nonetheless, the rule of law is one of the greatest inventions of mankind—a great stride along the path toward combining integration and freedom.

In separating the function of law enforcement from all

other functions we have divided societal activities into two big categories forming two levels of the hierarchy. Within its framework, each category has its own intricate structure—its own hierarchy. Consider any administrative system—the executive branch of a government for example. Here the hierarchy is formed by the command relationship. The chief has authority over his subordinates, and control is largely a matter of issuing orders and directives. But these orders, unlike those issued in a slave-holding society, are concerned only with official duties, and even then they are regulated by law. Nonetheless, this is a commander-subordinate relationship; and from it flow quite a few difficulties and defects that are usually labeled "bureaucratism."

The basic method of avoiding bureaucratism is to adhere strictly to structural-functional parallelism. One must find, for each level of the hierarchy, that specific method of functioning which will make it possible to effectively control the preceding level without replacing it. The organization of control is an extremely creative and extremely difficult job; it demands a tremendous amount of conceptual work. One must build a hierarchy of concepts and the parallel structural hierarchy in such a way that one can describe the control functions of each level, and indicate its task, in terms of the corresponding concepts. If this job is not done right, the inevitable result is a bureaucratic chaos in which each department head either oversteps the bounds of his authority or tries to shift responsibility to the next higher level.

But in addition to the purely practical aspect of the way a hierarchy functions, there is another aspect. Imperfect as we are, we are capable of abusing the authority conferred upon us. Many organizations, in order to prevent such abuses, have provided a supplementary level in their structure: one which does not issue directives but merely keeps check on the activities of the other levels. In a general way, this solution is fully in keeping with the principle of structural-functional parallelism; and it has proven helpful. Yet as experience has shown, it is not enough, In this set-up, the watchdog agency is too close, both structurally and functionally, to the agencies being checked on. As they constitute a single system, they find a common language and ways of cheating that are acceptable to both of them. In order to break out of that vicious circle, Western society invented a new solution: freedom of the press. The press, and the public opinion it guides, constitute a metasystem with respect to all levels of all hierarchies, both executive and judicial. Its functions therefore differ radically from those of all other levels. Journalists and writers do not issue orders; nor are they obligated to keep watch on anyone. Their motives and methods are of a quite different order. Yet they look into everything and keep watch on everything. They have no direct administrative authority to encourage or punish anyone; yet they *do* encourage and punish people, either through public opinion or by getting information to the judicial authorities.

In the manufacturing area, the integration of producers by means of the market offers a clear example of structural-functional parallelism. In contrast to barter (on the lower levels of the structure), exchange on the market among independent producers gives rise to a qualitatively new function, that of buying and selling, which involves such concepts as supply, demand, price, and cost. Commodity-money relations via the agency of the market have proven to be an amazing integrator, making it possible to assure—within the framework of the capitalist market—an unprecedented rate of production development, both qualitatively and quantitatively. Marx was quite right when he stressed that capitalism was a necessary phase in the development of society. But he felt that the abolition of commodity-money relations was essential in emerging from that phase and moving on to the next, socialism.

Socialism and communism are traditional enemies of the market, perhaps because money and the market are an integral part of capitalism, and the struggle against capitalism seems to be inseparable from the struggle against the market. But whatever its causes, hostility toward the market, and a determination to destroy it by means of governmental decrees, are typical of socialist barbarism—the result of mechanistic thinking and a total failure to understand the basic character of the evolutionary process. To replace market relations with pre-market relations (with barter in accordance with various plans, schedules, etc.) is exactly the same thing as to replace relations based on law with out-and-out command relations. For the commanders, this may mean (at first) a feeling of power, and intoxication with authority. But this is not the way to a "radiant future." On the contrary, this is regression; and it is anticybernetic. Progress, constructive evolution, is achieved by the creation of new levels of the control hierarchy. This means that market relations should not be abolished but controlled. One example of such control is Keynes's approach to the State's regulation of the economy with the aid of fiscal policy. Another is the state's participation in the market as a producer and consumer, and the state regulation of prices. Both are forms of control, provided that they do not violate the basic principle of the market's functioning. This approach is cybernetic; and it has demonstrated its effectiveness. In this case, the state's control functions are exercised *over* the market and not *in place of* it. And these are qualitatively new functions whose description requires new concepts, as is demanded by structural-functional parallelism.

By contrast, the nationalization of industry, as it has been carried out in the Soviet Union, means that the state *takes the place of* the market: it becomes the owner of all property, and controls it as one gigantic business. At all structural levels, the methods and functions are about the same: structural-functional parallelism is either totally lacking, or is at best feeble. This is a mechanistic and not a cybernetic approach. The resulting system is unwieldy and incapable of development. It is also, politically speaking, totalitarian. In its early stages, so long as the control hierarchy is not too much strained, such a system may show good results, because of its ability to mobilize (and therefore exploit) human and natural resources. But in time these indexes must inevitably fall off. This is something we have actually observed. Attempts to improve the functioning of the

Soviet economic system by means of reforms are attempts to restore the lost structural-functional parallelism. First came the attempt to increase the role of monetary relations by introducing *khozraschet* (self-supporting management). Then, in the 1960s, a feeble and plainly unsuccessful attempt was made to raise the level of economic freedom by bringing it close to the market level. All these things only prove yet again the validity of cybernetic laws.

Three Levels of Social Integration

Thus in the cybernetic model of integration, the conflict between integration and freedom is solved from a position of structural-functional parallelism. Like any other dialectic contradiction, this one does not lend itself to final solution. Rather, it can be solved only in the dynamic evolution of social structures and functions. In the process, the contacts among people become ever closer. People become increasingly necessary to one another, and learn better and better how to understand one another. At the same time, the "junction point of individuals" constantly moves up in the control hierarchy. The junction point of individuals is that obligatory element which limits a person's freedom in society; that which he must accept if society is not to break down. There is no lessening of this obligation as history progresses, but it does become more *abstract*, and therefore leaves people more freedom.

In the sphere of social relations, progress consists in elaborating concepts and methods of control which make it possible to create that abstraction, and to link it with the concrete acts of individuals.

As examples of clearly distinguishable control levels in the contemporary Western society let us indicate the executive authority, the legislature, the judicial institutions, and the free press in the sphere of politics, and industry, market, and state control of the monetary system in economics. Humanity had to travel a long, hard way before such concepts and methods were worked out.

Before trying to guess what the future holds, let's take a look at human history from a greater remove. In prehistoric times, integration took place essentially as it did among other animals—not yet as an object of thought, or of conscious human effort. With the beginning of civilization, conscious, purposeful social integration began as well. We can distinguish three levels, three mechanisms, by means of which integration can be affected: (1) direct physical coercion; (2) economic necessity (i.e., the necessity to secure the means of survival); (3) free integration guided by the spirtual culture of society.

The social order in which the first kind of integration is basic is called *slavery;* in the second case, what we have is *capitalism;* and the social order in the third case I call *socialism.* (As is often the case, the same word is used to mean both the social movement, and its ideal.)

Slavery and Capitalism

Under *slavery* we may lump both the slave-holding system and medieval society. In both cases, direct physical compulsion to work for the master is the basis of the social order (and it hardly matters whether the master kills the slave or merely flogs him half to death).

Capitalism presupposes a state based on law: one in which everyone is equal before the law, and no one can force another to work for him by means of physical coercion. The worker and the capitalist enter into a voluntary contract. And although the "voluntariness" is very relative on the worker's part (he must sell his labor in order to survive) it need hardly be shown what a great stride toward freedom capitalism represents as compared to slavery.

Capital is the means of production. Hence capitalism is the sovereignty of the means of production. A capitalist society is one in which the chief aim is to produce material wealth. Naturally, this does not rule out the possibility, for certain people and groups of people, of having both personal and group aims which go well beyond the framework of economics. But *economics remains the basis of social integration:* it determines the way human beings coexist, the rationale for a unitary coexistence, and the nature of their most important social institutions.

Capitalism becomes possible at a certain stage in the development of productive forces. Let us use (as Marx did) the letter *C* to designate what is put into one production cycle by the means of production (or constant capital), and a *V* to represent what labor puts into it. In the production cycle, the relative value of C and *V* in the sum $C+V$ varies with the development of the productive forces. Specifically, the share represented by *C* grows, while that represented by *V* decreases. So long as *C* is much less than *V*, labor is the basis of production; and the direct and most simple way of organizing labor—physical coercion—creates slavery. But at a certain stage in the development of industry, *C* becomes decisive. Moreover, the coefficient of production expansion (the ratio between the final product, which we designate as *P*, and the expenditures of $C+V$) begins to increase rapidly. As a result, the means of production begin to develop on their own, as it were. Although the human labor represented by the term *V* remains necessary, it is no longer the determining factor: it is now easier to hire a worker than to procure the means of production. Capitalism thus starts to grow exponentially, and the worker becomes "an appendage of the machine," to use a Marxist expression.

Classical capitalism represents the kind of society in which relationships among human beings are almost entirely economic ones effected via the market (and in particular, the labor-power market). In such a society, there are no producers' monopolies and no trade unions. Classical capitalism was analyzed by Marx, who reached a conclusion as to the maximization of the average rate of profit under those conditions. In other words, classical capitalism is a system which, with the given means of production, assures a maximum of industrial growth. This attribute of capitalism is a result of competition on the market, so that everyone who wants to survive must join in the race. That share of the final product, *P*, which goes for consumption (in particular, to pay for labor) becomes minimal; and that share of it which is put back into production becomes maximal. Every potential for increasing labor productivity is sought out and utilized.

Classical capitalism is an idealization—an extreme case which, in its pure form, does not exist and never did. But for a certain period of time, European capitalism was close to it. Then, under the influence of both economic and noneconomic factors, it underwent a substantial evolutionary change. In particular, owing to the workers' collective struggle for higher wages, the level of consumption has long since exceeded the minimum necessary to a maximal growth of industry, and it continues to rise. Even today, however, the nations of Western Europe and North America cannot be called anything but capitalist. Unquestionably, the main features of the social order are determined by the capitalist system for the production and consumption of material wealth.

The Transition to Socialism

Capitalist society has been subjected, and is being subjected, to criticism which is largely justified. But if we scrutinize that criticism, we see that it is a criticism of capitalism's defects and not an exposé of a real evil. At any rate, such is the case with responsible, well-founded criticism: it does not so much point out the existence of something harmful as show the lack of something useful—even essential. The power of money? But money is a means of securing necessities of life and keeping industry going. Money cannot but have power, because it is indispensable. What is unfortunate here is not that money means power, but that *only* money means power. The race for profits? But in itself it's a fine thing; it's a striving for maximum industrial growth—a goal upon which the so-called socialist countries base their policy. But it's bad if the race for profits is the *only* stimulus and regulator of economic development. The concentration of power in the hands of the big property-owners is often criticized, but in a large and closely-knit economic system, *someone* must have lots of economic power; just as in a large state, someone must inevitably have great political power. But of course it's too bad if there are no means by which the public can keep check on that power.

The transition from capitalism to socialism is a metasystem transition. It presupposes not the destruction of the preceding control level of the system but the construction of the next one. (It should be noted, however, that this does not preclude some *reconstruction* of the preceding level.) Revolutionaries like Marx and Engels called upon their followers to destroy capitalism down to its very foundations, and to build socialism on its ruins. Of course by "ruins" they did not mean the ruins of machines and buildings: they did not propose destroying the means of production. To the contrary, these were to serve as the material foundation for the new society. It was only social relations that were to be destroyed down to their foundations. Here we glimpse the "materialist" (read "mechanistic") background of the nineteenth century, in accordance with which only *things* have authentic existence, possess inertia, and require effort for their creation, while relationships are something ethereal and derivative. But a cybernetician of the twentieth century knows that the system of relationships is the reality—a reality whose creation demands tremendous creative work. For a cybernetician, to destroy a market or a "bourgeois" right is just as barbarous as to destroy machines and railroads.

Private Ownership of the Means of Production and the Labor Theory of Value

In order to justify the destruction of something, one must find in it some real evil—some essential vice. Marx found such a vice in the private ownership of the means of production, which in his opinion was in irreconcilable conflict with the social nature of production. The theoretical foundation for Marx's opinion was Adam Smith's labor theory of value. Marx developed it into an integral part of his own ideas.[18] According to Marx, the true "value" of a commodity (which he distinguishes from both "use-value" and exchange value), is the amount of "socially necessary labor" expended in making the commodity. Paradoxically, this theory arose and gained recognition at a time when capitalism was beginning to flourish; i.e., just when the theory had been proven erroneous. Indeed, the product of the production cycle is, roughly speaking, proportional to the sum $C+V$. In the precapitalist era C was small, and hence it could be considered that the production cost was proportional to the labor, V, expended. The product was produced by labor. But in the capitalist era it was C that was decisive: machines produced the product. Then why did Marx need the labor theory of value? To show that the capitalist was *robbing* the worker.

If we grant that the final product is proportional to $C+V$—i.e., $P=k(C+V)$, where k represents the coefficient of reproduction—then the surplus product, or surplus value, will be proportionate to $C+V$: $m=P-(C+V)=(k-1)(C+V)$.

But then it turns out that the owner of the capital C, is entitled to at least a proportionate share of the surplus value. In order to avoid that conclusion, Marx distinguished between "use-value" and an alleged "value" determined by the amount of labor time expended. He then postulated that the value contained in C simply passes as is into the finished product, while the surplus value, m, is proportional to the expended labor, V; and the coefficient of proportionality, m/V, he calls the rate of surplus value. This is of course a purely metaphysical postulate which has no real meaning. It is precisely the "use-value" of a commodity, its material form, which is the value for whose sake it is produced, and which takes part in the process of price-formation on the market.

Surplus value reflects an attribute of developing material systems: their capacity to increase their mass with the passage of time, and to produce new material forms. As for the labor-time embodied in the commodity, it remains invisible when the latter goes on the market: it affects the price only indirectly—through its effect on supply. And of course there is no reason at all to multiply the labor time by the rate of surplus value: time, unlike material objects, cannot reproduce itself.

In attempting to compute the rate of surplus value, we must take into account the final product, which is proportional not to V but to $C+V$—a fact which gives rise to many contradictions and absurdities in Marx's theory. These absurdities become especially evident when we are dealing with the work of an organizer or the invention of new machines, automated production lines, etc.

One thing in Marx's reasoning that should be noted is that in doing battle against capitalism he bases his argument on the concept of property, addressing himself to the proprietary instinct and by no means trying to rise above it. To rise above it means to see, and explain to others, that property is simply a way of controlling the material component of civilization: one which, like any other form of control, may be transformed gradually. To take such an approach means to favor reforms: a graduated income tax, a high inheritance tax, limits on the right to own large amounts of property, etc. But for a revolutionary there is no worse evil than reform, and no stronger term of abuse than "reformism." The Marxists prove that the capitalists *rob* the worker; i.e., that they take away his property; that the surplus value, which in a capitalist society is regarded as belonging to the capitalist, *really* belongs to the worker. This metaphysical "really" preserves the mystique of property, and is based on it. The resultant slogans of reciprocal plunder—"exploit the exploiters," "steal back what has been stolen"—find, in different segments of society, support that is inversely proportional to culture.

The Evolution of the State

Thinking of the era which would follow the socialist revolution, Engels wrote as follows:

> State interference in social relations becomes, in one domain after another, superfluous, and then dies out of itself; the government of persons is replaced by the administration of things, and by the conduct of processes of production. The state is not "abolished." *It dies out.*[19]

Indeed, if in accord with the Marxist doctrine we take the state to be exclusively and primarily an instrument for the coercion of some groups of people by others, the state should—and will—wither away. But this interpretation of the concept of the state is a vulgar, demagogic simplification. The state is usually taken to be the totality of instruments of social integration. A society cannot do without those instruments. How well perfected they are is another matter.

The character of the state depends upon the material and spiritual culture of the society, and is transformed along with that culture. So long as the society has no idea of law or rights, and so long as it is not recognized that this idea extends to each human being, the state cannot be anything but a feudal or slave-holding system. So long as the society has not elaborated an idea as to how to organize integration on a basis different from production and consumption, the state will remain a capitalist system. The evolution of the state is geared to the pace at which society, in its searching and its struggles, discovers new modes of integration assuring more freedom to the individual. Like any kind of evolution, this one is a *complication,* not a simplification—and therefore not a withering away. The control methods of the lowest level—physical coercion and sometimes even killing—remain available to the state. Progress means reducing the extent to which these measures are applied. But whether they can be done away with entirely remains an open question.

In the liberal and socialist thought of the nineteenth century, control over human beings was considered an unmitigated evil. The ideal social order was not a multilevel system of relationships that had constantly to be maintained with the aid of special institutions but something fundamentally simple—something that would happen on its own if only there were no coercion, no "government." This notion, typical of the chemo-mechanistic background conception of reality, makes the anarchists Godwin and Kropotkin akin to the liberal Spencer and to Marx and Engels. (Of course it makes them akin to the two last-named only until they get into power!) Kropotkin wrote:

> . . . Once the State has reached the point at which it is no longer capable of imposing forced union, union will arise of itself, in accordance with natural needs. Overthrow the State, and the federative society will surge up from its ruins, truly *one,* truly indivisible, but free and growing in solidarity because of its very freedom.[20]

It happens as follows:

> Instead of plundering the bakers' shops one day, and starving the next, the people of the insurgent cities will take possession of the warehouses, the cattle markets—in fact of all the provision stores and of all the food to be had. The well-intentioned citizens, men and women both, will form themselves into bands of volunteers and address themselves to the task of making a rough general inventory of the contents of each shop and warehouse. . . .

> In forty-eight hours millions of copies will be printed of the tables giving a sufficiently exact account of the available food, the places where it is stored, and the means of distribution. . . .
>
> Let the towns send no more inspectors to the villages, wearing red, blue, or rainbow-coloured scarves, to convey to the peasant orders to take his produce to this place or that, but let them send friendly embassies to the country folk and bid them in brotherly fashion: "Bring us your produce, and take from our stores and shops all the manufactured articles you please." Then provisions would pour in on every side. The peasant would only withhold what he needed for his own use, and would send the rest into the cities, feeling *for the first time in the course of history* that these toiling townsfolk were his comrades—his brethren, and not his exploiters.[21]

The Division of Labor

One cannot read the above without smiling; and the Marxists also chuckle at Kropotkin—at his naïveté and his unrealistic predictions. They claim that only Marx put the doctrine of the state's withering away on a "realistic" and "scientific" basis, relating it to the destruction of classes. Actually, though, the doctrine of the destruction of classes offers nothing new, as compared to the pictures painted by the single-minded utopians and anarchists. The absence of classes is, of course, possible only in a society where there is no division of labor—something about which the founders of Marxism wrote again and again. But the idea of abolishing the division of labor is more than utopian: it is an absurdity.

In "The German Ideology" we read:

> For as soon as labor is distributed, each man has a particular, exclusive sphere of activity, which is forced

> upon him and from which he cannot escape. He is a hunter, a fisherman, a shepherd, or a critical critic, and must remain so if he does not want to lose his means of livelihood; while in communist society, where nobody has one exclusive sphere of activity but each can become accomplished in any branch he wishes, society regulates the general production and thus makes it possible for me to do one thing today and another tomorrow, to hunt in the morning, fish in the afternoon, rear cattle in the evening, criticize after dinner, just as I have a mind, without ever becoming hunter, fisherman, shepherd or critic.[22]

Here, as in almost all of his specific examples, Marx looks not to the future but to the past. Thus the examples illustrating the labor theory of value do not seem absurd because they are taken from a sphere where the role of machines and invention is not yet great. Likewise, in the examples given above, we have the archaic occupations of hunter, fisherman, shepherd, and the comical profession of the "critical critic." If we replace these occupations with more modern ones, we get a picture of "Communist Man," who designs a new model of a computer today, and will be found, at a dizzying height, welding steel girders tomorrow. It will be possible for him to operate on a patient with a stomach ulcer in the morning, lecture on quantum mechnics in the afternoon, sing arias in the evening, and do some translations from classical Greek after dinner. Such a picture hardly requires commentary.

It is sometimes argued that with the growth in labor productivity, when only a negligible amount of time will be given to producing the necessities of life (and, consequently, to doing obligatory labor), conditions will be such as to permit a classless, structureless society in which there will be no division of labor, and the roles of all individuals will be alike. However, the division of labor is not due to the goal or result of work but to its complex and collective nature.

In scientific work, for example, the goal is not the production of consumer goods, yet a division of labor exists nevertheless, and is increasing. Integration and specialization are indivisible: they are two aspects of one and the same trend. Such was the case when multicellular organisms were formed; and such is—and will be—the case when people are combined into a society. So long as society exists, the division of labor and a hierarchical system of control will also exist.

There are two varieties of egalitarianism: one demands an equality of right; the other demands an equality of share. The former affirms that all people, from birth, have equal rights to social property and to share in all aspects of social life. This kind of egalitarianism is fully justified from the viewpoint of evolutionism, since any kind of inequality imposed on a person for reasons having nothing to do with his specific personality reduce the creative potential of society. A negative attitude toward all privileges acquired by inheritance—in particular the inheriting of capital—has always been, and will always be, a characteristic trait of socialism. But it does not follow that each and every person's actual participation in social life, and his share when the results of societal activity are distributed, should be equal, as is demanded by the second variety of egalitarianism. Naturally, society should strive to assure optimum living conditions, and to satisfy all of its members to a maximum. But *as a principle,* the equality of share has no reasonable justification. Indeed, such a principle has a deleterious effect on society, and can be implemented only by destroying society.

Social Integration in the USSR and the West

If by "property" we mean not some mystical link between people and things but the highest level in the hierarchy for the control of objects, then property will exist as long as the division of labor exists (a point stressed by Marx). Nationalization is not the abolition of property but its transfer into other hands.

Viewed in terms of economics, the Soviet social system is state capitalism. The state, in the person of its great overlords, is the owner of a huge system of industrial and agricultural production. In fact, it is the sole proprietor in the country, except for some peasants who own tiny personal plots of land. (*Kolkhoz* property does not count: in theory, it belongs to the commune, but in fact it belongs to the State.) The state-as-producer enters into market relations with the population: it buys labor and sells manufactured products. It strives to expand production to a maximum, and in general behaves like a dyed-in-the-wool capitalist. Since it has virtually absolute monopoly (its only competitors are those people who sell produce on the market), the state itself sets the prices of commodities; it sets wages as well.

In the United States there are antitrust laws to prevent capture of the market by monopolies and the foisting of jacked-up prices on the consumer. And workers have the right to strike for higher wages. In the Soviet Union, the state-as-capitalist is in the kind of position that Western capitalists can only dream of. (On the other hand, these hothouse conditions have a corrupting effect. Spared the necessity of competing on the market, the state-as-producer—along with each and every one of its structural components—knows no necessity for vigorously seizing all opportunities to increase economic efficiency. This applies first of all to the matter of introducing new equipment and technologies, and improving product quality—those two eternal worries of the Soviet industrial leaders. Moreover, the state can allow itself the luxury of promoting people not for their job skills but for "devotion to the cause of the Party.")

But there is more to the life of a society than its economic aspect; and the economic structure is not the equivalent of the social structure. State capitalism is an essential feature of the Soviet way of life, but the main instrument of social integration in the USSR is the Communist Party; i.e., a noneconomic phenomenon. The Party hierarchy, not the economic hierarchy, plays the leading role. For all the importance of economic development, Party unity—and unity around the Party—is an even more important factor. Indeed, it is the decisive one. And when that unity is at stake, the leaders unhesitatingly sacrifice the economy.

Moreover, the power of the Party hierarchy is exercised not by means of naked, direct coercion recognized as such by everyone (as happens in a slave-holding society) but by means of fostering, via the propaganda machine, the kind of thinking that serves the leaders' purposes. The mechanism of social integration in the USSR is not limited to physical force or economic coercion but exploits essentially the sphere of culture.

In the bourgeois-democratic states the organs of power are likewise formed by noneconomic associations (political parties); and often the government is as much a one-party affair as is the case in the Soviet Union. But here the relationship between the economic system and the political parties differs radically from that in the USSR. The reasons why citizens of capitalist countries join one or another party are their own business—and are subject to sudden changes. The basis of social stability is private ownership of the means of production—something recognized by the great majority of the population and protected by law. In the USSR, by contrast, it is the Party structure and the Party ideology which serve as the basis for stability, while the management of the economy is subject to sudden changes in structure and personnel. The Communist ideology is not based on any of the traditional religions with their metaphysical transcendentalism. Integration is understood in the most earthly and direct of all possible senses of the word: moral and political unity, carrying out the will of the Party, etc. Thus, Soviet totalitarianism is a sort of hybrid between slavery and socialism.

It is in the socialist element of the Soviet totalitarianism that its strength lies. This social order is not an absurdity, not a happenstance, but something much more dangerous: a perversion. The danger of totalitarianism lies in its *resemblance to socialism.* Substances completely foreign to a living organism, those which do not resemble any of the substances figuring in its metabolism, are as a rule excreted by the organism without their having done it any great harm. But when a substance is similar—but not identical—to some compound important to the organism's metabolism, it "deceives" the organism, and sometimes proves to be a virulent poison. Such is the case with totalitarianism in the global social "superbeing."

The reforms carried out in Western capitalist countries during the past few decades (governmental regulation of the economy, high income taxes, constant growth in welfare payments, etc.) have definitely socialist origins. But I suspect we shall have a long way to go before we reach the line separating capitalism from socialism, because all these reforms affect only one sphere: the production and distribution of material wealth. And socialism is a cultural phenomenon: a religion and a way of living in accordance with that religion. Suppose that tomorrow, in some country, people build an automatic production system that without any help from human beings can produce all manner of goods and distribute those goods strictly equally—or even "according to need." Or with a tenfold surplus! That would still not make such a society a socialist one. To the contrary, it might be suspected that it would start to degenerate, or to become totalitarian. We do not yet know any other mechanisms of noneconomic integration than the totalitarian.

Valence Bonds and Mass Bonds[23]

Ties between people in a society always represent some kind of influence or force at work between them. The movement toward socialism is an upward shift in the center of gravity of these forces and influences—upward from violence through economic necessity to the sphere of spiritual culture. And within that sphere, there occurs an upward shift from simple imitation and exchange of information on the empirical level toward ever-closer intellectual and emotional contact, which is a precondition to cultural progress.

Close intellectual and emotional contact between people requires time and effort. The number of such ties into which a person can enter at one time is limited. I shall call them *valence bonds* by analogy with the bonds between atoms, which form as the result of an exchange of electrons, and whose number is therefore limited. Valence bonds (*v*-bonds) between people are personal and individualized. They are relationships that presuppose close spiritual contact, mutual understanding and trust, and an exchange of the most complex (and perhaps the most vague) thoughts and feelings. Love, friendship, and creative collaboration are examples of such bonds. This is the most human mode of social intercourse (perhaps the *only* human mode in the fullest sense of the word)—one in which what is properly human unfolds to the full in a person, and one without which it cannot unfold. A *v*-bond is essentially bilateral. At the same time, one of the partners in such a bond may lead (or exemplify something), and the other may be led—e.g., in relations between parents and children.

The highest number of *v*-bonds into which a person can enter (his "valence") may vary from person to person. Let us take some average of it and designate it as v^{max}, bearing in mind that it is defined by the order of magnitude only. We may set $v^{max} = 10$. Indeed, it is hard to imagine a person with hundreds of friends. On the other hand, a person capable of friendship with only one person is rather the exception than the rule.

I use the term "mass bonds" (*m*-bonds) for those relations which are not *v*-bonds. One person may have a great number of such bonds (or contacts), and thanks to the mass communications media, that number is in principle unlimited. The relations a person has with passersby on the street, or with other passengers in a bus, are examples of *m*-bonds.

The President of the United States has *m*-bonds with all those citizens who hear and see him make a speech. A priest has *m*-bonds with all his parishioners who listen to his sermons, and from time to time come to him for confession. A policeman has *m*-bonds with people on his beat. A superficial, "nodding" acquaintanceship is also an *m*-bond.

We have an inherent need for *v*-bonds, which we have inherited from the social organization of our primate ancestors—an organization that was based on individualized bonds between community members. This mode of organization was characteristic not only of human forebears but of many other vertebrates, as we learn from a remarkable book by Konrad Lorenz, one of today's most outstanding specialists in animal behavior.[24] It is the most complex mode of social organization in the animal world.

Before discussing individualized bonds, however, let us examine the three other types of animal communities Lorenz describes.

(1) The most primitive type of society is the *anonymous flock* or *herd*. We find it, for example, in the case of herrings, lemmings, and many ungulates. Animals in a herd feel an attraction for one another, recognizing members of their species by the insignia common to them, and making no distinction among individuals. The attraction exercised by the herd on one animal, or on a small group of them, "is tremendously strong, and . . . increases with the size of the herd, probably in geometric proportion."[25]

(2) The second type of society has a certain structure that the herd lacks. Here, certain forces will bond a pair of individuals, a male and female, who produce offspring and rear them. But those forces are determined exclusively by the distribution of the individuals over a territory. Rather than bonding individual *X* to individual *Y*, they bond the individual inhabiting location *A* with an individual of the opposite sex inhabiting the same location. When, the territorial distribution changes for some reason, the bond is painlessly broken and replaced by another. This is true, for example, of the South European green lizard and the white stork.

This kind of relationship may be called "functional," since the individuals enter into it merely to perform a certain function, and either can be replaced.

(3) The third kind of social order involves living in clans, or extended families. Brown rats and social insects such as bees live in communities of this type. The number of individuals in a clan is too great for them to recognize one another, and in most cases membership in the clan is detected by smell. Clans fight fierce battles with each other. Animals who stray into an alien clan are usually killed.

(4) We turn now to the fourth and highest type of society, that based on individualized bonds. Each such bond is an independent phenomenon (although, of course, the mechanism remains the same): it ties specific individual *X* with specific individual *Y*. Individuals *X* and *Y* may or may not be of different sexes. Lorenz calls such relationships among animals friendship, since the mechanism and meaning of these phenomena in humans are the same as in the higher animals. And he uses the word "group" to designate an aggregate of individuals tied by bonds of friendship between members of pairs. The rudiments of individualized bonds are found in certain fishes; they are more common among birds (jackdaws, geese), and even more common among mammals—the wolf being the classic example. Lorenz describes with much feeling the friendship between wild grey geese (greylags).

Valence bonds between humans of course involve more than those relations of friendship available to animals. The friendship relations figure as an important biological component, whereas culture brings new elements and dimensions into *v*-bonds. For a cybernetician, it is important to note that when the brain of an animal develops to the point where it can reliably distinguish many different individuals of its own species from one another, a new type of social organization arises and becomes more widespread: a type base on individualized bonds. Like *v*-bonds among atoms, individualized bonds make it possible to build structures as complex as one wants—structures that amount to more than a colony of ants or a herd of cattle. These structures may be at once strongly bonded and flexible—capable of transformation. Therein lies the difference between individualized *v*-bonds and mass bonds, and the significance of their emergence in the process of evolution.

The Model of Intersecting V-Hierarchies

The President of the United States is freely elected by general voting. His speeches can be heard and viewed by every citizen; his decisions affect all Americans. This is a mass-bond. Modern democratic states, with their millions of citizens, are based on such bonds. Valence-bonds have an upper limit of v^{max}. Is it possible to build, on the basis of *v*-bonds, a social system which is a unitary whole although consisting of millions of individuals? Yes, it is—but only if that system has a clearly defined multilevel hierarchy.

The following schema is a model for decision making and control in a society based on *v*-bonds.

In the life of a human being, and of human society, one can distinguish several important aspects—those having to do with everyday living, industry, scientific research, or politics, etc. For each there is a corresponding system of *v*-bonds by means of which society makes and carries out the necessary decisions. Let us call those systems "*v*-hierarchies." The total number of aspects selected—and, consequently, the total number of *v*-hierarchies—should not be great: probably somewhere between two and eight.

The formation of each *v*-hierarchy takes place as follows. Initially, all of the citizens are broken down into groups of *v* persons each. (Here *v* is substantially less than v^{max}, and probably comes within a range of four to eight.) It is assumed that in the group, as a result of active contacts, *v*-bonds have been formed between the two members of each pair. The group must be formed on a strictly voluntary basis (a process which of course is not simple and which takes a good deal of time). When the groups are all formed, each one of them (we shall call them "zero-level" groups) selects one *representative.* These people will be the first-level representatives. They will form first-level groups, again based on *v*-bonds between the members. A first-level representative will remain a member of the zero-level group, and will take part in its activities. Thus he will participate in the work of two groups simultaneously. The first-level groups will elect a second-level representative, and so on until at the summit there is but a single representative.

The hierarchy will not remain permanently fixed. At any time (or at certain fixed intervals: this question, like many others, I am leaving unconcretized) a group on the *i*-th level may recall its representative and replace him with another. (But a representative from the *i*-th level who has risen to the $i + 2$nd level, cannot be recalled without the agreement of the corresponding group on the $i + 1$st level). Since deciding that a person is unworthy takes much less time than deciding he is worthy, a high-level representative who has committed an act that has met with unanimous censure may skid down to the bottom of the hierarchy in the wink of an eye. Moreover, contacts among members of various groups (since such contacts have not been prohibited, they will certainly take place) may result in a change in the makeup of the group, which may also affect upward and downward movement in the hierarchy. Mass-bonds, needless to say, will be preserved, and will play their own role. Thus when a person has written a widely read book, it will have an effect on the society as a whole (and presumably on his own movement through one of the *v*-hierarchies).

Each group of representatives will make decisions affecting all representatives and rank-and-file members of the group who took part in its election. The activity of a *v*-hierarchy—and in particular, the relationships among levels—must be based on the principle of structural-functional parallelism. I cannot concretize this idea, since I am building a purely abstract schema. I should assume, however, that in any given political v-hierarchy the use of physical force would be authorized only by the group to which the individual in question belongs. (The group's representative would of course count as a member of it.)

Let us now make a few simple mathematical computations in order to be sure that our system is not in conflict with actual statistics characterizing contemporary human society.

Let N represent the number of members of the society. The height of the hierarchy, represented by h, will have the following relation to n and v.

$$v^h = N \text{ or } h = \log N / \log v$$

Suppose that $v = 5$ and $N = 250{,}000{,}000$. Then $h = 12$. Let us assume that at each level the formation of a group takes six months (allowing for the time required to establish enduring valence bonds). Then the formation of the entire v-hierarchy will have been completed in six years.

Let us now take up the problem as to the total number of v-bonds into which each member of our hypothetical society will enter. In each hierarchy, a member will enter into $v-1$ bonds with his fellow members of the group on the zero level. If he is elected representative of the first level, the number of his bonds will be $2(v-1)$. If he rises to the second level, it will be $3(v-1)$, etc. The chief of the hierarchy will have $h(v-1)$ bonds (as many as on the $h-1$ level, since there will be no one else for him to bond with). In our example, $h(v-1) = 48$.

Thus the higher a person rises in a certain v-hierarchy, the more v-bonds he will have. This has two important consequences. First, it puts greater demands on highly placed representatives. Second, it hampers upward movement through other v-hierarchies—a healthy trait of our system.

I call this schema a model of intersecting v-hierarchies because every member of society is involved simultaneously in several systems of relationships—hierarchies. Nor is any parallelism assumed in the structure of these systems. To the contrary, opposing tendencies will arise: persons having more contacts and obligations in one hierarchy, will have fewer in others. Thus the number of v-bonds that different people have will be more or less equalized.

It is not hard to calculate that the average number of bonds per citizen in one v-hierarchy is v (assuming that N is much greater than unity).[26] It only slightly exceeds the minimum number of bonds, since as the representatives rise in the hierarchy, their number decreases in geometric progression.

Let r represent the number of hierarchies. When $r = 3$, then 15 valence bonds are required of the average citizen. It would be advisable to set up just enough v-hierarchies so that the total number of bonds would be equal to the maximum number of valence bonds into which the average person can enter. Earlier, we designated that number as v^{max}. Thus we obtain the following relation among the quantities r, v, and v^{max}: $rv = v^{max}$. As we could see, this relation is satisfied with realistic values of all the quantities involved.

A Comparison of Two Systems for Decision-Making

The model of intersecting v-hierarchies is not a blue print for a new type of society but merely a schema for the making and implementation of decisions. Let us now contrast this model with another system or decision making—one that is now in use almost everywhere, and that many people regard as the only one admissible in a democratic society: direct, general elections.

To set up v-hierarchies for decision making is a longer and more complex procedure than direct voting. On the other hand, a v-hierarchy provides a constantly functioning mechanism that not only makes decisions but *elaborates* them. It is all very well to vote when your mind is already made up and you know exactly what you are voting for. But what if it has not been made up? We have all been in situations where a complex question had to be decided at a meeting: the endless, senseless arguments that arise make it almost impossible to grasp the gist of the matter, with the result that no reasonable solution is found. The kind of work that must be done to solve complex problems can *only* be done among a small group of people. And in order for that work to be really creative and effective, there must be valence bonds among the members of the group. This precondition is especially important in solving social problems, most of which are not formalized and are closely linked to personal interests and emotions.

Voting no doubt came into being as a substitute for fighting, and it will forever bear the stamp of its origin. Voting is a kind of weapon, whereas a valence hierarchy is a tool. There is no justice in subordinating a minority to the majority: this is only a very simple way of avoiding bloodshed. Coercion remains coercion, even if it is the result of voting. In societies of the Western type, relations between the majority and minorities of all kinds—especially ethnic minorities—become more complicated in proportion as coercion is increasingly regarded as undesirable. Voting does not solve any problems. The solution of a controversial problem demands work: analyzing the causes, and building a metasystem that unites the conflicting systems and eliminates the conflict. The process of building a *v*-hierarchy compels people to do that work, and suggests ways of solving the problem.

From the viewpoint of formal organization, there is nothing new in the model of intersecting hierarchies: it represents voluntary cooperation among citizens, plus the self-government resulting from that cooperation. I do, however, see something new in combining this organizational form with the requirement that all contacts in it be *v*-bonds, which means limiting the number of persons who elect a representative. In modern social organizations, *v*-bonds play a positive role: if it were not for the personal ties based on friendship, mutual understanding, and trust, it is likely that not a single large social organization could function effectively. When it comes to the culture of a society, progress means above all improving the conditions that give rise to *v*-bonds, and increasing their role.

But so far, it is not they which form the structural skeleton of the state. The only structural unit based on *v*-bonds is the family; and there is no doubt that it has demonstrated its importance to society. Even so, from the formal point of view the family is based on contractual relations between the husband and wife, and on kinship relations linking other pairs of individuals. It is the mere fact that, as a rule, these relations are the result (in the former case) or the cause (in the latter case) of *v*-bonds, which gives the family its remarkable strength. And when there is nothing left of a family but the form itself, that family ceases to be a boon and becomes a heavy burden.

This distinction between the formal (or official) and the personal has taken such deep root in us that many people think it is a conceptual contradiction—an antinomy. But in fact there is no insurmountable contradiction here: it is simply that the organizational form must be flexible enough to accommodate the twists and turns of personal relationships. I have used "simply" as a grammatical connective: working out such organizational forms is actually a very complex matter.

In Defense of Hierarchies

In the democratic countries of today, it seems to me, there is one big obstacle blocking the way to a genuine fusion of the social and the personal. That obstacle is what I call the pseudodemocratic bias or prejudice toward hierarchies. The feeling is that a good democrat must be the enemy of any and all hierarchies; otherwise he is an "elitist," which is worse than anything. The concept of the hierarchy is identified with coercion and suppression.

In the perspective of history, this is perfectly understandable. Since ancient times, hierarchies have been set up with the aim of governing by force. The struggle for freedom and democracy has taken the form of a fight against the hierarchy of the regime. But to explain a bias or prejudice is not to justify it. We all must come to understand the simple truth that it is not the *existence* of a hierarchy (i.e., in the language of mathematics, a relation of partial ordering) that is the evil but the governing *principles* it employs. A mob provided with no sort of hierarchy is nevertheless capable of the worst kinds of coercion and violence to individuals.

The concept of a hierarchy by no means includes the idea of oppression or suppression. For a cybernetician the word "hierarchy" has positive emotional connotations. He always tries to discover or set up a hierarchy, because hierarchy is organization—it is structure. Large systems can be organized only hierarchically. The antithesis of hierarchy is chaos, not freedom. Even when you've turned to the dictionary for the word you need, you are profiting from the application of the hierarchical principle: in this case the ordering of words and their retrieval based on the precedence of some letters over others. Here no one letter "suppresses" or "oppresses" another. And if there were no hierarchy, you'd have to look through all the words in the dictionary every time you used it!

Since the value of v lies somewhere between one and ten, in a society with millions of members a v-hierarchy has considerable height. Here is where the pseudodemocratic prejudices come into play. A person wants to have a hand in governing the country "himself," and not through a hierarchical chain. Yet for all that he has to delegate his authority to someone else, which means setting up some kind of governmental hierarchy. Since he looks upon the hierarchy as an evil, he strives to keep it as small as possible. And he favors direct elections on all levels so that he can at least have the consolation that *he himself* is delegating his authority. Such is the origin of hierarchies based on mass bonds, which have both the defects of the hierarchy and those of the crowd—the human herd.

"Personal" delegation of authority in direct elections involving thousands and millions of voters—and consequently their supposed "personal" participation in government—is of course an illusion. This kind of government has, as a matter of fact, the result that personal participation and personal influence are eliminated. Like an unstructured mass phenomenon, it engenders a specific kind of determinism based on the law of large numbers. The way the voters will react to a given stratagem in an electoral campaign can be predicted with a good measure of certainty. The personality of each voter therefore loses its significance. There is only one way in which an individual person can have any real influence on events, and that is through some structure or hierarchy (of a party, of the mass media). And because those contacts in the hierarchy are *m*-bonds and not *v*-bonds, the phenomenon known as the *alienation* of the individual from society arises. The *m*-bond is too weak—it is a defective, impersonal relationship. The democratic societies of today are thus still too reminiscent of the anonymous herd. They need not to oppose hierarchies, but to introduce and improve them.

It is interesting that in contemporary systems of government the height of the hierarchy is nonetheless great, so that for influence to move from the bottom to the top it must pass through a great many *m*-bonds. (One wonders in what respect such a system is better than one built on *v*-bonds.) It is also interesting that the ratio between the number of people on one level and the number of them on the next, is especially great in the lower part of the hierarchy, and decreases as one moves upward. This makes it possible for *m*-bonds to develop into *v*-bonds on the upper levels. The result is corporative solidarity among the leaders at the top, while the gap between the summit and the lower levels remains wide. This does not, of course, help to overcome alienation.

The mechanism of the *v*-hierarchy provides each citizen with the best opportunities for influencing society as a whole, i.e., for governing (controlling) society. First, because each new, creative idea must be scrutinized and recognized in a context of valence relationships, or else it will not be recognized at all. Second, the *v*-hierarchy is the fairest way of gaining access to influence. Actually, in a society where valence-bonds are not formalized, and the formalized (official) contacts are not of the valence type, real access to influence is through chains of informal valence-bonds ("old boy" networks). These bonds have, as it were, an underground existence. And often they form closed circles comprising a few people—circles to which access from the outside is either impossible or extremely difficult. A valence hierarchy, on the other hand, links each citizen with the summit, and with any other citizen.

The absence of closed circles in a valence hierarchy is also significant in connection with yet another important aspect of a society's life: crime. Groups which are isolated (in the sense of *v*-bonding, at any rate) from the rest of society are a constant source of crime. Perhaps the only way to sharply reduce crime in a country whose populace numbers many millions, with diverse social, cultural, and ethnic elements, is to organize an all-embracing system of *v*-hierarchies.

By way of conclusion, I should say a few words about the downward flow of information, which leads to the unity of human wills and actions. It is plain that the *v*-hierarchy makes it possible to secure a high degree of unity: a valence bond is a strong and flexible tie enabling a combination of freedom and integration. But the realization of that possibility depends not only on choosing this or that organizational schema but on the culture of the society as a whole. And it depends above all on that stratum of the culture which determines the highest goals of the individual. A society which does not have social integration as its goal will not move toward socialism. And it will have no unity.

One Last Word About Terminology

My concept of socialism is unusual in many respects. It may well be that some people who favor socialism will find the sense in which I use the word quite unacceptable, and will declare "that is not socialism!" Others who share my views to some degree may also prefer not to call those views "socialist." Finally, many readers will deem it incorrect to call socialism a form of religion. I must admit that in declaring so categorically that socialism is a religion, I did so in order to lay special stress on the profound unity between these two cultural phenomena. But if a final choice of words is to be made, it would be, probably, better to say that socialism is religion's successor, and not a new form of it.

The link between real, historical socialism and the principle of social integration is for me beyond doubt. Freedom has always been favored by socialists, in words if not always in deeds. Then what name should one give to a conception based on the formula "social integration plus freedom" and to the social order which embodies it? "Socialism" seems the most natural and accurate name. Earlier, I mentioned the similarity between my conception and "ethical socialism." One might also call it "cybernetic socialism," because of the important—even decisive—role that cybernetics plays in it. Another term that could be used to designate this approach is "evolutionism."

Perhaps some readers will be disappointed by the lack of concreteness in the notions about socialism that I have offered them here. And in fact I did examine societal problems using the most general concepts—from the viewpoint of philosophy. But that kind of thinking is vitally necessary. Philosophical concepts and achievements synthesize concepts and achievements from all spheres of activity. Each person has his own approach to them. Mine is that of a physicist and cybernetician.

Part III
Totalitarianism or Socialism?

The Struggle for Ideas and the Struggle for Power

Whereas totalitarianism, in its assault on society, moves from the outside inward, proceeding from the seizure of power through restrictions on exchange of information to the transformation of thought and will, the liberation from totalitarianism must move in the opposite direction. It must begin with changes in the way people think—in their social consciousness. These will lead to an increase in the volume of information processed, freer expression of ideas, and fuller public disclosure of facts about the society. This will make it possible to democratize the government and to combat abuses of power successfully.

Such an approach is the only one feasible. Its alternative is stagnation or cataclysm (like that of the Revolution of 1917). A cataclysm of that kind would very probably take a huge toll in human lives, and it is extremely doubtful that it would help to build a better society.

We can distinguish two aspects of societal conflicts: the struggle for ideas, and the struggle for power. Usually, each of these aspects is regarded not as an end in itself but as a means of achieving some other goal; e.g., accumulating personal wealth, or improving the general welfare. But it is still a fact—and an important one—that both the struggle for power and the struggle for ideas are forms of self-expression and self-affirmation. The struggle for power is a much more ancient, pre-human form of self-assertion. Domination of a group assures an animal the first place in feeding and mating, and hence in transmitting its own genetic code to posterity. The struggle for ideas, on the other hand, is a specifically human phenomenon—the assertion of one's individual personality on the social level. When one struggles for the recognition of his ideas, one is fighting for the perpetuation of his personality in the way of life to be adopted by posterity.

These two kinds of struggle are closely interwoven in the fabric of a society. In struggling for power, a person relies on certain ideas; in struggling for ideas, a person often relies on power (or comes into conflict with it). Even though these two forms overlap, a distinction can still be drawn between them. The struggle for power is associated with a lower level in the universal hierarchy of control than that for ideas. From the viewpoint of the system's evolution, it is extremely important that the struggle for power be subordinated to (become merely the inevitable consequence of) the struggle for ideas. When the struggle for power becomes an end in itself, it leads to anarchy or tyranny—never to the constructive evolution of society. If we want to affirm certain ideas in life, we must choose, from among all the conceivable approaches, the one which is least associated with a change in the power structure. Otherwise the struggle for power will usurp the place of the struggle for ideas.

The One-Party System Is a Partyless System

Those persons critical of the first version of this book were most disturbed by my opposition to the struggle for a multiparty system in the Soviet Union. I proposed that the matter of political liberties be separated from the struggle for political power among parties representing the interests of large social classes. I suggested that the Communist Party be viewed as the prospective intellectual and spiritual integrator of society, functioning under conditions of broad political and civil liberties; this would be to accept in theory what the present regime claims has already been realized in practice. A multiparty system would by no means guarantee democratic freedoms; nor would the existence of such freedoms necessarily engender a multiparty system. One can try to find ways of resolving social contradictions that would not raise them to the highest government level, and that would not intensify artificial conflict among politicians.

Although on the whole my little book was well received among dissenting intellectuals, they were virtually unanimous in disagreeing with me on this point. The reaction of one rather well-known cybernetician (whom I did not know) was rather typical. I was told that when he was asked what he thought of my book, he said: "It's terrible! He comes out for Communism and the single-party system!" (One interesting detail: unlike me, that cybernetician is a member of the Communist Party.)

I got another interesting reaction when I had the temerity to send the manuscript to the journal *Kommunist.* I realized, of course, that they would never publish it, but I wished to make it plain that the book was in no way a covert undertaking, that it was constructive, and that I was fully prepared to listen to criticism. And I did get criticism from an official Party source—an editor on the staff of *Kommunist* who served as house reader of the manuscript. He explained to me that it could not be published because it lacked the "class approach" (i.e., a readiness to serve the interests of the ruling class, and to put those interests above the truth); in this he was rather accurate. With respect to one-party and multiparty systems, he said: "Strictly speaking, why should there be only one party? A country can have several parties equally devoted to the cause of Communism. Poland, for example, has several political parties."

Now that the Italian and French Communists have announced their resolute adherence to the multiparty system, my position strikes many of my friends as an anachronism which is not even justified on tactical grounds. But I still hold to my position, and I feel that it meets with opposition because it is ahead of its times rather than behind them. So I intend, now, to set forth my position more circumstantially than I did in 1968.

First, let us define terms. Many of my critics have pointed out that the phrase "one-party system" is essentially meaningless because, by definition, "party" means "a part"; so that the word has meaning only when there is more than one party.

I agree that the term is nonsensical. Historically, it arises when one party gets into power and then bans all the others. Once the existence of several parties has become a thing of the past, the "party" ceases to be a party and becomes an all-embracing political system or network. The Soviet system of today is not a one-party system; it is a partyless system. In the Soviet Union there are no political parties, but only a single political network that is indistinguishable from the state.

I do not intend to justify barring access to power by all other parties. I do think, however, that our future lies in a partyless system with a single political network. And if that is true, a reformist or gradualist movement must naturally expect to have a program which does not call for a seizure of power by force of arms or by fighting for votes, but for a transformation of the social consciousness that would increase the freedom and humanization of society as a whole, and of the political network in particular. This is the kind of program that the Czech Communists had in 1968—the one called "socialism with a human face."

Let us first look at the prospects. The most common argument for the multiparty system is that political liberties and an effective check on power can be achieved only when there are several competing parties, each potentially able to drive out the ruling party (or coalition). The single-party system, my critics say, inevitably leads to the abuse of power. Any political organization, whether it is called a party or a network, that has full political power and no competitors is doomed to stagnation and corruption; it cannot resist the deleterious effect of power. Regardless of the distribution of power among various social groups, regardless of who represents whom, there must be at least two independent political parties. One need only glance at the political systems in various countries to realize that wherever we find a multiparty (and in particular a two-party) system, we also find political liberties; and that wherever a one-party system has been adopted, the tyranny of a party-state apparatus rages.

This link between the one-party system and tyranny undoubtedly exists; but it does not prove anything, since the causal sequence is as follows: the absence of freedom leads to rule by one party, and not vice versa. A society in which the idea of political liberties has not taken root cannot sustain a multiparty system, even if such a system does chance to be established through a whim of history. Such was the pattern that developed in the Third World countries which became independent after World War II. This shows once again that in determining a society's political system, it is that society's *culture* which plays the decisive role. If a society is unable to keep its political liberties, it is not really very important what form the tyranny takes: whether it is absolute monarchy, an overt military dictatorship, a single-party system with farcical elections, or a multiparty system like that in Poland, which the critic on the staff of *Kommunist* so thoughtfully cited to me.

Speaking of prospects, we must assume that the idea of respecting basic individual rights has long since taken root in the society's culture, and that no one intends to encroach upon the democratic way of governing a country, even if only because such attempts offer little chance of success. Can one affirm that under these conditions a multiparty system will inevitably prevail?

Keeping watch on those in power, or those aspiring to power, is of course essential. But the chief factor here is not a pluralism of parties. It is broad public disclosure of information, vigorous mass political activity, and an unwillingness on the part of society to tolerate breaches of ethics. It is often claimed that when several parties are competing, there are always people with an interest in discovering mistakes or malice in the actions of leading politicians. But in a partyless system, there are even more such people. If, for example, a country has two parties of equal strength, one-half of its politicians (those belonging to the party in power) will show restraint in criticizing the leadership. But if there are no parties, each politician can gain by exposing the mistakes of another. In this respect, one can compare a partyless system with a system of scientific institutions. When a scientist makes a discovery or proves a theorem, his impatient colleagues will hasten to verify his statement, or to refute it or refine it. The same thing will happen in a political system organized along the lines of the scientific establishment.

A multiparty system is a two-edged sword. On the one hand, it helps to expose deceit; on the other hand, it creates a climate for more deceit in favor of group interests, and for a new conservatism. Of these two effects, the latter is quite obviously the stronger. In a free society, it only takes one person to expose deceit; but to practice it requires collusion.

In science, a division into parties is unacceptable: scientists are offended if told they are guided by sectarian interests. And of course no one would even consider splitting up all scientific institutions into two or three discrete parts in order to combat deceit or stagnation. The totality of all scientific and educational institutions forms a single whole, a single system. And this by no means leads to stagnation, corruption, the suppression of individual initiative and creative freedom, or to the elimination of pluralism and its replacement by uniformity. Why cannot a single political network function just as well? In a society where the basic ethical and democratic principles are as solidly ingrained as are the basic principles of scientific method in the life of scientists; where infringements of political freedoms are just as unthinkable (and presumably just as stupid) as infringements on free scientific investigation, the division of all politicians into several different parties would seem artificial and quite needless.

Politics and Science

But can one compare politics and science? It is more usual to contrast them: science consists in striving toward a truth common to all, while politics consists in a struggle for power—for personal and group interests.

There is rather good reason for making this contrast; but to make it is not to entirely answer the question. Politics is the art of social integration; and the basic contradiction in social integration—that between the personal and the societal—is reflected in two supplementary aspects of politics: the struggle for personal or group interests, and a striving toward the common interest (the common good). In assaying the second aspect, we refrain from defining the concept of the common good or goal (which two things, in the final analysis, are identical). Whether or not there is unanimity on that score in a society is a question pertaining to another stratum of culture. It is a religious question, not a political one. In politics, the question is this: Given a certain goal, or a certain definition of public benefit, how should society (and above all, the production system) be organized so as most quickly to achieve that goal, or a maximum of public benefit? This problem is essentially scientific. It is in no way different from the problem of seeking the truth (or, more precisely, the closest approach to the truth) posed by science. Hence we may call these two aspects the *struggle for interests* and the *striving for truth*. It is almost the same distinction as between the struggle for power and the struggle for ideas, but in objectified form. The struggle for power is the most direct expression of the struggle for group interests. The struggle for ideas is an expression of the aspiration toward the truth.

The level of a society's development—the degree of its integration—determines the relative importance of these two aspects of politics. An underdeveloped society lacks any notion of a common goal for groups of people with no direct links among them—not to mention the notion of a common goal for all humanity. Common interests are limited to those of small, closely knit groups. Also, under primitive conditions of production, each person or group can get more for himself or itself by snatching a morsel from someone else, than by working for the common cause. (This is seen most plainly in the extreme case when there is no production at all, and people compete like animals for the gifts of Nature.) In such a society, politics is reduced to a struggle among interests—Hobbes's "war of all against all." As society becomes more integrated and production more complex, the struggle of all against all becomes less and less profitable for all its members taken collectively, and for each person individually. In modern industrial nations, revolution has become *economically unprofitable,* even for those lowest on the social ladder. This is true not only of revolution but also of certain less radical modes of struggle for group interests. Thus I am not at all sure that today strikes are economically profitable for workers in advanced countries. They can result in higher wages, but they make for more inflation. The example of England gives one food for thought. But even if it is true that strikes are still profitable, the time will undoubtedly come when they will cease to be so.

The party system reflects an approach to politics as a struggle among interests: it teaches the citizen to see politics as first and foremost a clash of interests. A partyless system teaches one to see politics as first and foremost a common cause—a striving for the truth. Under conditions of a "war of all against all," a multiparty system is the inevitable and legitimate consequence of democratic freedoms. But as society moves toward socialism, the party system must give way to one with no parties. For this to happen, it is not necessary that the competition among interests disappear entirely from politics; that will never occur. It is necessary only that a striving for the truth be recognized by society as the more important of the two aspects. And here again, science may serve as an example.

Science as an abstract concept embodies a pure striving

for the truth. Science as a real societal phenomenon represents, like politics, a close interweaving of that striving with a struggle among interests. Science as actually practiced is a system with a definite structure, and a definite hierarchy of prestige and power. Scientists have the same vices and weaknesses as other people. In particular, it is typical of them to deceive both themselves and others by representing personal and group interests as a striving for the truth. And since we cannot take a scalpel and anatomize a living person's brain and behavior, we can by no means always tell whether the latter is determined by an aspiration toward the truth or by personal interests. Yet science remains partyless.

If a single political network is modeled after a scientific-educational system, it will serve as the basic instrument of social integration, supplying cadres for the legislative, executive, and judicial branches of government, and probably also for the top posts in the industrial hierarchy, since the big problems of industry are inseparable from social problems. The separation of the political network from the above-named hierarchies, like that among these kinds of power themselves, of course can not be eliminated in any case—at least not before we find a more perfect (and obviously more complex) solution to the problem of governing according to the principle of structural-functional parallelism.

The party system in politics is gradually becoming an anachronism. In the era of the French Revolution, the division of society into three estates naturally resulted in the representatives' being divided into three parties. In a modern democratic society there is no division into estates: all citizens have equal rights. Nor is there any sharp distinction between classes in the Marxist sense. The "classical" workers or capitalists have been outnumbered by people who cannot, except by Procrustean methods, be fitted into any one class. The dividing lines among classes are becoming increasingly eroded. Of course this does not mean that the division of labor is being eliminated; to the contrary, it is constantly increasing. And this is precisely why social roles are becoming more and more diversified. Social roles now form a continuous spectrum, and to break it down into only a few categories would be an arbitrary and forced procedure.

Under these conditions, the natural thing to do is to build a single political network that can accommodate the entire spectrum of social roles. A fixed division into parties, unchanged over decades, is an artificial phenomenon preserved as something vestigial. We have a situation in which parties begin to exist for their own sake. They cease to be an organic part of one class or estate, and become autonomous professional organizations concerned less with who votes for them than how many. The party's goal is neither to represent anyone's interests nor to strive for the truth—but to contend for power.

One can never rid politics of either personal greed or the struggle for power. We are even less able to draw a clear line between politician's aspiration toward power for the sake of truth, and his aspiration toward truth for the sake of power than we are for a scientist. A human being is not a machine (at least not one designed by us); but a political party *is* a machine. Then why should we design machines whose chief function is the pursuit of power? Would not a political system be improved if we admitted only those organizations whose chief goal is not power? Essentially, such is the state of things in science. In science, differences of opinion and division into factions take place in connection with specific problems—factions are formed and dissolve as some problems are solved and others arise. And such will be the case, too, in a political network under a partyless system. When factions exist not in connection with specific problems but as autonomous entities, we have the kind of situation that scientists regard as a perversion. Yet in a multiparty system, this is taken to be the norm.

In politics, unlike science, the ideal goal is not merely the truth—i.e., the common good conceived or defined in a certain way—but serving the interests of each citizen, regardless of ideas held in common. This is beyond doubt. But what is the best way to do it? In a society with a high culture and a great variety of social roles and types, are not each person's interests adequately served by their free participation in politics? I can conceive of a synthesis, in a socialist political system, of the two decision-making processes discussed earlier: the struggle among interests would be waged by means of universal suffrage, and the harmonizing of interests effected via intersecting valence hierarchies.

Political parties contending for power take on the traits of military organizations, with a need for party discipline, secretiveness, etc. In a single political network all this becomes superfluous, since as a whole that network is not opposing any other organization. It may allow itself to be altogether open and liberal. It has no need to restrict the development of different factions, or even to *register* them in any way. (Once again, the comparison with a scientific network suggests itself.) It might be said that where there are broad political liberties, a partyless system is neither a system without parties nor one with a single party: it is one with an indeterminate number of parties.

Here we come up against a paradox that may be called *systemic relativity*. When we compare the single-party and multiparty systems, using those concepts in the most general sense, the difference between them is seen to be merely relative. In a multiparty system the political parties are not isolated: each studies the political programs of its rivals—not to mention coalitions, parliamentary politics, etc. Thus one can say that in their totality they form a single political system or network. On the other hand, a single political party or network, under broad democratic freedoms, will in fact be made up of various groups, factions, and parties. The real difference between these concepts consists in the conception of political life implied by them: by what goals they set. The goal implied by the multiparty system is the struggle for power; that implied by the partyless system is the struggle for ideas.

Revolution or Reformation?

> In struggling to defend human rights we ought, I am convinced, first and foremost to protect the innocent victims of regimes installed in various countries, without demanding the destruction or total condemnation of those regimes. We need reform, not revolution.[1]
>
> Andrei Sakharov

In democratic countries with multiparty systems the transition to a partyless system must not, however, come about by a ban on political parties—or all but one. That would be a gross violation of democratic freedoms, and one can predict with near certainty that it would be followed by still more violations which will result in the tyranny of a ruling bureaucracy. The Western communist parties' recognition of the multiparty system are an acknowledgment of democratic freedoms and should be welcomed. The transition to the partyless system should be made under the influence of forces within the sphere of culture and not that of politics. It is likely that the movement of the public consciousness toward socialism will entail an increasingly negative attitude toward interparty conflict in its traditional (and often very ugly) forms—a conflict justified by the saying "all's fair in love and war." Such being the case, one can foresee two ways in which things may develop:

(1) We shall witness the formation of a super-party system financed by the state—the embryo of, and the basis for, a future political network enabling all citizens, regardless of their views or party membership, to be politically active. Under such a system, an ever-greater number of politicians will prefer not to be members of any party, and will create new ways of combining and limiting the latter's functions. To belong to a party will become unfashionable; and parties,

like the Marxist State, will not be abolished but will "wither away."

(2) One party (most likely founded on a coalition of several) will become so pluralistic, and will assure its members such favorable conditions for activity, that it will attract and keep all politicians of any degree of influence. Such a system will be nominally multiparty but actually single-party (and hence partyless), since the party will have become a single political network serving all segments of society.

The Bolshevik Party, soon after seizing power, banned all other parties. It is not surprising, therefore, that in the USSR the concept of democratization is usually associated with a restoration of the multiparty system—if not as a priority task, then as the ultimate goal. In his book *My Country and the World,* Andrei Sakharov puts the introduction of the multiparty system on his list of essential reforms. Roy Medvedev, a Marxist, also favors the multiparty system. He writes:

> I hope to see the growth of democratic movements representing various shades of opinion. And I do not rule out the possibility of a new socialist party's emergence—a party that differs from our present-day Social Democratic and Communist parties. Such a socialist party could form a loyal and legal Opposition to the existing leadership, and thus indirectly make for the renewal and normalizing of the CPSU. Since it would not be a successor to the old Russian socialist parties, the new socialist party could base its ideology only on those principles of Marx, Engels, and Lenin that have stood the test of time. Since it would not be hampered by the dogmatism typical of our official science, it would be free to develop a theory of scientific socialism and scientific communism that would meet the requirements of our time, and would take into account the experiences our country has gone through. And since it would bear no responsibility for the crimes of the past few decades, it could be more objective in evaluating both the past and the present of our society, and could work out socialist and democratic alternatives for society's development.[2]

I take a different view in the matter of a multiparty system. To develop the theory of scientific socialism freely, to evaluate the past and present of our society objectively, and to work out the socialist and democratic alternatives for its development simply does not require a political party. This is instead the task of a scientific institute or a group of authors associated with a publishing facility. A political party is an organization contending for power. To ignore this is merely to increase the number of unstated facts—already huge enough, as it is.

Under the conditions prevailing in the Soviet Union, the demand for a multiparty system is quite a revolutionary one. If the basic democratic freedoms were suddenly introduced in the USSR tomorrow, along with that free competition among parties that is usual in democratic countries, the CPSU as it is now constituted would most likely fall from power. This is clear to everyone—to Party leaders and outside observers alike. And it accounts for the political blind alley the USSR is now in. Democracy is identified with free elections under a multiparty system, which in turn is practically identical with loss of power by the ruling bureaucracy. Hence the bureaucracy's dread of any kind of democratization—any exchange of ideas and information—and its desperate resistance to minimal reforms. A demand for elementary individual rights is regarded as a call to revolution—to the overthrow of the government.

But is there a nonrevolutionary road to democracy? I believe there is. In my view, the way to achieve reform is, first of all, to draw a clear line between the struggle for power and the struggle for ideas, and to relinquish power in favor of ideas. This means giving up demands for a multiparty system in the immediate future—for the period of time it will require for basic individual rights to take root. For that matter, since the desirability of a multiparty system in the future is at best doubtful, any plans for such a system might just as well be taken off the agenda. The ideal kind of reformation would be the gradual transformation of the CPSU—in response to the evolution of social consciousness and behavioral norms—

into the single political network of a genuinely socialist State. Those democratic freedoms the Soviet citizen must have of course include freedom of association. But even in the most democratic of societies, not all types of association are permitted (association for the purpose of committing theft, or overthrowing the government by force of arms, for example). I think it would be quite logical to rule out any possibility of forming an association with the aim of seizing power by means of the vote. (I have used the word "seized" to emphasize the similarity between taking power by force of arms and taking power by force of the ballot. In an age when the mass consciousness is manipulated by propaganda, one should bear in mind the relativity of the difference between these two methods. It suffices to recall the mechanism by means of which Hitler came to power.)

No one can predict whether or not this idealistic approach to democratization will be taken. But it is important to know that it exists, and that whether it is taken depends upon us alone.

The Experience of Tsarist Russia

It is easier to deny reforms are possible rather than to effect them. And such denial has one of two aims: to justify passivity or to propagandize the revolutionary approach as the only feasible one. The latter position is of course that taken by the Bolsheviks in Tsarist Russia. "The worse, the better," was their slogan. The people they regarded as their worst enemies were not the obtuse reactionary officials who blocked reforms, but the reformers: those who were trying, without destroying the system, to better the lot of the poor, to put a stop to scandalous practices, and to get the nation on the track of gradual progress. The Bolsheviks labelled all these things "deception of the toilers" aimed at weakening the revolutionary spirit.

For a long time after the Revolution, the Bolshevik concept of political change remained the only one that was tolerated (and the only one that was regarded as universally applicable). From early childhood Soviets were reared in the conviction that in any society, the power belongs to a certain class and serves the interests of that class. No substantive changes are possible unless the ruling class is replaced by another. Since the ruling class will never yield up its power without a fight, substantive changes in a society can be effected only by armed revolution.

The unwillingness of blue-collar workers in the West to make a revolution has gradually led to a change in the programs of the Western communist parties—a shift toward the idea of coming into power by parliamentary means. As a result, Soviet propaganda has had to recognize this approach as feasible in principle. But for the rest (and the rest is what counts most) its concept has remained unaltered.

What, then, will that concept lead to as regards Soviet society? First of all, to a debate as to which class has the power in the USSR. If one believes the official line that the power in the Soviet Union is held by the workers and peasants, then change is possible only in the sense of "a conflict between the better and the merely good." Some Western leftists still take that position. The Soviet Union is a workers' and peasants' state, and that is the main thing. Hence it must be a cause for rejoicing and a model to be imitated. Certain details and slight defects, such as the millions martyred in the Stalin era, or the "re-education" of dissidents with injections of neuroleptic drugs, are unpleasant; but they do not change the main thing.

Those who do not want to put up with these "slight defects" and try to explain them from a Marxist position tell us (as does Milovan Djilas) that it is the Party bureaucracy (the "new class") that really holds the power. From this it follows that the only hope for change lies in seizing power from the CPSU. And since parliamentary modes of contending for power do not exist in the USSR, the only recourse is to set up illegal organizations with the aim of overthrowing the regime. This is of course the Bolshevik position transposed to our time. It is clear to everyone, however, that this approach has little chance of success. Hence in practice the Bolshevik position yields no other result than that a person throws up his hands and does nothing.

If I were to explain my own position in terms of prerevolutionary Russia, I would probably be counted among the Constitutional Monarchists—not owing to any love for the new Communist "dynasty," but because I believe that the best chances for the democratization of the Soviet Union lie in gradual transformation without abrupt changes in the existing power structure. I reject all forms of Bolshevism not merely because I am opposed to violence as a matter of principle but also because I reject the entire ideology of Marxism-Leninism on which the Bolshevik approach to politics is based. In particular, I do not believe that preaching violence against the ruling class—be it landowners, capitalists, or the Party bureaucracy—can lead to anything but senseless destruction. Real social progress consists in a change of ideas, not of power.

The parallel between reformism in Soviet Russia and reformism in Tsarist Russia has a solid basis. After going through a bloody revolution and civil war, the nation has reverted to a power structure and social consciousness which are more reminiscent of traditional Russia than of the revolutionary times; it is again facing the problems that Russia faced in the nineteenth century. One finds the same all-powerful, highly centralized bureaucracy, the same tyrannical exercise of power, the same disdain for basic individual rights by rulers and the ruled alike, and the same intolerance toward ideas not approved by the higher authorities. The mentality of the Soviet bureaucrat is the same as it was in Tsarist days. As for that bureaucrat's worldview, the trappings may have changed but in essence that view itself has changed very little. As before, its foundation is the triad of orthodoxy, autocracy, and national character. Today, however, the "orthodoxy" is called Marxism-Leninism; autocracy has become "the leading role of the Party"; and instead of "national character" we have "the moral and political unity of the Soviet people."

I am convinced that when a Soviet official sees a movie about revolutionaries in Tsarist Russia, he identifies with the Tsarist officials and not with the Bolsheviks. After all, what does he have in common with those demagogues who are plotting revolution in order to undermine a state created by the thousand-year-old history of Russia? To destroy order and return the country to a condition of bloody chaos?

Russian history teaches us that two conditions must be met before a reform becomes possible. First, strong social pressure for reform must be exerted on the regime. A society that cringes before its rulers engenders tyranny on the one hand and destructive extremism—Bolshevism—on the other. Russia has always lacked that combination of firmness and moderation which is necessary for reforms. Until we acquire such a combination, we shall swing from one extreme to the other instead of moving straight ahead.

Second, the regime must learn to stop fearing reforms and learn how to effect them in time. Such a policy would not weaken the regime, but rather strengthen it. In social science courses given in the Soviet Union, the professors quote Marx who held up the English bourgeoisie as an example of the exercise of power without blocking reform. But in their own policies, the Soviet leaders imitate not the English bourgeoisie but the worst examples from Russian history.

Stabilizing totalitarianism leads to catastrophe. Ossification and stagnation cannot continue indefinitely. Sooner or later, as the result of some external or internal cause, the society will be destroyed—and that destruction will be horrible. Blind dread of ideas in action, plus resistance to political and economic liberalization, are leading the nation to the abyss.

The communist regime in Russia is thus repeating the Romanovs' fatal mistakes. For that matter, there is more than one way to correct the Romanovs' mistakes. One dissenter told a KGB agent: "Even under the tsars there was more freedom than now!"

To which the agent replied: "And so they got a revolution!"

That reply was not devoid of logic. It shows, once again, who is who in the new Russia. And presumably, it reflects the views of some portion of the Party apparatus—in any case, those of the leaders.

Well. Self-reproducing totalitarianism is virtually in a steady state already; the possibility of its staying that way for generations is not to be ruled out. But the KGB agent failed to take two things into account:

First, steady-state totalitarianism is possible only under absolutely steady conditions—no change may take place quantitatively or qualitatively. Any changes, even quantitative, require new solutions, new creativity—something the totalitarian society is incapable of. This is not understood by the Party bureaucrats, who lack the necessary culture and philosophical scope. Apparently they sincerely believe that a society which has banned freedom of thought can go on indefinitely, "meeting the constantly growing demand."

Second (and fortunately), the world is not yet entirely totalitarian; it has not yet stopped developing. And since we live in that world, we cannot ignore it—a fact that places certain restrictions on those aspiring toward eternal darkness.

It was not because they granted "too much" freedom that the Romanovs perished. Although there was more freedom then than now, there was certainly not very much of it. What doomed the Romanovs was their inability to carry out the necessary reforms in time, and the alienation between the state and the educated vanguard of society. A specifically Russian social phenomenon arose: the intelligentsia, the educated segment of society, which is in conflict with the state. The state was not the only culprit in this conflict. The writers who contributed essays to the anthology *Landmarks*[3] brought many well-founded charges against the intelligentsia. In a prophetic way, they pointed out those traits of the Russian intelligentsia which, in the final analysis, led to the Bolshevik terrorism. Yet the basic blame must undoubtedly be put on the tsarist regime.

And now we see that the Soviet State is taking the same suicidal path that led to the demise of the tsarist State. (Ah! If it had been only the state and nothing more!) By denying its citizens their elementary civil rights and liberties, it is deepening and perpetuating that conflict between the regime and the culture in which a society cannot develop normally. Can it really be possible that history has taught Russia nothing?

The Inertia of Fear

Neither of the two preconditions to gradual democratization—pressure from below and a capacity for reform from above—is being met in the Soviet Union—primarily because of fear. Or, more precisely, the inertia of the fear that came into our lives under Stalin. The fear that paralyzes our society is that of Stalin's victims; the fear that paralyzes the authorities is that of Stalin himself. Having come to power as a result of a reign of terror without precedent in history, Stalin suspected everyone of secretly hatching plans for vengeance. To him, every person was a potential enemy. Obviously, that is still the mentality of the top leadership. The harsh and senseless repression of the dissidents (who have no intention of ousting the leaders from their swivel chairs), is testimony to that mentality. At the same time the repression regenerates and reinforces this way of thinking. A vicious circle is formed. In order to break it, there must be at least *some* trust between the regime and society, so that a line can be drawn between the struggle for ideas and the struggle for power. But with the shroud of fear and lies that now envelops us, reaching even the minimum of trust that would be necessary is a hard task. The regime is so much in dread of the real problems now facing the country, that it doesn't even want to call them by their right names: it prefers to deny obvious facts. That is the policy of an ostrich, hiding his head in the sand because he is afraid.

Debate with a Bolshevik

Needless to say, the process of democratization will necessarily entail certain changes in the Party–State hierarchy. Persons plainly unable to function under changing conditions will have to leave the political scene. But if the reforms are effected skillfully and gradually, they will not threaten the ruling elite as a whole. A human being is teachable. He is quite able to adapt his work or his way of life to changing conditions. Why should we assume that in that respect a Party worker differs radically (almost biologically) from other people? The mastodons will of course have to die out; but society will only benefit from that.

At this point I hear a Bolshevik (one of the current variety) objecting: "All this is idealism and illusion. The class interest of the Party leadership consists in changing nothing in the slightest degree. They have grown up under certain political conditions, and have become used to them. They are quite content with their lives. What do they need with democratization, which will disturb their tranquility, force them to somehow try to deal with new conditions—to demonstrate their righteousness or other virtues at public meetings? To risk failure in free elections. Making them go along with democratization is like making a wolf eat cabbage. It goes against their class interest."

This objection is outwardly plausible. It is nevertheless faulty, it presents a partial truth as a whole one. The effect pointed out by my imaginary adversary undoubtedly takes place. Certainly the top officials' desire for a tranquil life obstructs democratization. But to conclude from this desire that democratization is impossible one must make several assumptions.

First, one must assume that the ruling elite, as a class, has no aspirations other than to lead a tranquil life. But that is untrue even within the framework of a strictly Marxist approach. A class interest is one engendered by the *function* of that class in society. According to Marx, a capitalist strives for profits not because he is greedy, but because that is his role in society—in the production system. If he behaves otherwise, he goes bankrupt and ceases to be a capitalist. Similarly, the function of the Party–State apparatus is to govern the country. And it fulfulls that function, although by no means in the best way: by leaning heavily on fear and a wide range of punishments, while not providing the conditions essential to the development of the national economy and culture. There is still more to it. If the ruling class does not change its style of governing, the result will be either ossification, with inevitable destruction from without, or a revolutionary explosion from within. And neither of these corresponds to the class interest of the power elite. What *would* be in its interest is gradual democratization—freeing the people's creative energies while yet preserving the elite's ruling position and power.

It is a difficult path, however, and the power elite fears that it may prove unable to contain the process of democratization within certain limits. Thus it prefers not to take any steps at all in the direction of democratization. But what relationship does that bear to the *social function* of that elite? Its inability to find an acceptable solution in a complex situation (in particular, to find a means of democratization while retaining its own power) cannot in any way be deduced from its social functions or social interests. If people fail to strive for what would be ideal for them because of laziness, cowardice, or stupidity, we should say so and not pass off human weaknesses as class interests.

The second assumption implied in the Bolshevik's viewpoint is that the classes of society are rigidly separated—each with its own culture and ethics, each at bitter war against the others, defending its class interests. This view does not reflect reality; it is a Marxist vulgarization of it. A society's culture is something indivisible, and influences all classes and members of society. Classes are not monolithic; and the class struggle is by no means the only factor determining the development of society (it is not always even the most important one). The grouping and division of people on the basis of their psychological traits, worldviews, and character traits are no less important than the division into classes; and they affect all social strata.

Marxists usually try to represent social change as the result only of an armed struggle by the oppressed classes against the power elite, while ignoring those changes which take place among the ruling classes as a consequence of cultural evolution. Yet the latter are at least as important. And if culture does not evolve, the lot of the oppressed may not improve despite periodic uprisings. The history of European civilization definitely indicates that cultural evolution, not force, is decisive. Improvement of weapons and transportation has made it physically possible for a small segment of society to keep all others in complete submission. Technically, this has become easier than in the Ancient World. Yet if certain deviations are left out of account, European civilization has shown a constant trend toward less use of force by the ruling elite. On the other hand, totalitarianism in Russia and China shows vividly how successfully, with Western technology and without the Western cultural traditions, people can be kept in subjugation.

According to Marxism, changes in social relations result from the development of material culture: for example, at a certain stage in the development of the productive forces, it becomes more profitable to collect rent from a free tenant farmer than to have a serf. But is that really the cause of the abolition of servitude? A more important and direct effect may be observed all around us (unless of course we close our eyes and invent a "materialist," pseudoscientific explanation). In and by itself, the evolution of social consciousness—under the action of forces which cannot be derived from material production, despite all the efforts of the Marxists—changes both the ideas and methods of a ruling class that no longer wants to, or can afford to, use the old recipes.

The example of the British raj comes to mind. It cannot

be shown—even by the most clever sophistry—that it was in the "class interest" of the British civil service and military forces to leave India. If they had been firmly resolved to stay there at any price, and if they had resorted to the same repressive measures (or harsher ones) they had employed in the nineteenth century, I doubt that India could have gained its independence. I have no wish to underrate the importance of the Indians' struggle for independence. I maintain merely that the decisive factors in that struggle were ethical and ideological. If economic and military factors had been decisive, the British would not have left India. They had the physical capability to stay there.

The preconditions to democratic reforms are to be found in the way we think. Essentially, social consciousness penetrates all the strata of society. Thus one must not, using the Bolshevik frame of reference, put all the blame on the "new class." In a country where world-famous scientists anxious to curry favor with the regime, are capable of smearing Sakharov, their only honest and courageous colleague, what can be expected of Party and government officials?

No one can convince me that there are certain "objective" reasons why gradual democratic reform is impossible. This is merely an excuse for failure to act. Whether we in the Soviet Union follow a course of action that opens up prospects for a future worthy of humans, depends solely upon us. And if we fail to follow such a course, there will be no justification for that failure.

The Human Rights Movement

That Soviet citizens have been brought up in the belief that "economics is the base, while ideology and politics are the superstructure," is reflected in their attitude toward anyone who decides to speak out on sociopolitical issues.

They demand first of all a specific plan for economic reforms—preferably with charts and long columns of figures. Any other approach is regarded as "frivolous." After all, politics is a reflection of economic interests. So how can citizens support someone if they don't know what specific plans that person has in the area of economics? And if the person has no such plans, what is there to talk about?

Actually, under today's conditions, it is precisely this economic approach that is frivolous. The social philosophy I have set forth implies the necessity of liberalizing the economy, stepping up the role of private initiative, and revising the economic system along the lines of structural-functional parallelism. But I have no intention of concretizing those general principles. The economic system is huge and very complex, with a great many indirect, tangled linkages; and any serious attempt to modify that system requires a detailed study of it. It is not just that I am not a professional economist. I venture to say that even a very knowledgeable economist could not, on his own, provide a well-founded and sufficiently concrete plan for economic reform. What is needed is the kind of study produced by a large collective with freedom to discuss ideas and exchange information. Also needed is experimentation on a broad scale. These conditions are political, and until they are fulfilled, Soviet economic problems will not be solved. The stumbling block here is politics, not economics. And the same thing applies to the concrete problems of legislation, government administration, etc. Any serious discussion of them, or search for a solution to them, is possible only when the most basic civil and political rights of the individual are respected. The problem of individual rights ranks first among all other problems.

What is meant by "the basic rights of the individual" are the following, set forth in four articles of the United Nations Universal Declaration of Human Rights (adopted December 10, 1948):

> Article 5. No one shall be subjected to torture or to cruel, inhuman or degrading treatment or punishment.

> Article 9. No one shall be subjected to arbitrary arrest, detention or exile.
>
> Article 18. Everyone has the right to freedom of thought, conscience and religion; this right includes freedom to change his religion or belief, and freedom, either alone or in community with others and in public or private, to manifest his religion or belief in teaching, practice, worship and observance.
>
> Article 19. Everyone has the right to freedom of opinion and expression; this right includes freedom to hold opinions without interference and to seek, receive and impart information and ideas through any media and regardless of frontiers.

In the Soviet Union, the realization that it was necessary to defend basic human rights has given rise to a movement which by now has a history of more than a decade. It unites people of the most varied political and philosophical views. It is not a political party, and has no formal membership, organization, or leadership. It does not even have a definite name. Formerly, it was usually called "The Democratic Movement." Today it is most commonly called "The Human Rights Movement." Nonetheless, it really exists; and despite its minuscule membership relative to the population of the USSR, it is a significant social phenomenon. Those who belong to it (the "dissidents") have such common bonds as a rejection of totalitarianism, protesting specific violations of human rights, and an interest in underground literary works. *The Chronicle of Current Events* may be regarded as the movement's press organ.

Since the Soviet Human Rights Movement has no definite organizational structure, it cannot be said to have a definite program. It has only general principles shared by the majority of its participants. Within the framework of those principles, each dissident expresses his own views and suggestions.

I should like to suggest the following rough plan for democratic reforms—one deliberately set forth not in terms of specific legislative acts or governmental decrees but in general terms. Hence it is rather a schema of measures than a detailed plan for them.*

1. Stop judicial and psychiatric persecution for exchanges of ideas and information; for criticizing the social system and the regime; for preaching religious beliefs; and for declaring one's wish to leave the USSR. Assure public access to all open trials, and permit cameras and tape recorders.

2. Proclaim amnesty for all political prisoners, defined by Amnesty International as: "People detained anywhere for their beliefs, color, ethnic origin, religion, or language, provided they have neither used nor advocated violence."

3. Abolish prior censorship of the press and other mass media.

4. Permit the free movement of persons and the free exchange of information with all countries in the world. In particular: Permit person to go abroad freely and return to their own country; permit the free sale of foreign newspapers, magazines, and books; stop the arbitrary retention of letters and other materials sent by mail to and from foreign countries; stop the jamming of radio broadcasts and the disruption of telephone service.

With respect to all the above kinds of information exchange, orders for prohibition or seizure must be based only on a decision handed down in an open trial.

Implementation of the reforms listed in these four paragraphs could be carried out very quickly without any risk to the system or the regime. Strictly speaking, this was the obligation the Soviet Government undertook at the Helsinki conference. Fulfillment of that obligation would do much to enhance the USSR's prestige abroad, and would open up new and favorable prospects in relations with the West. The next two matters require more time, and a certain degree of caution.

* The concretization of that schema goes beyond the framework of my aims in this book, and would be meaningful only on the political level, in the process of collective discussions. (It would be desirable to have representatives of the regime take part in such discussions.)

5. Introduce a slate of several candidates for each office in the elections to all Party and state bodies, in lieu of the present farce in which one candidate is "elected."

6. Tolerate all associations of citizens who do not advocate force and do not have the status of political parties; enable them to function normally. In particular, allow associations to have their own independent publications and printing presses.

It would of course be fine if all these steps were initiated from above. But one can hardly count on such an initiative. There must be pressure from below. And that would require the exercise of one's civil rights without "prior permission." The Soviet state claims to be free and democratic. Hence to a rather high degree, the struggle for human rights means taking those claims and putting them into action.

Even with the restriction on associations mentioned above, the freedom of associations which are independent of Party and state remains the most difficult point. But without freedom of association, it is ludicrous to talk about human rights or democracy. Several independent associations have been founded within the framework of the Human Rights Movement. Their members are constantly arrested or compelled to emigrate. But the organizations persist, and one may hope that new independent organizations will be founded, again and again. They should not necessarily set political goals; there are more varied aspects of life for them to take up. Take the pollution of the environment, for example—something that disturbs everyone. Government agencies can hardly assure thorough and objective monitoring, because the struggle for a clean environment is not in their interest but in that of private citizens. For this, we need independent public organizations.

Transportation safety is another such problem. In the Soviet Union, airplane disasters are reported in the press only if the fatalities include foreigners. The statistics on these disasters are not published. Obviously, the government is afraid that if the Soviet citizens get to know the statistics, they will refuse to fly in airplanes.

One engineer told me: "I never fly in airplanes. You know why? Because I work at a plant where airplanes are built, and I know *how* they are built."

Secrecy about disasters certainly contributes to their increase, because it makes it possible a coverup of their underlying causes. Here we have exactly what Soviet propaganda calls "sacrificing the interest of the toilers to the interest of the monopolies" when referring to capitalist countries. In fact, the government's refusal to publish statistics on disasters and their circumstances, amounts to its murder of its own citizens. There is no way to correct this situation without setting up independent public organizations as watchdogs. Finally, every factory or plant, and every municipal economy, has many problems that can be solved only if there are independent watchdog organizations. Also, associations of scientists or artists, can play a very important role in professional activities.

In many respects, the struggle for human rights is harder than a revolutionary struggle for power. But it leads to alterations in the way people live and think that are salutary and enduring. Rather than a "struggle," perhaps it should be called "work." This work is hard, long, and—under present-day conditions in the Soviet Union—dangerous. But it is the only way to arrive at a truly human existence. It is democracy in action—democracy for the masses. The advanced nations of the West, having set out on that course, are stubbornly pursuing it. And there is no other course for the Soviet Union.

East and West

> Today, on all continents and in all parts of the world, there are on-going "circles for studying the great ideas of our leader, Comrade Kim Il Sung," institutes "for

> research on the works of Comrade Kim Il Sung," and "Kim Il Sung readers' clubs." The movement for studying the leader's ideas has grown beyond the framework of discussion groups and is expanding on the scale of a general zonal and continental movement.
>
> *Koreya* (Korea) 229 (10), 1975

> The speech by Comrade Leonid Ilich Brezhnev, General Secretary of the CPSU, was not yet over, but England's tremendous, all-embracing interest in it was growing from hour to hour. . . .
>
> It goes without saying that in England today, there is not a single London newspaper which has not given front-page space to accounts of the work being done by the Forum of Soviet Communists—usually accompanied by a photograph of the CPSU General Secretary on the rostrum.
>
> *Komsomolskaka pravda*, Feb. 26, 1976

If the Soviet Union were the only country on earth, it is quite possible that the steps it has already taken along the path to steady-state totalitarianism would be irreversible. But the actual situation in the world is not quite so gloomy. The nations of the Free World still hold the leading position in the global economy and in culture; and so long as they keep that position the triumph of totalitarianism cannot anywhere be regarded as final. Totalitarianism has not yet become a worldwide norm: the countries under its sway must still take world public opinion into account.

The kind of demands that the evolving global society imposes on all countries cannot be met by a stagnating totalitarianism. It is therefore likely that sooner or later some fresh air will blow into the Soviet Union and China—unless the totalitarian countries adopt a policy of rigid isolationism. But how real is that possibility?

However hard the Communist world tries to convince itself and others that today the prevailing winds are from the East, it realizes that *Westernization* (the absorption and spreading of the culture that arose in Western Europe) is now embracing the entire world. As it spreads, Western culture in turn absorbs certain of the Eastern cultures' traits. This is of course very important to the future global civilization. But it does not alter the fact that in the culture now taking shape, the active force is the Western culture and not the Eastern. The totalitarian countries are outlying areas of the civilization now being formed; and this accounts for the basic stance taken by people in those countries vis-à-vis the people of the West. That attitude is compounded of a painful awareness of their inferiority, and a healthy awareness of their vigor—their urge to overtake the West. Prolonged, consistent isolationism in this situation is unthinkable.

For the totalitarian countries, as for those of the Third World, the West is the only natural measure of all things. The boasting one finds in Soviet propaganda—the claims that the "socialist" countries have become the center of world culture—is yet another device serving the main goal of that propaganda: to "disinform" the public. To some degree the propaganda has succeeded (one sometimes hears the same kind of boastfulness from "the man in the street"), but deep within themselves, everyone knows where the yardstick is. The leaders, too, know this, and are therefore greatly concerned that the study of their "great ideas" expand "on the scale of a general zonal and continental movement," and that in Western countries their as-yet-unfinished speeches provoke a "tremendous, all-embracing interest" that "grows from hour to hour." Also, that not a single metropolitan daily fail to publish their photos.

Two circumstances play a role in the Soviet leaders' great and still-increasing sensitivity to public opinion in the West. First, Soviet society has passed from its revolutionary phase into its steady-state phase. In the revolutionary phase of a society, much is condoned as temporary and transient. The heat of passions is so great that external influences are ignored. During such periods, a certain degree of isolationism is inevitable. But the steady-state phase imposes new demands for relations with the rest of the world, and the importance of those relations grows.

Second, certain segments of Western society important to the Soviet Union have undergone a change of mood. The Soviet State has never been indifferent to its image in the Western world. That state in fact arose as a "breach in the chain of world capitalism"; and the slogan of world revolution remained current for many years after November 1917. It is a mistake to think that Stalin was not concerned with the USSR's prestige in the West. He was and he had it. In those segments of Western society he counted on for support (the workers and leftist intellectuals) that prestige was immense, despite the atrocities committed by Stalin's regime. The wish to believe that the first socialist State in the world really existed was so great that people refused to face obvious facts, and applauded the hangmen. The Molotov-Ribbentrop pact of 1939 was of course extremely damaging to Soviet prestige. But the defeat of Nazi Germany, the Soviet people's heroism in the war, and their great sacrifices, rehabilitated the regime in the eyes of many people in the West, even though this was not logical. Greater influence accrued to the foreign Communist parties, all of which at the time regarded the CPSU as the only model worthy of emulation, and glorified it. In 1945 Theodore Dreiser requested of William Z. Foster, chairman of the CP of the U.S., that he be accepted into the Party. He wrote that his belief in the greatness and dignity of man had always been the guiding principle of his life, and that logic of his life and work had led him to the Communist Party. And that at a time when the massive technology developed by the Stalinists for crushing man and destroying his dignity had become the foundation of the new society's stability!

It was not until after Khrushchev's immortal 20th Congress of the CPSU in 1956, where he disclosed some of

Stalin's crimes, that, gradually, the scales began to fall from people's eyes. No longer would the regime receive surefire applause, and in order to maintain its prestige the leadership had to make concessions to public opinion.

Political and cultural relations with the outside world necessitate economic relations as well. To avoid lagging too far behind the Western standard of living, the USSR imports wheat; to keep pace with scientific and technological advances, it imports computers; to avoid looking like savages, it follows Western fashions and provides its elite with foreign clothes, footwear, cosmetics, and household utensils. The West thus has a special kind of glamor for the Soviets. An opportunity to go abroad—especially to Western countries—is one of the chief lures used by the authorities to attract and nurture obedience in a certain part of the intelligentsia.

None of the top leaders in the USSR would try systematically to curtail or cut off contacts with the West; he would find no support for such a move. In the struggle for power, isolationist slogans may be useful; they can hardly be distinguished from an appeal to "tighten the screws." Thus a politician may say, "The people have been spoiled. And it's all because of contacts with the West."

One can assume that this kind of demagogy will be employed to get some people dislodged from their positions and replaced by others. But anyone who took such language seriously would be naïve: it is merely a tactic used in fighting for power. As soon as the new people are in the saddle, the logic of things compels them to mend and strengthen contacts with the West. (I am not considering, here, such specific problems as relations with China, although they play a role that is far from negligible.) Such was the case with Khrushchev; such is now the case with Brezhnev; and such will be the case with their successors in the foreseeable future.

The Triumph of "Realism"

The West is by no means using all of its potential for influencing—through trade and culture—the Soviet Union in the area of basic human rights. No one in his right mind would call, today, for the use of force (or threats of force) regardless of the ratio of military potential between the two super-powers. Obviously, the agreements aimed at lessening the danger of armed conflict are a great feat of political intelligence and common sense. But it is the lawful right of every human community to disseminate its ideas via peaceful, friendly contacts. And if that community really believes in the truth of its ideas, to disseminate them is both its right and its duty. The idea of the freedom of the individual person is a great one, and it is a cornerstone of Western civilization. The West's passivity and lack of persistence in spreading that idea testifies to a crisis in Western civilization—a failure of nerve.

Blue jeans and pop music easily cross national borders. Their influence is constant—no doubt because they are always in evidence. But when a person from the West gets into contact with the Soviet system, he politely hides his ideas in his pocket. It is considered a mark of good breeding, during professional contacts between people from the different "camps," to assure each other from time to time that one has no intention of involving the other person in a "political" argument. When a Soviet scientist visiting America senses that the conversation is taking a hazardous turn, he will say, "Well, now, that's a political matter."

"True enough—let's drop it," the American will agree readily—perhaps apologetically. "Let's not talk politics. You have your views, and I have mine. But science is neutral. Let's drink to more scientific contacts—to friendship between our nations!"

Mutual satisfaction and complete agreement. Friendship between nations. Détente. But here is what I want to know:

Does the American realize that even though science may be neutral, he, in taking that position, is not at all neutral but is supporting totalitarianism? Does he realize that in divorcing himself from what (following his Soviet colleague) he calls "politics," he is actually divorcing himself from ordinary decency and basic ethical principles? Because for the Soviets, everything outside the sphere of physiological functions and his boss's orders at work is politics. Morality? Politics! Humanity? Politics! Conscience? Politics! Plain, simple sincerity free of political considerations (and if it isn't free of them, what kind of sincerity is it?) is labeled "abstract" sincerity that is ideologically faulty. It was that language which was used to criticize an article written by a journalist, V. Pomerantsev, and titled "On Sincerity in Literature." It was published during the first phase of the "thaw" after Stalin's death. The critic writing about it in *Literaturnaya gazeta* said:

> The Soviet public has already, on good grounds, judged V. Pomerantsev's essay, "On Sincerity in Literature," to be ideologically faulty, written from an idealistic viewpoint, and in favor of abstract sincerity as against the principles of ideological significance, the Party spirit in literature, and the criterion (*sic*) for the faithful reflection of reality.[4]

Soviet citizens are divided into two categories: the first-class citizens are permitted to travel abroad; the second-class citizens are not. First-class citizens are completely reliable, tested people—people whose superiors are sure they will accurately carry out all orders given them, and will never take the liberty of showing their true faces (if indeed they have any). This applies both to their behavior abroad and to the way they behave at home, since a trip abroad is a reward which has to be earned.

"If you sign the letter against Sakharov, you can go. If you don't sign it, you can't." These words were actually spoken to a research associate at the institute where Sakharov was working. Such is the method of selecting those who are permitted to appear on the international stage. And the world community sanctions such choices. Handshakes. Applause. Toasts.

In recent years the wave of protests in the West against Soviet persecution for one's convictions has been swelling, and it is producing consequences. Among scientists, the mathematicians have been the most vigorous. In particular, it was through their efforts that Leonid Plyushch was finally discharged from a psychiatric hospital. Again, during preparations for the Fourth International Conference on Artificial Intelligence (held in Tbilisi in September 1975), some American members of the steering committee threatened the Soviet organizers of the conference with a boycott if Professor Alexander Lerner (who had been dismissed from his post after applying for permission to emigrate to Israel) were not allowed to attend the conference and read a paper he had written.

But such actions are in a sense "atypical": they are initiated by individual fighters for human rights—against the wishes of the majority. And it is not by those actions that the atmosphere of cultural and scientific relations is determined. That atmosphere is still such that the persecution of dissidents and the strangling of creative freedom are considered to be the "internal affairs" of the totalitarian countries—affairs in which a Westerner must not interfere. So long as that atmosphere continues to exist, cultural exchanges will strengthen totalitarianism. As a lesson to the younger generation, the Soviet authorities put docile persons on the international stage, and bury the disobedient ones alive. The Western countries accept without a murmur the totalitarian rules of the game in cultural, scientific, and other exchanges.

Steady-state totalitarianism needs international recognition, and it is getting it. Totalitarianism has become one of the legitimate modes of societal existence. The representatives of totalitarian culture—these cogs of a machine which pulverizes human consciousness—travel all over the world without experiencing the slightest inconvenience. Indeed, they are everywhere honored and respected. Totalitarianism has become a norm. So far, it is one norm among others. But will it not become, tomorrow, the *only* (the "uniquely scientific," the "uniquely progressive") norm?

The Western public's recognition of totalitarianism as a norm is welcomed in Soviet and pro-Soviet propaganda as a "realistic approach," "political realism," or "the triumph of realism." The word "realism" is exploited with gusto. But of course it must be taken to mean an accommodation to the reality of totalitarianism. And the same term is exploited by the capitulators in the West. So long as it has a positive connotation (one associated with sober-mindedness and wisdom), yielding up positions will almost look like victory.

And there is yet another concept that serves as a constant pretext for jobbery. That term is "impartiality."

Impartiality in a Polarized World

Western public opinion has often been inclined—in its striving toward misconceived "impartiality" and "neutrality"—to yield ground voluntarily in the ideological struggle against totalitarianism; to sacrifice vitally important ideas. This is shown in the reaction of some circles to the awarding of the Nobel Peace Prize to Andrei Sakharov—a great event in the struggle for human rights and in East-West relations.

An editorial (October 16, 1975) in the prestigious scientific journal *Nature* stated:

> The award of the Nobel Peace Prize to Academician Andrei Dmitrievich Sakharov took nearly everyone by surprise. No doubt he could at one time have been considered a candidate for a Physics Prize, but few had thought of him in the context of a Peace Prize. So was the action of the Oslo committee an inspired gesture aimed at expanding the horizons of "peace" to include human rights

> as the "only sure foundation for a genuine and long-lasting system of international cooperation"—as the citation read; or was it simply a political act, such as can be carried out from the relative safety of Scandinavia, designed to cause a certain amount of embarrassment to the Soviet Union?
>
> First, let it be said that Sakharov's record, initially as a physicist, then as a proponent of restraint in weaponry, and finally as a social democrat fighting for civil rights, has been admirable. If the year's award is controversial, the controversy is not centered around the personal qualities of Academician Sakharov in any way. Furthermore, it is undeniable that the award of this prize will have done much to encourage Sakharov, if encouragement were needed, to continue his work.
>
> So far so good. But even if the West can, on the whole, view the award as given for human rights work, the Soviet Union undoubtedly views the award as a piece of political cynicism supportive of troublemakers. If the Nobel Foundation were a political outfit devoted to the supporting of Western ideals that would matter little—but Nobel Prizes would then have the significance only of Stalin Prizes. By aspiring to have a global significance Nobel Prizes must be free of the sort of ambiguity and polarization that this year's prize generates; and not only this year's—recent awards to Willy Brandt, Le Duc Tho and Henry Kissinger have all in their different ways been political and arguable.[5]

I was overjoyed by the decision of the Nobel Committee, since in 1975 there was no one more deserving of a Nobel Peace Prize than Academician Sakharov. The citation for the Peace Prize stated that the observance of civil rights on a global scale is the only sure foundation for peace. With a closed society, there can be no genuine peace. Sakharov's contribution to the cause of human rights is a contribution to the cause of peace. And it is more significant than those solemnly proclaimed undertakings that are violated the day after they are signed. Also, it should not be forgotten that in awarding the Peace Prize, unlike the other Nobel prizes, what counts is not simply a particular piece of work—a scientific discovery, an artistic creation—but the recipient's personality as a whole and his influence on his contemporaries. Andrei Sakharov has created a new model of behavior; the full extent of his influence will be revealed only in the future.

These considerations, which for me are beyond doubt, are by no means obvious (so far as I know) to the broad public in the West. The Nobel Committee's decision was no trifling matter; it demanded considerable courage, and it provoked pleasant astonishment.

By contrast, the reaction of *Nature* came as an unpleasant surprise to me. I would have been happy to read and consider any arguments regarding Sakharov's contribution to the cause of peace, but there is nothing of the sort in the article. Sakharov personally is given high marks; the only reason why *Nature* criticized the Nobel Committee's decision was that it provoked the dissatisfaction of the Soviet Union. Thus it doesn't matter what role Sakharov has played in international affairs. It doesn't matter whether he deserved the Peace Prize or not.

But since the Soviet authorities look upon Sakharov as a "trouble-maker," he should not have been awarded the prize.

And this is called neutrality? Impartiality? In that case, what is partiality? And what is *servility*, the worst kind of partiality, arising from the fear of force?

When *Nature* compares the Nobel Prize with the Stalin Prize, the argument is at first blush convincing. Indeed, it would be most undesirable for the Nobel Prize to be like the Stalin Prize. But upon closer analysis the persuasiveness of the argument is dissipated. For this analysis we must return to the concept of impartiality.

In the contemporary world, we find two opposed ideologies, and two political blocs. Each side wants humanity as a whole to accept its ideology and structure life in accordance with its model. In this situation, what is political impartiality? Does it exist at all? The Eastern and Western ideologies supply opposite answers to this question.

Western ideology affirms that impartiality exists and in

certain situations is essential. The human mind possesses the capacity to look at itself from the outside: to consider its system of ideas, values, and goals from the viewpoint of a broader metasystem. In particular, a person can disregard his own goals, however passionately he actually strives for them, and analyze things as if he did not have those goals. This is impartiality. Without it there would be no science, and the intelligent correction of social goals would be impossible.

Totalitarian ideology affirms that there is no such thing as impartiality (at any rate none in matters associated with the life of society) nor should there be any. The individual's every thought and every action directly serves the goals of that camp to which he belongs. Impartiality is either deceit or self-delusion. Usually, a person who talks about impartiality is one who has secretly gone over to the enemy.

The difference between a Stalin Prize and a Nobel Prize is that Stalin Prizes are bound to be politically partial, both in the intent and in realization, whereas Nobel Prizes should and can be impartial, in intent. Of course human beings are imperfect and in the realization of that intent, occasional partiality and other deviations are inevitable. However, the intent itself, and the fact that the resources of Western civilization include a definite tradition and understanding of impartiality, compel thinking people throughout the world, including Soviet citizens (and even the Soviet leaders!) to regard Nobel Prizes very differently from the way they regard Stalin Prizes.

This regard will not change as a result of one or two controversial cases, since it is based not on a statistical analysis but on an understanding of the difference between the Western and Eastern ideologies. It would require great efforts to change this attitude. As for the case in question, to refrain from awarding a prize to Sakharov for political reasons (as *Nature* would have preferred) would have constituted a deviation from the idea of impartiality. People expect that the Nobel Committee will be guided strictly by its view of the candidate's contribution to the cause of peace, without regard to any political aims whether those of the Committee or of any other party.

In the *Nature* editorial we find a strange phenomenon: gentlemen plainly belonging to the Western side, in an apparent striving toward impartiality, are actually calling for political discrimination in favor of the totalitarian side. The cause of this phenomenon may be found in that fundamental point I mentioned earlier: the authentic concept of impartiality is wholly a Western concept. Pseudo-impartiality, which in fact amounts to a lack of principle, leads to renouncing the authentic concept of impartiality as alien and unacceptable to the Eastern side, and to its replacement by political pragmatism—or putting it more simply, a constant concern not to anger Moscow. In many cases (and the award of the Nobel Peace Prize to Academician Sakharov was one of them), an impartial approach leads to results that are unfavorable to the totalitarian camp. At such times pseudo-impartiality serves as a defense for the theory and practice of totalitarianism.

As to the ultimate reason for the West's yielding ideological ground, there can scarcely be two opinions: the reason is fear. When a person in the West tries to be impartial, he easily disregards his own political ideals and goals (following the best Western traditions). But to disregard the existence of an armed totalitarian camp and a Third World attracted toward it, is not so simple. As a result, the scales are weighted on the side of totalitarianism. This is the psychological basis of a Munich-style policy of appeasement.

The editorial in *Nature* concludes with these words:

> We have noted before that Nobel Prizes often leave a trail of devastation behind them. This is particularly so of the Peace Prize; it is time that the Nobel Foundation seriously looked at other ways of supporting its very worthy ideals.

From that part of the editorial quoted earlier we can see that these other methods must not, in the journal's opinion, engender "polarization." But how can we avoid polarization in our polarized world when even the concept of impartiality is rejected by one of the sides? Obviously, only by showing partiality toward that side.

Nonpolitical, impartial organizations of global scope, like the Nobel Foundation and Amnesty International, are vitally necessary to the modern world. Ideologically and organizationally, they can be based only in the West. By definition, there can be nothing of the sort in the East. A mixed East-West organization may prove capable of compromise but never of impartiality. Even under Western conditions, however, it is no easy job to preserve impartiality. Criticism of such organizations that is based on an examination of their concepts and decisions in matters of substance, is indispensable and constructive. Criticism engendered by cowardly political conformism is destructive.

The Weakness of the West

> And nonetheless, until I myself had reached the West and had spent two years looking around this part of the world, I had no notion of how very badly the West *wants* to be blind to the world situation—no notion of the extreme degree to which the West has already become a world that has lost the strength of its will, which is paralyzed in the face of danger; and above all, a world dispirited by the necessity of defending its freedom.
>
> Alexander Solzhenitsyn[6]

Today, few people in the West harbor any illusions about "the land of victorious socialism," but the size of the threat posed by totalitarianism as a world phenomenon is still far from being realized. Russia was the first nation to fall into that pit; then it dragged several others in after it. Obviously, only a person who had actually been imprisoned in the pit can understand what kind of place it is, and how hard it is to get out of it. A tourist cannot. When such a person tells a Westerner about it, he shrugs in disbelief, trying his best to ignore the pit's existence.

Sakharov and Solzhenitsyn have often warned of how serious the totalitarian threat is. The latter has said: "I'm not criticizing the West—I'm criticizing the weakness of the West." He has been harder on the British than on anyone else, and it has stung them to the quick. His talks on the BBC in March 1976 were discussed throughout the country. Some very prominent people took part in the roundtable discussion of those talks organized by the BBC in its "Panorama" series. They included former Prime Minister Edward Heath, Senator Hubert Humphrey, former U.S. Defense Secretary James Schlesinger, and Dr. Joseph Luns, Secretary General of NATO. These people countered Solzhenitsyn's criticism with several arguments intended to show that the West is not really so weak—arguments dealing with military, political, and economic matters. But Solzhenitsyn's ideas on these subjects were only of secondary importance. The substance of his criticism was quite different.

As a writer, it is Solzhenitsyn's job to see what people "live by," in Tolstoy's phrase. It was such observations that led him to his conclusions as to the weakness of the West. Thus he did not find any strong belief in those higher values without which courage and unity cannot exist. What he saw was opportunism and fragmentation. And he made it quite plain that for him, it was in these things that the West's weakness lay.

If you compare that picture with the mechanistic, iron unity of the totalitarian machine, you will understand why Solzhenitsyn's talks are so apocalyptic. Totalitarianism is incapable of creating anything basically new. But the flow of scientific and technical information from the West compensates for that defect. And in the strictly military (or "politico-military") sphere, the totalitarian state has the advantages of unity, concentration, and discipline. It will not invent gunpowder, but it will use it better. And when you think about the coming biological revolution, your thoughts can be very gloomy indeed.

Western observers often describe the situation in terms as apocalyptic as those of Solzhenitsyn. In an article titled "A Question of Survival," Walter Lacqueur and Leopold Labedz have this to say:

> America and the other Western democracies face the most severe crisis in their history, a major economic depression coupled with the rapid decline of their influence in world affairs and paralysis and confusion on the domestic front. It has been building up over a fairly lengthy period, but one still looks in vain for a realistic analysis of the unique character of this crisis and a policy to overcome these difficulties. On the contrary, in the current discussions about the political predicaments and the economic situation there is an unfortunate tendency to single out one specific aspect of the crisis and to believe that it will go away as the result of technical manipulation or perhaps a summit meeting. The inclination is perhaps natural. In foreign policy, capitulation, especially if dressed up as a peace policy, is almost always more attractive than resistance. Pétain in 1940 had a great many supporters, and de Gaulle only a few. But there are crises and crises, and there is every reason to believe that the present one is quite unprecedented. It is a crisis of societies, of norms and values, of the disappearance of the consensus which held society together in the past. Comparisons with past crises are, therefore, not particularly helpful, and the hope that there will be a return to normalcy with an upturn in the business cycle later this year—or the year after at the latest—seems ill founded.[7]

These authors characterize the mood in the West as one of "pessimistic determinism." Prophecies of doom (say they) have a soporific effect, paralyzing the political will by presenting the decline of the West as inevitable. In the foreign policies of the European countries, a "narrow national egotism" prevails. This is paralleled, on the domestic scene, by a "growing pursuit of narrow sectional interests" by various groups of the population, regardless of the difficulties that creates for other groups, and for the nation as a whole. Great Britain is the "leader" in this respect:

> As the internal consensus is breaking up, there is growing anarchy in Britain with other European countries not far behind. One hesitates to apply the term *class struggles* to the struggles which now go on in many European countries; class struggles are inevitable in a society divided into classes, a natural concomitant of the democratic process. But the present situation is increasingly characterized by a novel phenomenon—the relentless pursuit of pay claims by some occupational groups in disregard not just of the general economic situation but of other, less well-paid groups without the means to assert their influence a similar way. Working-class solidarity is giving way to the law of the jungle, as small groups of professional people, technicians, or workers effectively paralyze whole industries against the wishes of the majority. It is a return to the practices of the medieval guilds coupled with an ideology (if any) of social Darwinism with an admixture of laissez-faire. But whereas in the Middle Ages there was an authority, be it the pope or the emperor, who had the power to impose order, authority in Western democratic societies has been weakened, and in some countries has been eroded altogether. Modern society, unlike the jungle, cannot function without a minimum of orderly conduct. Hence, the alternative to anarchy is the emergence of authoritarian regimes, unless reason, responsibility, and the awareness of long-term interest assert themselves in time to prevent a backlash.[8]

Marcuse

The outburst of rage in the Western leftist movement in the 1960s testified to the discontent among the young people of contemporary Western society who wanted change of one kind or another, and to a total failure to realize just what changes were needed, and how they should be brought about. A combination of these two traits, before they were embodied in the social actions of the New Leftists, was to be found in the philosophical writings of their ideological leaders—above all, in the works of Herbert Marcuse.

I have read only one of Marcuse's books, *One-Dimensional Man*, but that book alone is quite enough to give one a notion of an amazing phenomenon—a combination of passionate demands for change with a total lack of constructive ideas about change. *One-Dimensional Man* is a systematic critique of modern Western society. It is not necessarily required of such a book that it present any specific sociopolitical program. But the author's ideological position, and his philosophy, can be discerned rather clearly in his critique.

The amazing thing about Marcuse's book is the absence of any concept of *evolution*. Despite all his passion for change, Marcuse's philosophy is anti-evolutionary. For evolution is not merely a time sequence of changes but a sequence of changes subordinated to a definite, overall plan. To speak of evolution is to speak of such a plan. But we find nothing of the kind in Marcuse. What we do find is quite the opposite: a total failure to understand the nature and mechanisms of evolution. Without evolution there can be no revolution, since the latter is a subspecies of the former. A belief in "change for change's sake" can only engender senseless violence—which is what happened in the student riots of 1968. In the Introduction to his book, Marcuse writes:

> But here, advanced industrial society confronts the critique with a situation which seems to deprive it of its very basis. Technical progress, extended to a whole system of domination and coordination, creates forms of life (and of power) which appear to reconcile the forces opposing the system and to defeat or refute all protest in the name of the historical prospects of freedom from toil

> and domination. Contemporary society seems to be capable of containing social change—qualitative change which would establish essentially different institutions, a new direction of the productive process, new modes of human existence. This containment of social change is perhaps the most singular achievement of advanced industrial society; the general acceptance of the National Purpose, bipartisan policy, the decline of pluralism, the collusion of Business and Labor within the strong State testify to the integration of opposites which is the result as well as the prerequisite of this achievement.[9]

The first part of this excerpt disposes us favorably toward the author. If a society has lost its capacity for change, that is plainly bad. We envision the end of the road—stagnation and inevitable collapse. We are inclined to sympathize with a critic who charges society with this. But as we read further, we see that the author regards the integration of opposites as both the cause and the result of this standstill. He identifies the integration of opposites with the standstill. One can in no way agree with this. The integration of opposites is one aspect of the metasystem transition and an indispensable factor in development. Hence the mere presence of that factor does not in any way testify to a cessation of development—a standstill. In the process of development, the integration of opposites takes place because of the creation (and in the process of that creation) of a new level in the control hierarchy which coordinates opposite elements within the framework of the whole.

Let us take a very simple example. The development of the motor apparatus is accompanied by the appearance of muscle fibers whose contractions have mutually opposite results. This is true, for instance of the muscles which flex and unflex extremities in one and the same joint. The simultaneous contraction of these muscles would be senseless. A "struggle" between these "opposites" (to use Hegel's and Marx's terms), or a victory by one of them over the other, would not lead to constructive evolution. Significant evolutionary change (which is also revolutionary change) requires the creation of a rudimentary nervous system to control the contraction of the opposed muscles and make rhythmic movement possible. This is a metasystem transition involving the integration of opposites. It takes place *in the context* of a conflict between opposites, but is by no means confined to it, and is not its direct result. It requires a certain creative effort—requires *rising above* the conflict between opposites.

The integration of opposites does not mean the end of development, but only that the action is shifted to the next higher level. Now the nervous system will be perfected. The simple mechanisms of rhythmic movement will be integrated into a more complex plan of behavior. And here again, the process of development will take place by means of quantitative accumulation and qualitative leaps—metasystem transitions.

Only a person lacking any understanding of the process of evolution could attack "the collusion of Business and Labor within the strong State" as an obstacle to further advance toward "new modes of human existence." Actually, this is a necessary stage through which we cannot avoid passing—a step that must be taken in one way or another. And when that step has been taken we shall have to shift the point of application of our efforts to the next and higher stage—to the sphere of human relations, culture, and the highest goals.

If society is incapable of that shift—of that next metasystem transition—it *is* in fact doomed to a standstill. But if so, that standstill will not occur because of the integration of opposites on the level of material production, but because of much deeper causes in the sphere of culture. It is these causes which should be examined. Meantime, aggravating the conflicts in the production system—or the struggle against other modes of integrating opposites on the lower levels—can bring only regression.

Let us again use the example of muscles by way of explaining this point. When the mechanism for simple rhythmic movement has been developed, the next stage is adapting those movements to the current situation. This requires the presence of sensory organs to provide information on the outside world. Also required is a system for coordinating the movements—for assuring that they are made in accordance with that information. Does a "struggle of opposites" between the flexor muscles and the extensor muscles help to accomplish that task? The simultaneous contraction of opposed muscles is a spasm—something that hardly helps to coordinate movements. All of Marcuse's philosophy is a longing for spasms, and an attempt to provoke them—an attempt that has not been entirely unsuccessful.

His metaphysical mode of thought, and the vagueness of his notions about development, give rise to a false image suggesting that development is caused by the struggle between opposites—rather like the formation of a new substance via the interaction of "opposed" substances, such as acid and alkali. This image further implies that when the reserve of "opposites" is exhausted, development will cease. Marcuse becomes very distressed when he compares how things stand with the critique of capitalist society today, to how they stood when that critique arose in the first half of the nineteenth century. At that time the critique "acquired concreteness," being based on the struggle between two opposed classes, the bourgeoisie and the proletariat. Nowadays,

> In the capitalist world, they are still the basic classes. However, the capitalist development has altered the structure and function of these two classes in such a way that they no longer appear to be agents of historical transformation. An overriding interest in the preservation and improvement of the institutional status quo unites the former antagonists in the most advanced areas of contemporary society.[10]

It would seem that one should conclude, from this fact, that we must shift the critique's point of application—transpose it to new spheres and new levels. That would be the natural reaction of a healthy, creative intellect that sees criticism as an active principle transforming the world. But Marcuse draws no such conclusion. He thinks in terms of Historical Materialism, for which critical thought—indeed every kind of thought—is a reflection of social reality. Critical thinking does not create something new; it is merely a form in which objective social contradictions manifest themselves.

Marcuse writes:

> In the absence of demonstrable agents and agencies of social change, the critique is thus thrown back to a high level of abstraction. There is no ground on which theory and practice, thought and action, meet.[11]

But after all, the demonstrability of agents of social change depends upon the viewpoint from which the critique is made. If we postulate that development can only result from the conflict between the opposed interests of the bourgeoisie and the proletariat, and then find that the opposites have been integrated, we conclude (rather tritely) that development is impossible, and block ourselves off from any further investigation. The best that Marcuse can expect is an explosion—the destruction of society.

In his own words:

> *One-Dimensional Man* will vacillate throughout between two contradictory hypotheses: (1) that advanced industrial society is capable of containing qualitative change for the foreseeable future; (2) that forces and tendencies exist which may break this containment and explode the society.[12]

The possibility of constructive evolution is rejected even as a hypothesis. There is no such concept—only the status quo or a spasmodic tension between opposing forces which breaks the existing regulators and throws society back to the Golden Age of Marxist critiques (the first half of the nineteenth century).

If on the one hand Marcuse's Historical Materialism makes him cancel out the role of creative thought, on the other hand it causes him to make a fetish of technology and technological progress. It is the same kind of fetishism we find in official Soviet Marxism, but with a minus sign. Marcuse sees modern industrial technology as the root of all evil; or, more precisely, as the source of stagnation.

> In this [industrial] society, the productive apparatus tends to become totalitarian to the extent to which it determines not only the socially needed occupations, skills, and attitudes, but also individual needs and aspirations.[13]

And again:

> By virtue of the way it has organized its technological base, contemporary industrial society tends to be totalitarian. For "totalitarian" is not only a terroristic political coordination of society, but also a non-terroristic economic-technical coordination which operates through the manipulation of needs by vested interests.[14]

A person can write about totalitarianism in this way, and entertain this notion of it, only if he denies that man is able to rise above his environment, or at any rate denies the importance of that ability in historical development. Because technology changes only the *milieu* of each individual and nothing more.

From a biological viewpoint, this new milieu is not less but more favorable for life in its higher forms. It assures satisfaction of biological needs, increases longevity, and provides more leisure time. If under such conditions those forms of life we are observing display a tendency toward stagnation rather than development, the causes are to be sought not on the material-technological level but on that of ideology and politics. In particular, the totalitarian blind alley is an ideological and political phenomenon. It arrests development by the massive physical suppression of free thought and creativity. Here the individual is opposed not by a passive environment but by an active human force. So long as no such opposition or active suppression of freedom exists, one cannot call a society totalitarian, because that would mean changing the essence of the concept. (Comrade Marcuse simply does not know what real totalitarianism is!)

Even though the New Left movement has proven incapable of making a constructive contribution to the evolution of society, it is (nevertheless) of evolutionary origin. It has shown that (primarily among the young, of course) society contains an evolutionary potential—a need to go beyond the limits of the given, to effect a metasystem transition. Marcuse's critique is based on the conceptual apparatus of Historical Materialism, which dooms it to sterility. But I fully understand his intentions and feelings. The essence of his charge against Western society is that, of all the aspects of evolution, it has preserved only one—scientific and technological progress—while in all other respects it has ceased to evolve and has lost its creative potential. Obviously, it was this that attracted students to his philosophy.

The chief target of his critique, then, is the individual's lack of inner freedom from society—the lack of that "private space" that is indispensable to creativity. Because of that lack, both man and society are becoming "one-dimensional"; they are losing that dimension "perpendicular" to the order of things:

> Today this private space has been invaded and whittled down by technological reality. Mass production and mass distribution claim the *entire* individual, and industrial psychology has long since ceased to be confined to the factory. The manifold processes of introjection seem to be ossified in almost mechanical reactions. The result is, not adjustment but *mimesis:* an immediate identification of the individual with *his* society and, through it, with the society as a whole.
>
> This immediate, automatic identification (which may have been characteristic of primitive forms of association) reappears in high industrial civilization; its new "immediacy," however, is the product of a sophisticated, scientific management and organization. In this process,

> the "inner" dimension of the mind in which opposition to the status quo can take root is whittled down. The loss of this dimension, in which the power of negative thinking—the critical power of Reason—is at home, is the ideological counterpart to the very material process in which advanced industrial society silences and reconciles the opposition.[15]

If we leave aside the satanic role that Marcuse assigns to industrial technology and scientific progress, his charge that modern Western society is "one-dimensional" very likely has a basis. In any case, Marcuse's critique has in this respect a forward orientation and not a backward one. And in the last part of *One-Dimensional Man,* where he sketches some possible alternatives, the general orientation of his thought is likewise forward. He conceives of one alternative as a "transcendent project" (almost a metasystem transition); i.e., a program going beyond the limits of what is accepted and recognized in societal life. It is also a pleasure to read those passages in which Marcuse gives the imagination its due as a factor in historical development. The New Leftists' slogan "power to the imagination," their serious attitude toward utopian thought, and the call for "redefining needs"—such things have always struck a responsive chord in me. It seems to me indisputable that any solution to the problems facing contemporary society demands radical change and a break with many of the notions and principles that today's public opinion regards as absolute and not subject to revision.

But merely to recognize the necessity for a "transcendent project" is not enough. One must endow that project with at least some rough lines; and that assumes a definite theory as to the causes of the present situation. Although Marcuse makes some corrections to Marx's theory of value and his concept of alienation, his own theory remains Marxist. He seeks (and assumes he will find) the causes of the drop in society's creative potential, and of the flourishing of consumerism, in the mode of production: industrial technology, class relations, etc. I regard this as nonsensical. The mode of production is important as a milieu, a background, but it does not determine the course of events. For example, the environment may be more or less favorable to the development of pathogenic bacteria; but the nature and course of the disease are determined by the kind of bacteria present, not by the environment. And until we ascertain what kind they are we shall make no headway in curing the disease. In this example, as everywhere else, we see one and the same law at work: the lower levels of the hierarchy create the conditions; the higher levels determine the course of events.

The situation that has provoked the criticism from the New Left may, I think, be described in more direct terms as the culture's lack of a supreme goal. Or at any rate, of the kind that would satisfy the young people and be accepted by them as supreme. We are witnessing, in contemporary Western society, the erosion of that stratum of the culture (the *religious* stratum in the broadest sense of the word) which provides answers to questions about the meaning of life. Hence that segment of the culture concerned with material production and consumption is occupying an ever more dominant position, and is becoming the highest level in the hierarchy of ideas and behavior plans. It is precisely here, in the historical erosion of the culture's religious stratum, and not in one or another monstrous trait of the modern mode of production, that we find the cause of that phenomenon known as "the consumer society." That dimension "perpendicular" to reality, whose disappearance Marcuse writes about, is the dimension of higher goals.

In a consumer society (and here I am in complete agreement with the New Left's critique) the higher goals are set not by people but by the production apparatus. People no longer create and command; they merely place themselves into the milieu they have created. Society becomes incapable of constructive evolution.

From this view of the situation, it follows that a constructive critique of modern industrial society must begin with a look at the question of the supreme goal. That question is central. And it is a bottleneck: the measure of successful forward movement in dealing with that question is the measure of forward movement in solving all other problems.

Marcuse virtually ignores this question. He gets around it with some rather vague remarks about a "more human" way of life; and, like Whitehead, talks about "perfecting the art of living." Other authors do the same thing. It is as if they all proceeded from the assumption that the problem of the meaning of life will solve itself, and that the answer to the question is more or less clear to everyone, and so there really is no such question. But there is. And in this age, when we have learned how to produce necessities on a scale undreamed of by our forebears, it has become an especially burning one. For the first time in human history, it has become a question *for the masses* and not merely for a tiny elite.

We are faced with a choice. Such is our nature that our goals, our needs, our desires are not something fixed, or something handed down to us from above. To a large extent, they depend upon the supreme goal that we, on our own, set for ourselves. Then what supreme goal shall we choose? The kind of society we shall have depends upon how we answer that question.

Toffler

As a sort of complement to Marcuse's high-brow language and reasoning, let me review a bestseller book written by a journalist for millions of unsophisticated readers—*Future Shock* by Alvin Toffler.[16] Having chiefly the U.S. in mind, Toffler draws a picture of an industrial society becoming a "post-industrial" one. The dynamics of that transformation, the scope and swiftness of the changes, stagger the imagination. Herewith a few paraphrases of scattered passages.

More and more throw-away articles are being manufactured. Paper napkins. Cardboard trays. Handkerchief-type tissues. A toothbrush with the paste already on it, which you throw away after using once. Thousands of new consumer and other products appear on the market every year.

The mobility of the population—both in terms of travel, and in the sense of changing homes—is constantly increasing. In 1967, 108 million Americans traveled 360 million miles. The average car owner in the U.S. drives 10,000 miles a year. Four million Americans go abroad every year. Spain alone is visited by 1.5 million vacationing Germans each year. Every year, 37 million Americans change their homes, usually because of a new job. In each new edition of the Baltimore telephone directory, more than half of the names have changed.

New companies are formed, and old ones reorganized, at a dizzying rate. In 1967–69 the Questor Corporation bought eight companies and sold two. More flexible and dynamic forms of organization are being used in industry, science, and social life. The traditional stable bureaucracy is giving place to ad hoc organizations, which die a natural death after they have accomplished their assigned task. When the Lockheed Corporation obtained a contract to build 58 giant military transport planes, it set up a special organization of 11,000 people to coordinate the production of 120,000 parts for those planes—parts manufactured at the plants of 6,000 companies.

Scientific developments are becoming a central part of all peoples' lives. Already, more than 13,000 Americans have pacemakers; another 10,000 have had heart valves made of synthetic material implanted surgically. In the works are implantable hearing aids and artificial arteries, kidneys, and lungs. The biological revolution is almost upon us. The agenda includes genetic engineering (producing animals with specific hereditary traits); the reproduction of an entire human organism from the nucleus of a single somatic (not germ) cell (an organism genetically identical to the donor of the cell nucleus); the growing of a human embryo outside the mother's body; and the production of "Cyborgs"—hybrids that are part human and part machine:

> Today we struggle to make heart valves or artificial plumbing that imitate the original they are designed to replace. We strive for functional equivalence. Once we have mastered the basic problems, however, we shall not merely install plastic aortas in people because their original aorta is about to fail. We shall install specially-designed parts that are *better* than the original, and then we shall move on to install parts that provide the user with capabilities that were absent in the first place. Just as genetic engineering holds out the promise of producing "super-people," so, too, does organ technology suggest the possibility of track stars with extra-capacity lungs or hearts; sculptors with a neural device that intensifies sensitivity to texture; lovers with sex-intensifying neural machinery. In short, we shall no longer implant merely to save a life, but to enhance it—to make possible the achievement of moods, states, conditions or ecstasies that are presently beyond us.[17]

As labor productivity increases, the percentage of people employed in the production of necessities will decrease. A small percentage of the U.S. population supplies the nation with the food it needs. The proportion of people employed in industry is decreasing, while the share of those in the service sector is growing. But the service sector, as it exists today, will likewise soon cease to expand. Here, too, automation will result (and already is resulting) in huge labor savings. The emphasis is shifting to esthetics and psychology.

> We shall also witness a revolutionary expansion of certain industries whose sole output consists not of manufactured goods, nor even of ordinary services, but of preprogrammed "experiences." The experience industry could turn out to be one of the pillars of super-industrialism, the very foundation, in fact, of the post-service economy.
>
> As rising affluence and transience ruthlessly under-

> cut the old urge to possess, consumers begin to collect experiences as consciously and passionately as they once collected things. Today . . . experiences are sold as an adjunct to some more traditional service. The experience is, so to speak, the frosting on the cake. As we advance into the future, however, more and more experiences will be sold strictly on their own merits, exactly as if they *were* things.[18]

And yet in reading Toffler, one very soon begins to feel depressed, because in all this rapid movement, this haste, this pursuit of "experiences," something very necessary and important is lacking: a meaning, a purpose.

Only in the last 40 pages of a 500-plus page book, does Toffler deal with the question of the purpose of activity. And when he does, he discusses not really purpose but a procedural question: How to set goals "democratically" (something I shall return to later). In the rest of the book, where Toffler describes the processes that are taking place in today's society (and will take place in the near future), the notion of a goal is quite simply lacking, as if such a notion did not exist. As if the reader should not or could not, put to himself the question that is fundamental for any intelligent being: *Why?*

We see the tremendous acceleration in the turnover of things; but we are offered no judgments as to what is good in all this, and what is bad. We see a tremendous increase in people's mobility, an ever-faster shifting from place to place. Also, Toffler believes that relationships among people are becoming ever more transient; but we don't learn how the Americans themselves feel about it. We are told of plans for refined sensual gratification; but we do not learn whether this is all that the post-industrial society will be able to offer us, or there will be something else. As for spiritual culture, it is completely ignored. Not a single word is said about literature, art, philosophy, religion; or about their influence on the society of the present and that of the near future. It remains unclear to a foreign reader, whether spiritual culture actually plays no significant role in American society, or whether this omission reflects only the author's view of things.

At the very beginning of his book, Toffler sets forth his subject as follows:

> This book is about change and how we adapt to it. It is about those who seem to thrive on change, who crest its waves joyfully, as well as those multitudes of others who resist it or seek flight from it. It is about our capacity to adapt. It is about the future and the shock that its arrival brings.[19]

In the picture that Toffler paints, change is seen as something external both to the individual and to society as a whole. It is not man who creates change in his striving for certain goals, but change that creates man and forces him to adapt to it. (Presumably, change is determined by "the objective laws of the movement of matter," although this Marxist formulation is not found in the book.) And whoever cannot adapt to change falls a victim to "future shock." Says Toffler: "Future shock is the dizzying disorientation brought on by the premature arrival of the future. It may well be the most important disease of tomorrow."[20]

(How curious that people living in the same society at the same time, see completely opposite things in it! Marcuse sees lack of change, stagnation, and calls for change at any cost. Toffler sees a superabundance of change, and sets up plans to help people adapt to it. What the two have in common is that neither offers any concept of constructive change—of evolution.)

According to Toffler, then, only the conformist, has a chance of remaining mentally healthy in this "Brave New World." Of course Toffler does not use these epithets: he is enthusiastic about the future. This leaves me somewhat puzzled as to his way of thinking. Is his stance a literary device like that of the anti-utopians? Or does he think this spectacle of energetic fuss devoid of higher purposes should arouse positive feelings?

Whatever Toffler's thoughts about this may have been, his book struck me as the gloomiest of anti-utopias. The usual thing in an anti-utopian work is to present a society in a state of eternal stagnation. Toffler, however, performs a very instructive experiment. Instead of using the future as a setting, he describes the present, and keeps intact all the intensity of change that is characteristic of it. Then he projects certain changes into the near future—making predictions that are altogether sound and plausible. He takes away, however, any purpose from those changes, and leaves it up to the reader to judge the results.

The concept of creativity vanishes at the outset. It is amusing, by the way, that the word "creativity" is not even deemed worthy of a separate listing in the index. If you look for it, you will find: "Creativity, *see* Imagination." But imagination is hardly the same thing as creativity. The latter implies going beyond the limits of the individual: from the subjective into the objective sphere. Imagination may serve as a tool of creativity; but then again it may not. It may well run idle, engendering "experiences" and nothing more.

Life without creativity is a distressing spectacle. Essentially, it is the same thing as the torpor in Huxley's and Orwell's classic anti-utopias. Almost everyone is familiar with one of the first experiments which demonstrated that there are pleasure centers in an animal's brain. An electrode was implanted in the brain of a rat, so that an electric current could be sent to the desired point. When the rat pressed down on a pedal, the circuit was closed and the rat experienced pleasure. Once the animal had made this discovery, it began to press down on the pedal continuously. Are we to share the rat's fate? It is dismaying to read such prophecies by Toffler as the following:

> Future experience designers will, for example, create gambling casinos in which the customer plays not for money, but for experiential payoffs—a date with a lovely and willing lady if he wins, perhaps a day in solitary confinement if he loses. As the stakes rise, more imaginative payoffs and punishments will be designed.

A loser may have to serve (by voluntary preagreement) as a "slave" to a winner for several days. A winner may be rewarded by ten free minutes of electronic pleasure-probing of his brain. A player may risk flogging or its psychological equivalent—participation in a day-long session during which winners are permitted to work off their aggressions and hostilities by sneering, shouting at, reviling, or otherwise attacking the ego of the loser.

High rollers may play to win a free heart or lung transplant at some later date, should it prove to be necessary. Losers may have to forego a kidney. Such payoffs and punishments may be escalated in intensity and varied endlessly. Experiential designers will study the pages of Krafft-Ebing or the Marquis de Sade for ideas. Only imagination, technological capability, and the constraints of a generally relaxed morality limit the possibilities.[21]

The diversity of novel experiences arrayed before the consumer will be the work of experience-designers, who will be drawn from the ranks of the most creative people in the society. The working motto of this profession will be: "If you can't serve it up real, find a vicarious substitute. If you're good, the customer will never know the difference!" This implied blurring of the line between the real and the unreal will confront the society with serious problems, but it will not prevent or even slow the emergence of the "psyche-service industries" and "psyche-corps." Great globe-girdling syndicates will create super-Disneylands of a variety, scale, scope, and emotional power that is hard for us to imagine.[22]

Antireligion

The last 40 pages of *Future Shock* I mentioned make up a chapter entitled "The Strategy of Social Futurism." It begins as follows:

> Can one live in a society that is out of control? That is the question posed for us by the concept of future shock. For that is the situation we find ourselves in. If it were technology alone that had broken loose, our problems would be serious enough. The deadly fact is, however, that many other social processes have also begun to run free, oscillating widely, resisting our best efforts to guide them.[23]

Toffler finds incorrect planning, based on the principles of technocracy, to be the chief cause of society's going out of control. Technocracy takes the production of material wealth as its cornerstone. It engenders a drive to maximize production, while all other goals and aspects of life are ignored. But in our time, says Toffler, it is precisely these other goals and aspects which are taking on decisive significance and determining people's social behavior. Technocratic planning is "econocentric" and hence incapable of correctly predicting the social results of various decisions.

Toffler's critique of technocratic planning is accurate and well-founded. But I very much doubt whether planning can be blamed for the loss of control in society. Is it not more likely that the cause of the lack of control lies in the fact that there is no consensus as to any common goal (something which should be present in a free society), or no strict system of compulsion (such as is found in a totalitarian society)?

Toffler writes:

> Today, mounting evidence that society is out of control breeds disillusionment with science. In consequence, we witness a garish revival of mysticism. Suddenly astrology is the rage. Zen, yoga, seances, and witchcraft become popular pastimes.[24]

I doubt this explanation very much. Is it not more probable that these crazes are fostered by dissatisfaction with the system of values, and by a search for higher spiritual values?

I completely agree with Toffler that a new strategy for solving social problems is needed. But what strategy? What kind of value system is needed?

> In its historical time and place, industrial society's single-minded pursuit of material progress served the human race well. As we hurtle toward super-industrialism, however, a new ethos emerges in which other goals begin to gain parity with, and even supplant those of economic welfare. In personal terms, self-fulfillment, social responsibility, aesthetic achievement, hedonistic individualism, and an array of others vie with and often overshadow the raw drive for material success. Affluence serves as a base from which men begin to strive for varied post-economic ends.[25]

Toffler is quite correct in saying that the goals of economic welfare are being supplanted by an "array" of other goals. But if that array, or horde, does not form a system, a hierarchy, and hence has no commander-in-chief, life will be aimless and depressing. And society—if it is possible at all—will be out of control.

Having many goals means not having any one goal. Sensuous pleasures are marvelous and indispensable. But that cybernetic system called a human being is so constructed that in addition to sensuous pleasures and a diversity of experience, it needs a certain supreme goal. Without it, the human cybernetic system breaks down. You get bored. You get sick or old before your time. You become a neurotic. You go insane. You commit suicide.

An article published in the *Readers Digest* in 1976, begins as follows:

> Despite its extraordinary variety of diversions and resources, its frenzy for spectacles and its feverish pursuit of entertainment, America is bored. The abundance of efforts made in the United States to counter boredom have defeated themselves, and boredom has become the disease of our time. No authority is willing to guess at the number of people who are bored, but there are millions, and the number is growing.
>
> Young people are particularly subject to boredom. Dr. M. Robert Wilson, psychiatrist-in-chief at the Constance Bultman Wilson Center, in Faribault, Minn., who

> specializes in problems of the young, estimates that as many as 20 percent of American adolescents are handicapped by significant boredom and depression. This handicap often leads to loss of self-esteem and, in extreme cases, to suicide. In fact, suicide has risen drastically among adolescents in America; the rate has doubled among 15- to 25-year-olds since 1960, and suicide is now the second leading cause of death among teenagers.
>
> One of the most grisly mass killings in recent American history—the Charles Manson "family" murders—was committed, in the opinion of some experts, as a result of boredom.[26]

Toffler's book exemplifies a doctrine that might be called *antireligion*. It is the liberal democratic doctrine transplanted from the sphere of politics to that of culture. The credo of antireligion goes as follows: The goals a person sets for himself are his own business, and to meddle in them is unethical—tantamount to physical coercion. The establishment by society of a hierarchy of goals is not to be tolerated, and a socially defined concept of a supreme goal is even less to be tolerated. It is almost the same thing as the dictatorship of the bureaucracy, or of the Supreme Potentate.

Antireligion arises in a liberal democratic society as a result of religion's collapse. Liberal democracy came into being within the framework of Christian culture as a means of achieving a supreme goal organically tied to definite notions about human life. It has since metamorphosed from a means into an end in itself. Politics is encroaching on culture. Some kind of agreement as to goals is indispensable in a society, so agreement as to the absence of a supreme goal replaces the agreement as to its presence that characterized religious society. But this symmetry is very relative. The presence of a supreme goal assures social integration. Its absence, elevated to the status of a principle, leads to society's disintegration.

> Acceleration produces a faster turnover of goals, a greater transience of purpose. Diversity or fragmentation

> leads to a relentless multiplication of goals. Caught in this churning, goal-cluttered environment, we stagger, future shocked, from crisis to crisis, pursuing a welter of conflicting and self-cancelling purposes.
>
> Nowhere is this more starkly evident than in our pathetic attempts to govern our cities. New Yorkers, within a short span, have suffered a nightmarish succession of near disasters: a water shortage, a subway strike, racial violence in the schools, a student insurrection at Columbia University, a garbage strike, a housing shortage, a fuel oil strike, a breakdown of telephone service, a teacher walkout, a power blackout, to name just a few. . . .
>
> This is not to say no one is planning. On the contrary; in this seething social brew, technocratic plans, sub-plans and counter-plans pour forth. They call for new highways, new roads, new power plants, new schools. They promise better hospitals, housing, mental health centers, welfare programs. But the plans cancel, contradict and reinforce one another by accident. Few are logically related to one another, and none to any overall image of the preferred city of the future. No vision—utopian or otherwise—energizes our efforts. No rationally integrated goals bring order to the chaos. And at the national and international levels, the absence of coherent policy is equally marked and doubly dangerous.[27]

But why is there no integrated system of goals? Why is there no "vision"? Again, Toffler puts the blame on the technocrats. He tells us that three successive presidents—Eisenhower, Johnson, and Nixon—set up special organizations to work out a system of goals for planning. But all these attempts were unsuccessful because (in Toffler's opinion) they bore "the unmistakable imprint of the technocratic mentality."[28] That is, they evaded what Toffler regards as the basic question: Who is to set goals for the future? For Toffler, the "revolutionary, new" approach to goal-setting that is needed consists in making that process more democratic:

> The time has come for a dramatic reassessment of the directions of change, a reassessment made not by the politicians or the sociologists or the clergy or the elitist revolutionaries, not by technicians or college presidents, but by the people themselves. We need, quite literally, to "go to the people" with a question that is almost never asked of them: "What kind of a world do you want ten, twenty, or thirty years from now?" We need to initiate, in short, a continuing plebiscite on the future.[29]

His idea is to convene, in each nation, in each city, in each neighborhood, democratic assemblies charged with defining specific social goals for the remainder of the century. Such assemblies could represent both geographic and social units. All must have equal rights in determining the future—prominent intellectuals and people who are inarticulate alike. He calls this scheme "anticipatory democracy," by analogy with "participatory democracy."

"To some," Toffler writes, "this appeal for a form of neopopulism will no doubt seem naive."[30] I must admit that I am of that number. The naïveté of the scheme borders on the absurd. It is like trying to prove the correctness or incorrectness of a mathematical theorem by means of a majority vote. The problem of a rational integration of goals—of a "vision" of the future—is a cultural problem, not a political one. It is solved not by voting, not by a compromise among interests, but by long, hard work in the form of creative activity, for goals can be rationally integrated only by introducing higher goals and values, and building a hierarchy of goals. Unlike lower-level goals ("I want a future with lots of honey in it, and pancakes with syrup, and a scenic view from my window"), the higher ones cannot be expressed in concrete concepts. They demand the creation of abstract and generalized images that must be given currency so that they enter into the life of the masses. This is the job of writers, philosophers, prophets, scientists, film directors, and many other creative people.

But what will Toffler's assemblies do? Coordinate orders for pancakes and for scenic views? The hallmark of true democracy is the general public's participation in culture and not just in plebiscites.

In the final analysis, the integration of goals requires one supreme goal. Certainly Toffler's intention to involve the masses in setting goals for the future is a sound idea, but the main feature in any such scheme must be the concept of a supreme goal, which essentially means the founding of a religious movement.

Goals and plans possess the property of forming a hierarchy, and they are determined from the top down: the goals and plans of the lower level are determined by those of the upper level, but never vice versa. This is of course all very "undemocratic," but there's nothing one can do about it. Such is the nature of goals and plans. Toffler, however, is unwilling to accept this fact. One of his strongest charges against the technocrats (pity the poor technocrats—the scapegoats for everything!) is that they plan from the top down and not from the bottom up:

> The continuation of top-down technocratic goal-setting procedures will lead to greater and greater social instability, less and less control over the forces of change; and ever greater danger of cataclysmic, man-destroying upheaval.[31]

This also accounts for the moral enthusiasm in Toffler's scheme, which he declares to be a "breath-taking affirmation of popular democracy."[32] Here the goals are determined from the bottom up, the only way acceptable to genuine democrats—fighters against technocrats, bureaucrats, hierarchies, and other vestiges of the accursed past. This is an example of violence being committed upon reality by political ideology—upon knowledge by the will. The Soviet people are familiar with many instances of that phenomenon. In the Soviet Union, the conformist toadies to the ruler; in the West, he toadies to mass man: the reader, the buyer, the voter. In the Soviet Union he declares that the key to all problems is Marxism-Leninism; in the West he says that key is democracy.

Toffler's "anticipatory democracy" provides a logical ending for his anti-utopia. During the first nine-tenths of the book we saw only the commotion of a world without a supreme goal. Now we get a kind of theoretical explanation of why a supreme goal is unnecessary—why all we need is to gather information as to what goals people *have*.

"Anticipatory democracy" is equality among ideas; it is an antireligion. Toffler's anti-utopia is a product of his antireligion. But there is one circumstance the author of *Future Shock* does not take into account. Whether this utopia can be realized depends, in a very serious way, upon the neighbors of the "post-industrial society." Because a society in which the most creative minds are engaged in erasing the line between reality and illusion, and getting their ideas from the Marquis de Sade, can hardly offer much resistance to totalitarianism.

It is interesting to note that Toffler's system of concepts, like any such system lacking the concept of creativity, is deterministic. He insists on the necessity of *studying* the future—a phrase I find quite unacceptable. In one passage he puts it very resolutely: "it is time to erase, once and for all, the popular myth that the future is 'unknowable.' "[33]

My own slogan is "The future is unpredictable." This divergence is of course a relative one: both parties to the dispute realize that predictions of the future are, first, possible; and, second, incomplete. The difference is a matter of emphasis; i.e., it depends on which aspect is placed in the foreground. Toffler sees the future in the light of individualism. Each member of society, finding himself in definite social conditions common to many people, is guided by his own personal interests. According to the law of large numbers, the result of the totality of these people's actions may be predicted with a great degree of accuracy. I, however, envisage society as a unified super-being capable of a creative act—the metasystem transition. The results of that act are unpredictable, because a metasystem transition involves self-description and self-knowledge. This means that all the predictions we make are information that we must take into account. (In mathematics, this corresponds to Gödel's theorem and other "negative" results.) We can predict the future only in the segments between one metasystem transition and another. For me, however, life's greatest charm is found precisely in these gaps in predictability—in these creative acts.

The Depoliticization of Socialism

It is my belief that the Western world can control the totalitarianism that it itself created only by depriving the latter of its monopoly on conscious social integration. In other words, totalitarianism can ultimately be conquered only by socialism. Needless to say, I do not have in mind those political parties which now call themselves socialist or communist. What I do have in mind is socialism as a cultural phenomenon, in the sense in which I defined it in part II.

Contemporary socialism, as a political phenomenon, does not incline one toward optimism. On the right wing we find the social democrats, for whom the idea of social integration is confined to the economic and financial spheres. It can offer no more attractive ideal than a consumer society. On the left wing we find the radical socialists, all of whom think in Marxist terms (which makes them potential or actual peddlers of totalitarianism and not fighters against it). Apparently, the negative element is prevailing over the positive one; the struggle for power is prevailing over the struggle for ideas.

It is most interesting to observe that the Communists, unlike the more moderate social democrats and socialists, have suddenly shown a strong tendency toward nationalism. Communism has become nationalistic.

How did that happen? After all, the Communists regard themselves as the most loyal followers of Marx. And whatever his faults may be, being a nationalist is not one of them.

The underlying fact is that the real force that has made Communism strong is its will for integration—that, and the resultant system of values and stress on organization. From the very beginning of their careers, Marx and Engels assumed that the proletariat constitute a unique, worldwide "people"—an ethos. In this sense, Marxism has always been an ideology of ethnic unity. But the twentieth century has shown very plainly that human beings much prefer to think of themselves as members of a nation rather than as members of a class. The division between classes has been eroded, but then it was never so clear as the division between ethnic groups.

The twentieth century has become the century of nationalism. After the decline of the great religions, the nation became the only—or, in any case, the most popular—basis of integration. Somewhat belatedly, even the Communists realized this. Ethnic integration is based on spiritual culture; and class integration on material interests. Ethos has proven stronger than class—something which once again shows the primacy of the spiritual principle in humanity. Not wanting to relinquish their culture medium, the Communists and the radical socialists have been backsliding into nationalism.

Even today, however, the left-wing Marxists apparently differ little from the Leninist Bolsheviks. This means that one can expect, if they accede to power, the same kind of thing we got in Russia from the Bolsheviks. Thus Leszek Kolakowski reports the following conversation with a Latin American revolutionary on the subject of torture in Brazil:

> I will quote to you a talk with a Latin American revolutionary who told me about torture in Brazil. I asked: "What is wrong with torture?" He said: "What do you mean? Do you suggest it is all right? Are you justifying torture?" And I said: "On the contrary, I simply ask if you think torture is a morally inadmissible monstrosity." "Of course," he replied. "And so is torture in Cuba?" I asked. "Well," he answered, "this is another thing. Cuba is a small country under the constant threat of American imperialists. They have to use all means of self-defense, however regrettable."[34]

I was reminded of that episode recently, when I was talking with a young Englishman—a non-Communist leftist. We were discussing the notion of the "historical compromise" that Berlinguer had just proposed.

"How do you feel," I asked him, "about a coalition between the Communists and the Christian democrats?"

He thought it over, and then replied: "That kind of coalition could be regarded as a positive phenomenon if in the future it made it possible to form a purely leftist government without any Christian democrats."

Well, I thought to myself, I wouldn't want to be in the same coalition with *those* boys! Because basically the young Englishman was thinking in the same terms as the Latin American Kolakowski had talked to. The approach is the same: a Leninist approach.

It may well be that Berlinguer does not think in those terms; but the Italian Communist Party consists of other people besides him. And in what terms do most of the Communists think? The Italian Communist Party constantly stresses its commitment to human rights, and the French Communists have recently been saying the same thing. Both openly condemn the treatment of dissidents in the Soviet Union. This marks a distinct shift in the international communist movement, and gives rise to the hope that ultimately that movement may play a positive role in history. But that will require the intellectual and moral rebirth of radical socialism. First of all, radical socialism must relinquish the nihilistic and destructive aspects of Marxism, and Leninist politicization too. But even that will not suffice. A complete overhaul of the theoretical baggage is essential, and so are new, lively ideas. Without this restructuring of its basis, the very "integrationism" of the left-wing socialist movement—its distinguishing and attractive trait—will inevitably engender the kind of integration that is mechanistic and totalitarian.

The present state of radical socialism is one that can be described only as intellectual and spiritual impoverishment. When I come across a non-Soviet Marxist magazine or book, I can't get over how much it resembles Soviet publications.

The same poverty of thought; the same dead phrases learned by rote; the same vulgar—almost cartoonish—politicization; and the same self-righteousness.

One more comment from Kolakowski:

> When I was leaving Poland at the end of 1968 (I had not been in any Western country for at least six years), I had a somewhat vague idea of what the radical student movement and different Leftist groups or parties might be. What I saw and read I found pathetic and disgusting in nearly all (still: not all) cases. I do not shed tears for a few windows smashed in demonstrations; that old bitch, consumer capitalism, will survive it. Neither do I find scandalous the rather natural ignorance of young people. What impressed me was mental degradation of a kind I have never seen before in any Leftist movement.
>
> I saw young people trying to "reconstitute" universities and to liberate them from horrifying, savage, monstrous, fascist oppression. The list of demands, with variations, was very similar all over the world of campuses. These fascist pigs of the Establishment want us to pass examinations while we are making the Revolution; let them give all of us A-grades without examinations. Very often there were demands for abolishing altogether some subjects of teaching as irrelevant, *e.g.*, foreign languages.
>
> In one place revolutionary philosophers went on strike because they got a reading list including Plato, Descartes and other bourgeois idiots, instead of relevant great philosophers like Che Guevara and Mao. . . . In another place, the noble martyrs of the world revolution demanded to be examined only by other students they would choose themselves, and not by these old reactionary pseudo-scholars. Professors should be appointed (by students, of course) according to their political views, students admitted on the same grounds. In several cases in the U.S. the vanguard of the oppressed toiling masses set fire to University libraries (irrelevant pseudo-knowledge of the Establishment). And all were Marxists, of course, which meant they knew three or four sentences written by Marx or Lenin, in particular the sen-

> tence "the philosophers have only interpreted the world, in various ways; the point, however, is to change it." (What Marx wanted to say in this sentence, it is obvious to them, was that it made no sense to learn.)[35]

Today, the ideological framework of socialism is limited to economics and politics, which looms large among the causes of socialist thought's pathetic state. Radical socialism attracts people with strong religious feelings, but it cannot satisfy them. In radical socialism, the religious element has a kind of underground existence, in organizational and political practice.

Only by understanding socialism as a phenomenon of spiritual culture—only by incorporating in it a religious concept of the world and humanity—can we get out from under the "consumer society." Neither a nonreligious liberal democratic society, nor a socialist democratic society, nor Soviet totalitarianism is capable of this. It is interesting that the officially proclaimed supreme goal of Soviet society is "the maximum satisfaction of the ever-growing material and spiritual needs of Soviet man." That is a very accurate formulation of what a consumer society is.

Marxism-Leninism preaches in theory (and puts into practice), an extreme politicization of all aspects of societal life. On every hand it sees (and where it does not see it, it plants it!) the struggle for political power. But what the world needs now is the opposite—a *depoliticization* of the most important aspects of life. The success of Amnesty International, and its growing influence, show that more and more people on Planet Earth are beginning to realize this. The basic idea of Amnesty International is to depoliticize the notions of individual rights and political rights, and to show that torture and other kinds of inhuman treatment of human beings are not to be tolerated. From time immemorial these matters have been classified as political. Now Amnesty International is shifting them to the sphere of universal morality—to the sphere of spiritual culture.

A paradox: How can one depoliticize the concept of *po-*

litical rights? But AI is doing it. It is doing it by means of refraining from *the struggle for power* and everything associated with it. It has completely and emphatically refrained from favoring one political regime or trend over another. And this strategy is working. Separating the problem of individual rights from the political struggle makes the former into a cultural question. In my view, this is one of the most promising developments of our times.

The creation of a genuinely socialist culture requires the depoliticizing of socialism. Probably we shall need extrapolitical socialist organizations, and ultimately a single, worldwide organization which, in addition to staying out of struggles for political power will, like AI, scrupulously refrain even from expressing any political preferences. Of course this does not mean that the members of such an organization, like the members of AI, should not *have* political preferences. It is plain to everyone that the people working with AI favor political regimes which more or less respect human rights, and are indignant toward regimes which crudely trample on those rights. But in their work within that organization, they set aside those pro and con feelings. Such, plainly, is the only road to human integration.

Cultural processes are slow; and therein lies the threat of totalitarianism. This is also the basic problem of our time. The ability of the contemporary West's transient culture to stand firm against totalitarianism is doubtful. Which will happen first? Will we get a renewed socio-economic-cultural system that will give the Free World the necessary minimum of unity and firmness? Or will socioeconomic conflicts, the lack of a common will, and the selfishness of separate groups lead to global totalitarianism?

The course of events in the Soviet Union will play the key role in the race between these two processes. Russia was the first of the developing nations to enter the totalitarian phase, and it has become one of the world's two superpowers. Its example—not to mention its direct political-economic influence—will largely determine the fate of other countries. If Russia proves able to begin humanizing and liberalizing socialism, and to get out of the blind alley of totalitarianism, that will be almost tantamount to a solution of the problem. On the other hand, the stabilization of totalitarianism in Russia will be the signal to step up totalitarian tendencies in other countries. Thus the problem of human rights in the Soviet Union goes far beyond the limits of its national problems: it is one of worldwide scope. In defending human rights in the Soviet Union, a Westerner is showing concern for the future of his descendants.

The Inertia of Fear and One's Worldview

> The reconstruction of our age, then, can begin only with a reconstruction of its theory of the universe. There is hardly anything more urgent in its claim on us than this which seems to be so far off and so abstract. . . .
>
> Every human being who calls himself a man is meant to develop into a real personality within a reflective theory of the universe which he has created for himself.
>
> Albert Schweitzer[36]

But no one can help us if we don't care for ourselves.

When Stalin died, I belonged to that minority of young people who rejoiced at his death, although neither they nor their parents had been heavily repressed. I say "heavily" because my parents had not been arrested, and by the yardstick of those times everything else seemed tolerable. But my mother was from a "middle-peasant" family that had been "dekulakized."[37] In her youth she had had to conceal her origins, and therefore lived in constant fear of exposure. My maternal grandmother was not only dispossessed during collectivization but witnessed the horrible famine in the Ukraine, when entire villages became extinct simply because the "people's" regime took away their last grains of wheat. I remember what she told about Stalin shortly before her death in 1945: "If I could, I would choke him to death with these hands of mine!"

Although for the last fifteen years of her life she had lived in the city, her hands were still those of a peasant—the kind of hands I had read about in Russian and foreign literature: tanned from the sun and wind, with swollen veins and joints.

My father, a professor of soil engineering, was emphatically a non-Party man. He clearly understood the meaning of what was happening, and he passed on that understanding to his children. One strict rule that I was taught early in my childhood was this: outside of the family circle, you never discuss politics, never mention the repressions, and never tell any political anecdotes.

After Stalin's death, however—and especially after 1956—everyone began to talk about politics. It actually became possible, without any great risk, to exert some kind of influence on one's social milieu, if only on the level of trade-union meetings, "wall newspapers," and philosophical seminars. I began trying to make use of that opportunity, and it seemed to me that every normal person should and would do the same. It seemed to me that such things as the struggle for the right to express one's opinion, for public disclosure of facts about our society, or for putting an end to the general practice of toadying to the authorities not only followed necessarily from ethical principles but should yield a spiritual gratification that would justify taking whatever risk was required. And I was astonished when I discovered that the great majority of the people I knew were unwilling to take any risk at all. The most one could count on was that they would be glad if the necessary changes happened by themselves.

In trying to understand this phenomenon, I got into long discussions and arguments. At first they were only about politics and economic matters. But gradually I came to realize that the basic causes determining peoples' behavior lay elsewhere. All the chains of reasoning, starting from concrete, local problems, passed through general political and socioeconomic problems and then, invariably, ran smack up against the basic question: What is the meaning of life?

Previously, I had thought that partial answers to that question (and each person finds some in one way or another; in my case, for example, I had long since decided to devote my life to science) were adequate both for oneself and for society as a whole. But now I realized that they were not. I realized that neither I nor my friends had the general criteria needed to make decisions. I am not referring, of course, to the kind of *formal* criteria that enable one to calculate the value of x, and if it turns out to be more than unity, to say yes, and if it is less than unity, to say no. In the final analysis, a person faced with an ethical choice makes his decision intuitively, in accordance with his own conscience. But intuition is not something hanging free in outer space. The way one's intuition works is determined by one's fundamental system of ideas and values. The question as to the meaning of life cannot be answered in one sentence or a few maxims. The answer to it is one's worldview.

But we had no worldview. We had available a few vestiges of the old and some embryos of the new, but nothing more. And the only discernible force in that vacuum was the inertia of fear: an inertia that was meeting with no resistance and hence had every chance of going on forever.

I refrained more and more from political arguments, and finally gave them up altogether. I learned that even slight differences in the vestiges of a worldview affect social behavior more than all sociopolitical discussion. Logic cannot help convince a person to make a moral effort if he does not know the purpose of his life, or if he knows that his life is not serving that purpose. Behind the critical utterances of such people, I could discern the nauseatingly familiar outlines of "the fig in the pocket."[38] In each argument advanced, I could not help seeing that it was built on the equally familiar law of the logic of self-justification. I realized that I had to synthesize my views of society with my notion of life's meaning—a notion which had previously seemed to me to be a profoundly personal matter. Lacking such a synthesis, I could not find a basis for making specific decisions. The lack of that synthesis meant a vacuum; and in a vacuum, motion due to inertia is never arrested. It became clear to me that the book I was planning—a book about the inertia of fear; or, more accurately, *against* inertia of fear—had to be basically a book about my worldview.

Probably no political revolution in history caused such a rupture of cultural traditions as the Revolution of 1917. In building his worldview, none of us can simply continue some filament of pre-revolutionary Russian culture. We can and should make use of such filaments; but it is not in our power to graft on dead tissue. We must begin from scratch, as people living in an industrial nation toward the end of the twentieth century. This is an experiment of worldwide significance.

I hope that the reader who feels the need for an integrated system of views has found my book interesting. The worldview toward which he is moving, or at which he has arrived, will coincide with mine in some respects, and differ from it in others. In any case, I am certain of one thing: any integrated worldview that can capture a person's interest *and* define the meaning of life for him, will be anti-totalitarian. It will prompt that person to social activism, because the life of Soviet society is degrading and absurd. It renders meaningless everything it touches; and it touches everything. Whatever occupation a Soviet chooses—science, the arts, the manufacture of goods, educating children, or anything else—he will find again and again that his attempts to do something significant will be blocked by totalitarianism. And if he really wants to do something, he'll have to crawl out of the shell of his narrow speciality. (Young boys and girls in totalitarian countries! Don't listen to your parents when they try to teach you the stock-in-trade wisdom of totalitarian man. They are good people, but they have been crippled by years of fear and degradation. They have your best interests in mind, but they are teaching you how to deprive life of meaning. Life is more interesting—and each individual's contribution to it is greater—than they think.)

Today, to struggle for human rights would be a real contribution toward restoring the health of Soviet society. In the final analysis, that struggle cannot be waged without open opposition to totalitarianism—outspoken demands that human rights be respected. No sophistry can circumvent that truth.

Each action in defense of human rights changes the situation in the Soviet Union to some extent. Every ethical act has at least *some* consequences. The Human Rights Movement has already made a breach in the blank wall of totalitarianism.

The dissidents' importance to societal life within the USSR consists in the fact that they are creating a new model of behavior which, merely by the fact of its existence, affects each member of society. Under the present conditions, being a dissident in the USSR means that one necessarily drops out of the system. But in the final analysis, the fate of the system depends upon those who remain in it. Slight changes in the thinking and behavior of many people are what is most needed today. And of course democratization requires that some tangible (not infinitesimally small) part of society strive vigorously for it.

A question one often hears when discussing the subject of human rights and democratization, is: "But what can I do?" In most cases, the question is insincere. The important thing is to *really want* change. Something always *can* be done.

The future is not predetermined. Neither in the case of a single individual, nor in that of society as a whole does there exist an invincible force which will inevitably cast him or it into the abyss. The future depends on *us*—on our collective will and intelligence. It is up to us to make life meaningful.

Notes

Preface

1. A neologism—trans.

2. M. K. Gandhi, *Gandhi's Autobiography: The Story of My Experiments with Truth*, trans. Mahadev Desai (Washington, D.C.: Public Affairs Press, 1954), p. 337.

I. Totalitarianism

1. Arkady Strugatsky and Boris Strugatsky, *Obitaemyi ostrov* (The Inhabited Island) (Moscow: Detskaya literatura Publishing House, 1971), p. 193.

2. The word here translated as "control" is *kontrol'* (meaning "monitoring," "checking," etc.) and not the much stronger *upravlenie* ("managing," "government," etc.) which is used elsewhere in the book with reference to cybernetic systems in expressions like "the control level"—trans.

3. Arkady Strugatsky and Boris Strugatsky, *Obitaemyi ostrov*, original version, *Neva* (The Neva), no. 5 (1969), p. 100. When the novel was being published in book form (see note 1) the phrase "the Unknown Fathers," which played a key role in the story, was apparently found to be too transparent, and was everywhere replaced by the rather meaningless "The Fire-Bearing Creators."

4. Valery Chkalov (1904–38) was a Soviet pilot who made several record-breaking nonstop flights, including one in 1937 from Moscow to Vancouver via the North Pole—trans.

5. Admiral Ivan Papanin (1894–?), a Polar explorer, was in 1937–38 chief of the first Soviet research station in the Central Arctic. P. P. Shirshov, E. K. Fedorov (Fyodorov), and E. T. Krenkel were members of that expedition—trans.

6. A degree roughly equivalent to the American Ph. D.—trans.

7. "Doctor of Sciences" is the highest academic degree awarded in the Soviet Union. The author of this book holds such a degree—trans.

8. "Deprivation of freedom" (*lishenie svobody*) was a phrase introduced into Soviet legal usage in the early days of the regime, to replace "imprisonment." It is still in use as a general term synonymous with "incarceration"; i.e., it covers both imprisonment and confinement in a forced labor camp—trans.

9. Yevgeny Zamyatin, *We*, trans. Mirra Ginsburg (New York: Bantam Books, 1972), p. 180.

10. "Member of the intelligentsia." In some texts (e.g., in historical writings), this word is often left in Russian as untranslatable. I have, however, elsewhere rendered it as "intellectual" or "educated person"—trans.

11. Speech at the 18th Congress of the VKP(b)—All-Union Communist Party (Bolshevik).

12. At the Herzen Pedagogical Institute in Leningrad—trans.

13. Bureaucratic jargon for a panel consisting of the three top-ranking persons (in a department, etc.): one from the administrative section, one from the Party section, and one from the trade-union section—trans.

14. *Otshchepentsy* (sing. *otshchepenets*), a word which might equally well have been rendered as "apostates" or "schismatics." Used as a derogatory term in official statements, it has stronger religious overtones than either of the two more familiar synonyms, *dissident* and *inakomyslyashchyi* ("he who thinks differently")—trans.

15. "A New Russia? A New World?", *Foreign Affairs* (April 1975):482–97.

16. This figure was given out at a seminar for anti-religious propagandists.

17. I have in mind a remark made by Prof. Henri Brugmans: "If you are a Marxist, or if you have at least accepted Historical Materialism, the least disputable principle of Marxism . . ." *See Proceedings of the International Symposium on the 50th Anniversary of the USSR*, published by the International Committee for the Defense of Human Rights in the USSR, Brussels, p. 18.

18. V. I. Lenin, *Sochineniya* (Works), 18:343.

19. René Descartes, *Traité des passions* (Paris: Union Générale d'Editions, 1965), p. 44. English translation, *The Philosophical Works of Descartes*, trans. Elizabeth Haldane and G. R. T. Ross, 2 vols. (London: Cambridge University Press, 1967).

20. See George Miller, Eugene Galanter, and Karl Pribam, *Plans and the Structure of Behavior* (New York: Holt, Rinehart, and Winston, 1960).

21. The MS was delivered, under contract, to the Sovetskaya Rossiya Publishing House in 1970, but was never published in Russian. An English edition was brought out by the Columbia University Press in 1977.

22. By "representations" I mean representations, in the brain, of some parts of the external world; i.e., mental images of outside phenomena.

23. *Volya*, which can mean either "will" or "freedom," or sometimes both together, here definitely means "will."—trans.

24. *Marksistko-leninskaya filosofiya. Istoricheskiy materializm* (Marxist-Leninist Philosophy: Historical Materialism) (3rd ed., Moscow: 1957), p. 5.

25. Franz Mehring, *Karl Marx*, trans. Edward Fitzgerald (New York: Covici and Friede, 1935), p. 61.

26. K. Marx, F. Engels, V. Lenin, *On Historical Materialism* (Moscow: Progress Publishers, 1972; New York: International Publishers, 1974), p. 284.

27. Preface to the book *Lyudvig Feierbakh* (Ludwig Feuerbach), *Sochineniya* (Works), vol. 2 (Moscow/Leningrad, 1926).

28. *Ludwig Feuerbach and the End of Classical German Philosophy*, in Lewis S. Feuer, ed., *Karl Marx and Friedrich Engels: Basic Writings on Politics and Philosophy* (New York: Doubleday Anchor Books, 1959), p. 205.

29. *Ibid*, p. 216.

30. *Ibid*, p. 223.

31. V. I. Lenin, "Report to the 5th Party Congress," *Sochineniya* (Works), 5th ed., 15:297–98.

32. Albert Camus, *L'Homme révolté*, (Paris: Gallimard, 1951). English translation, *The Rebel*, trans. Anthony Bower (New York: Vintage Books, 1956), p. 240.

33. *Marksistsko-leninskaya filosofiya*, p. 381.

34. *Lichnost'*, a word usually rendered as "person" or "personality"—trans.

35. Or "folk," "nation," etc.—trans.

36. M. M. Rosenthal, ed., *Filosofskiy slovar'* (Philosophical Dictionary), 3rd ed. (Moscow, 1972).

37. Jean Jaurès, *Introduction to the History of Socialism*, as quoted in Jean-Jacques Servan-Schreiber, *The American Challenge*, trans. Ronald Steller (New York: Atheneum, 1968), p. 75.

38. Harrison E. Salisbury, ed., *Sakharov Speaks* (New York: Knopf, 1974), pp. 118–25.

39. *Marksistko-leninskaya filosofiya*, p. 357.

40. Her salary was 100 rubles per month, or 90 rubles take-home pay after deduction of the income tax. Except for certain months of the year, the state price for apples is 1 ruble and 50 kopecks per kilogram.

41. K. A. Muravyova, *Chelevek i atmoshera* (Man and the Atmosphere) (Leningrad: Znaniye Society Publishing House, 1974), pp. 36–37.

42. Roughly equivalent to "washing one's dirty linen in public"—trans.

43. *Vertet'*: "to turn" or "to turn around," meaning to make someone dance to your tune—trans.

44. Vladimir Lifshits, *Naznachennyi den'* (The Appointed Day) (Moscow: Sovetskiy pisatel' Publishing House, 1968), pp. 68–69.

45. *Khronika tekushchikh sobytiy* (The Chronicle of Current Events) (New York: Khronika Press), nos. 28–35.

46. *Ibid*, no. 28.

47. *Ibid*, no. 30.

48. This section was written in July 1975. In September of the same year, Vladimir Osipov was sentenced to eight years of incarceration. In December, Sergei Kovalev was sentenced to seven years of incarceration and three years of internal exile. In April 1976, Andrei Tverdokhlebov was sentenced to five years of internal exile. In January 1976, as a result of pressure from world public opinion, Leonid Plyushch was given permission to emigrate. Valentin Moroz was among the five Soviet dissidents exchanged for two Soviet spies in May 1979.

Hundreds were arrested and tried on political charges in 1976–80, including 40 members of "Helsinki Watch groups," whose purpose was to monitor the compliance of the Soviet authorities with the humanitarian provisions of the Helsinki Accord signed in August 1975. Professor Yuri Orlov and Ukrainian writer Mikola Rudenko are among the imprisoned Helsinki monitors. Both are sentenced to seven years of hard labor to be followed by five years of internal exile. One must keep in mind that only a small fraction of political persecution in the USSR becomes known to the human rights activists and to the world at large.

II. Socialism

1. Albert Schweitzer, *The Philosophy of Civilization, Part II: Civilization and Ethics*, trans. C. T. Campion, 2nd ed. (London: A. C. Black, 1929), p. 16.

2. Igor Shafarevich in Alexander Solzhenitsyn, ed., *From Under the Rubble* (Boston: Little, Brown, 1975), p. 28.

3. This passage from Shafarevich's essay is translated directly from the original *samizdat* text, as quoted by Dr. Turchin—trans.

4. *Ibid*.

5. Solzhenitsyn, ed., *From Under the Rubble*, p. 62.

6. *Ibid*, p. 64.

7. *Ludwig Feuerbach and the End of Classical German Philosophy*, in Lewis S.

Feuer, ed., *Karl Marx and Friedrich Engels: Basic Writings on Politics and Philosophy* (New York: Doubleday Anchor Books, 1959), p. 221.

8. Albert Schweitzer, *The Philosophy of Civilization, Part I: The Decay and the Restoration of Civilization*, trans. C. T. Campion, 2nd ed. (London: A. C. Black, 1932), pp. 81–82.

9. V. I. Lenin, *Sochineniya* (Works), 4:236.

10. K. Marx, F. Engels, V. Lenin, *On Historical Materialism*, p. 180.

11. Albert Camus, *L'Homme révolté*, pp. 195–96.

12. *Ibid.*, pp. 220, 221.

13. As is usual in all of the sciences except mathematics, this is not a completely formalized definition, primarily owing to the lack of precision in the concept of "control." But it does permit of further formalization, if (or, more accurately, when) it is needed. Some day, surely, it will be needed; and then a productive method of formalization will be found.

14. A coinage of Teilhard de Chardin.

15. From the viewpoint of logic, the shift from qualities (attributes) to relations was a great stride forward: from one-place predicates to predicates with an arbitrary number of variables. On Hegel's dialectics in this connection, cf. *The Phenomenon of Science*, chapter 6.

16. From Mayakovsky's narrative poem, *Vladimir Ilich Lenin.*

17. Herbert Spencer, *Reasons for Dissenting from the Philosophy of M. Comte and Other Essays* (Berkeley, Calif.: The Glendessary Press, 1968), pp. 17–18.

18. My interest in Marx's labor theory of value in its relationship to Soviet society and in connection with Marxism's hostile attitude toward capital was prompted by two essays written by the Soviet author N. Rudenko, titled "The Energy of Progress" and "Farewell, Marx," which as of now exist only in *samizdat*. They are part-fictional, part-philosophical works in which Rudenko, following the Physiocrats, bases himself on the premise that surplus value is in the final analysis a product of solar energy which reaches the earth and is absorbed via photosynthesis. In his view, to combat capitalism is tantamount to combatting solar energy.

The disastrous effect of the labor theory of value on price formation in the USSR is well analyzed in K. Bourzhuademov's book, *Sketches of a Growing Ideology* (Munich: Ekho). (Bourzhuademov is the pseudonym of a Soviet writer.)

19. "Socialism: Utopian and Scientific," in K. Marx, F. Engels, and V. Lenin, *On Historical Materialism*, p. 194.

20. Peter Kropotkin, *Paroles d'un révolté* (Paris: Marpon and Flammarion, 1885), p. 117.

21. Peter Kropotkin, *La conquête du pain* (Paris, 1892), pp. 76–96. English edition, *The Conquest of Bread*, ed. Paul Avrich (London: Allen Lane, 1966), pp. 90, 100.

22. Erich Fromm, ed, *Marx's Concept of Man* (New York: Frederich Ungar, 1966), p. 206.

23. My ideas on the role of valence bonds and mass bonds in connection with social integration were published in an article titled "On the Mathematical Modeling of Social Integration" in *Modelirovanie sotsial'nykh protsessov* (Modeling Social Processes) (Moscow, 1970), pp. 92–103.

24. Konrad Lorenz, *On Aggression*, trans. Marjorie Kerr Wilson (New York: Bantam Books, 1967).

25. *Ibid*, p. 135.

26. Let $w = v - 1$. Now let us compute the total number of bonds. Each member of the hierarchy has at least w bonds, which yields a total of Nw bonds. All those who rise to at least the first level, and there will be N/v of these, will have an additional Nw/v bonds. Those who rise to at least the second level will have an additional Nw/v^2 bonds, etc. The total will be:

$$Nw(1 + 1/v + 1/v^2 + \ldots) = Nw\frac{1}{1 - 1/v} = Nv$$

Thus the average number of bonds is equal to v.

III. Totalitarianism or Socialism?

1. Andrei D. Sakharov, *Alarm and Hope* (New York: Vintage Books, 1978), p. 17.
2. Roy A. Medvedev, "What Is in Store for Us?" (On Alexander Solzhenitsyn's "Letter to the Leaders").
3. *Landmarks* (*Vekhi*), published in 1909, was an anthology of essays by a number of leading Russian thinkers (e.g., Nikolai Berdyayev, Sergei Bulgakov, Peter Struve, and Semyon Frank) who shared a belief that the radical Russian intelligentsia of the later nineteenth century had been uncritical in importing Western ideas—trans.
4. "On the Literary Criticism Department of *Novy Mir*," *Literaturnaya gazeta* (July 1, 1954).
5. "Peace is Too Politicized for Prizes," *Nature* (October 16, 1975), vol. 257.
6. Alexander Solzhenitsyn, "A Speech on the British Radio Network," *Vestnik Russkogo Khristianskogo Dvizheniya* (Herald of the Russian Christian Movement), no. 117 (1976), p. 137.
7. Walter Lacqueur and Leopold Labedz, "A Question of Survival," *Harper's Magazine* (1974), 251 (1502):20.
8. *Ibid.*, p. 22.
9. Herbert Marcuse, *One-Dimensional Man* (Boston: Beacon Press, 1964), p. xii.
10. *Ibid.*, pp. xii, xiii.
11. *Ibid.*, p. xiii.
12. *Ibid.*, p. xv.
13. *Ibid.*, p. xv.
14. *Ibid.*, p. 3.
15. *Ibid.*, pp. 10–11.
16. Alvin Toffler, *Future Shock* (New York: Random House, 1970; paperback edition: Bantam Books, 1971). Pagination is from the paperback edition.
17. *Ibid.*, p. 208.
18. *Ibid.*, p. 226.
19. *Ibid.*, p. 9.
20. *Ibid.*, p. 11.
21. *Ibid.*, p. 230.
22. *Ibid.*, pp. 232–33.
23. *Ibid.*, p. 446.
24. *Ibid.*, p. 450.

25. *Ibid.*, p. 452.
26. *Readers Digest* (February 1976), p. 51.
27. Toffler, *Future Shock*, p. 471.
28. *Ibid.*, p. 473.
29. *Ibid.*, pp. 477–78.
30. *Ibid.*, p. 479.
31. *Ibid.*, p. 477.
32. *Ibid.*, p. 477.
33. *Ibid.*, p. 461.
34. Leszek Kolakowski, *Encounter*, 44 (6):89–90.
35. *Ibid.*, pp. 91–92.
36. Albert Schweitzer, *The Philosophy of Civilization, Part I*, pp. 85, 90.
37. I.e., dispossessed and (in most cases) "resettled" in Siberia—trans.
38. An untranslatable idiom. To "give someone the fig" while keeping "the fig in the pocket," is to make a threatening gesture in a cowardly manner—trans.

Index